JUMPSTARTING
SOUTH ASIA

JUMPSTARTING SOUTH ASIA

REVISITING ECONOMIC REFORMS AND LOOK EAST POLICIES

Pradumna B. Rana
Wai-Mun Chia

OXFORD
UNIVERSITY PRESS

OXFORD
UNIVERSITY PRESS

Oxford University Press is a department of the University of Oxford.
It furthers the University's objective of excellence in research, scholarship,
and education by publishing worldwide. Oxford is a registered trademark of
Oxford University Press in the UK and in certain other countries.

Published in India by
Oxford University Press
2/11 Ground Floor, Ansari Road, Daryaganj, New Delhi 110 002, India

ISBN-13: 978-0-19-947928-3
ISBN-10: 0-19-947928-3

Typeset in Berling LT Std 9.5/14
by Tranistics Data Technologies, New Delhi 110 044
Printed in India by Rakmo Press, New Delhi 110 020

CONTENTS

Contents

TABLES, FIGURES, AND BOXES

Tables

Figures

Boxes

FOREWORD

In the bygone era, the Indian subcontinent and China were the most prosperous regions of the world. During the colonial days and the early decades of the post-colonial period, however, the Indian subcontinent became an economic laggard. Political conflicts also transformed the region into one of the least integrated parts of the world. It was only in the 1980s and the 1990s that the South Asian countries started to opt for greater economic openness and began the long process of aligning their economies with those of the rest of the world. These reforms propelled South Asian countries onto a higher growth path and their share of global GDP started to increase somewhat. It appeared as if the slow and minimalist annual growth rate of 3–4 per cent might be a thing of the past and the region would embrace close to double-digit growth on a sustained basis.

Unfortunately, these were false hopes. In recent years, the economic growth in South Asia has slowed down yet again. Since Indian Prime Minister Narendra Modi's election in 2014 on the promise of reforms, India is bucking the trend, but there are questions about how much he can deliver.

The weak external environment faced by emerging markets since the global economic crisis of 2007–9 is obviously one of the causes of this slowdown. But the authors of this book, one of whom has many years of experience at the Asian Development Bank, argue that the principal cause is domestic and structural, namely the slowing pace of economic reforms that were once the key drivers of the region's dynamism.

The authors argue convincingly that in order to jumpstart economic growth and deepen economic integration in the region, South Asian countries need to adopt a two-pronged strategy. First, they need to complete the economic program that they had begun earlier. After having plucked the low-hanging fruits of early macroeconomic and structural reforms, they need to focus on the more difficult and politically sensitive microeconomic reforms comprising sectoral and 'second-generation' reforms, mainly governance and institutional reforms. Next, they need to implement the second round of 'Look East' policies or the so-called LEP2 to link themselves to production networks in East Asia, their largest export market.

The authors provide a comprehensive list of reforms that each South Asian country has to implement. They also recommend a set of policy actions that South Asian countries should take to link themselves to production networks in East Asia and the world.

The book is timely and useful. It will help enhance the understanding of recent economic development issues in South Asia and how the region's trade and investment relations with East Asia could jumpstart economic growth and integration in the region and pave the way for an integrated Asia. It will be of value to a wide spectrum of readers, not only in Asia but also in other parts of the world. For those in academia, policy, development institutes, students, and even the general public, this volume is a welcome contribution to the growing literature on Asian economic development.

Singapore has played an important role in supporting development efforts in South Asia, mainly in India. I see opportunities for further collaboration between Singapore and South Asian countries, particularly in the areas of trade and investment facilitation, infrastructure and industrial park development, and financial services.

Ambassador Ong Keng Yong
Executive Deputy Chairman
S. Rajaratnam School of International Studies
Nanyang Technological University

ACKNOWLEDGEMENTS

Before retiring from the Asian Development Bank (ADB), Pradumna B. Rana was responsible for conducting research on Association of Southeast Asian Nations (ASEAN) and ASEAN plus China, Japan, and Korea (ASEAN+3), and working with policymakers in the region in helping them to implement the findings. Since his retirement, he has been trying to expand this vision to South Asia and integration between South Asia and East Asia or Pan-Asian integration. He has a number of publications including an edited book entitled *Renaissance of Asia: Evolving Relations between South Asia and East Asia*, published by World Scientific in 2012. The central argument of that book is that Asia's emergence and integration and the irresistible shift of economic power to the East are undoubtedly of keen interest, but they are not without precedence. If one looks at the economic history of Asia, one should really be talking about Asia's 're-emergence' and 'Asia's re-integration' or the 'Renaissance of Asia'. This is because, even in the previous eras of globalization, Asia was prosperous. Asia was also regionally integrated and globally connected.

The Academic Research Fund Tier 1 (AcRF Tier 1) grant that he won together with Wai-Mun Chia, the co-author of this book, for a 'Study of Economic Integration between South Asia and East Asia: Research and Perception' provided an opportunity for further research on the subject. The research was focused on the areas of domestic economic policy reforms, issues in designing and sequencing reforms, development of production networks and supply chains, cross-border physical infrastructure and information communication technology (ICT) connectivity. We are, therefore, grateful to the Ministry of Education in Singapore for the research grant. When we embarked on the journey, we had no idea that we would end up with a book.

This book owes much to many. We have benefitted from comments from many colleagues and friends. In particular, we thank Yothin Jinjarak of the University of Wellington and Aekapol Chongvilaivan of ADB. We are grateful for the support and encouragement of Ambassadors Ong Keng Yong and Barry Desker, and Professors Chong Yah Lim, Euston Quah, and Joseph Liow.

Pradumna Rana would also like to thank the Centre of Multilateralism Studies of S. Rajaratnam School of International Studies (RSIS) where he is based and its staff Ralf Emmers, See Seng Tan, and other colleagues.

A number of very valuable comments and suggestions given by two anonymous reviewers have greatly improved the book. Thanks are also due to Taojun Xie and Don Rodney for their excellent research support and for going over many drafts of the book. We continue to thank Changtai Li for his absolute reliability.

We also thank the editorial team at Oxford University Press for their help.

Finally, we both are grateful to our families for their continued support without which the book could not have been prepared.

ABBREVIATIONS

ADB	Asian Development Bank
ADBI	Asian Development Bank Institute
AFTA	ASEAN Free Trade Area
AIIB	Asia Infrastructure Investment Bank
AIM	ASEAN ICT Masterplan
AIS	Asian Information Superhighway
AMF	Asian Monetary Fund
AML	Anti-money Laundering
AMRO	ASEAN+3 Macroeconomic Research Office
APTA	Asia-Pacific Trade Agreement
ASEAN	Association of Southeast Asian Nations
ASEAN+3	ASEAN plus China, Japan, and Korea
BCIM	Bangladesh–China–India–Myanmar
BIMSTEC	Bay of Bengal Initiative for Multi-sectoral Technical and Economic Cooperation
BPO	Business Process Outsourcing
CAREC	Central Asia Regional Economic Cooperation
CECA	Agreement on Comprehensive Economic Cooperation
CGE	Computational General Equilibrium
CIAA	Anti-corruption Agency
CIB	Credit Information Bureau
CLMV	Cambodia, Laos, Myanmar and Vietnam
CMIM	Chiang Mai Initiative Multilateralization

ECU	European Currency Unit
EMS	European Monetary System
ERIA	Economic Research Institute for ASEAN and East Asia
ERPD	Economic Review and Policy Dialogue
FATF	Financial Action Task Force
FDI	Foreign Direct Investment
FSDS	Financial Sector Development Strategy
FTA	Free Trade Agreement
GDP	Gross Domestic Product
GLS	Generalized Least Squares
GMS	Great Mekong Subregion
GNI	Gross National Income
GST	General Sales Tax
GVC	Global Value Chain
ICT	Information Communication Technology
IDI	ICT Development Index
ILO	International Labour Organization
IMF	International Monetary Fund
IT	Information Technology
ITU	International Telecommunications Union
IWT	Inland Water Transport
LEP	'Look East' Policy
LEP2	Second round of "Look East" Policies
LNG	Liquefied Natural Gas
LPI	Logistics Performance Indicators
MCR	Minimum Capital Requirement
MIEC	Mekong–India Economic Corridor
MoAD	Ministry of Agricultural Development
MOU	Memorandum of Understanding
NAFTA	North American Free Trade Agreement
NIEs	Newly Industrialized Economies
NGO	Non-governmental Organization
NPL	Non-performing Loan
OECD	Organization for Economic Co-operation and Development

OGI	Overall Governance Indicator
PB	Production Block
P&C	Parts and Components
PNP	Production Network Participation
RCA	Revealed Comparative Advantages
RCEP	Regional Comprehensive Economic Partnership
REER	Real Effective Exchange Rate
RMB	Chinese Renminbi
RMU	Regional Monetary Unit
RTI	Right to Information
SAARC	South Asia Association for Regional Cooperation
SAFTA	South Asian Free Trade Agreement
SAPTA	South Asian Preferential Trading Agreement
SASEC	South Asia Subregional Economic Cooperation
SATRC	South Asian Telecommunication Regulator's Council
SCO	Shanghai Cooperation Organization
SDR	Special Drawing Right
SEZs	Special Economic Zones
SITS	Software and IT-enabled Services
SL	Service Link
SME	Small and Medium-sized Enterprise
SSR	South-western Silk Road
UNCTAD	United Nations Conference on Trade and Development
UNESCAP	United Nations Economic and Social Commission for Asia and the Pacific
VAT	Value-added Tax
WAPDA	Water and Power Development Authority
WGI	Worldwide Governance Indicators
WTO	World Trade Organization

INTRODUCTION, OVERVIEW, AND POLICIES

Context and Background

The seminal work of the late Angus Maddison (2007) has established that 2000 years ago, the Indian subcontinent or the modern day South Asia[1] and China were, by far, the richest regions of the world. Even in the early nineteenth century, South Asia's share of global gross domestic product (GDP) stood at about 20 per cent on purchasing power parity basis. This share, however, started to decline after the Industrial Revolution in Europe. After independence, India and other South Asian countries adopted some inward-looking development strategies that isolated themselves from the global economy. Their share of global GDP, therefore, continued to fall further. Subsequently, with the economic reforms of the 1980s and 1990s, South Asia's economic growth rate had shifted to a higher trajectory and its share of global GDP had also started to increase somewhat.

More recently, however, the pace of economic growth in South Asia has slowed yet again. Data from the World Bank presented in Table I.1 show that after peaking in 2006 in Maldives and Pakistan, in 2007 in Bangladesh, and Bhutan, and 2008 in Nepal, overall GDP and per capita GDP growth rates in most South Asian countries have softened. Similarly, in Afghanistan and Sri Lanka, economic growth peaked in 2012, and has softened since then. In India, GDP growth rate peaked

---

[1] Includes the member countries of the South Asia Association for Regional Cooperation (SAARC), namely, Afghanistan, Bangladesh, Bhutan, India, Maldives, Nepal, Pakistan, and Sri Lanka.

Table I.1 Average Growth in GDP and GDP Per Capita (Per cent)

	2006	2007	2008	2009	2010	2011	2012	2013	2014	2015	Pre-reform 1976–90	Post-reform 1991–2005
GDP Growth												
Afghanistan	5.6	13.7	3.6	21.0	8.4	6.1	14.4	1.9	1.3	1.5	N.A.	N.A.
Bangladesh	6.7	7.1	6.0	5.0	5.6	6.5	6.5	6.0	6.1	6.6	3.9	5.0
Bhutan	6.8	17.9	4.8	6.7	11.7	7.9	5.1	2.1	5.5	3.3	N.A.	6.0
India	9.3	8.6	3.9	8.5	10.3	6.6	5.6	6.6	7.2	7.6	4.8	6.0
Maldives	20.7	10.8	12.5	−5.5	6.0	8.7	2.5	4.7	6.5	1.5	N.A.	N.A.
Nepal	3.4	3.4	6.1	4.5	4.8	3.4	4.8	4.1	5.4	3.4	4.0	4.5
Pakistan	6.2	4.8	1.7	2.8	1.6	2.7	3.5	4.4	4.7	5.5	6.3	4.3
Sri Lanka	7.7	6.8	6.0	3.5	8.0	8.4	9.1	3.4	4.9	4.8	4.6	4.8
GDP Per Capita Growth												
Afghanistan	2.3	10.7	1.1	18.0	5.5	3.0	10.9	−1.2	−1.7	−1.3	N.A.	N.A.
Bangladesh	5.3	5.8	4.8	3.9	4.4	5.2	5.3	4.7	4.8	5.3	1.2	3.0
Bhutan	4.3	15.4	2.7	4.7	9.8	6.1	3.5	0.7	4.0	1.9	N.A.	4.6
India	7.6	7.0	2.4	7.0	8.8	5.2	4.3	5.3	5.9	6.3	2.5	4.2
Maldives	16.3	5.7	8.4	−5.0	3.9	5.8	0.4	2.6	4.4	−0.5	N.A.	N.A.
Nepal	2.2	2.3	5.1	3.5	3.7	2.3	3.6	2.9	4.1	2.1	1.6	2.2
Pakistan	4.0	2.7	−0.4	0.7	−0.5	0.6	1.3	2.2	2.6	3.4	2.9	1.9
Sri Lanka	6.9	6.0	5.2	2.8	7.2	7.6	8.3	2.6	3.9	3.8	3.0	3.8

Source: Data from World Development Indicators, 2015.
Note: N.A. means that data are not available.

in 2010 at 10.3 per cent but fell during the next three years. The Indian economy has been growing faster since 2014 but it is still not generating enough jobs. The International Monetary Fund (IMF) and the Asian Development Bank (ADB) have advised that in order to sustain this growth the pace of economic reforms should be accelerated in the country.[2]

The recent slowdown of economic growth in South Asia can be explained by two factors (Patnaik and Pundit 2014). The first factor is mostly due to the overall deterioration in the global economic environment facing South Asia. After the global economic crisis of 2008–9, economic recovery has begun in the industrial countries, but it is still nascent and there are only tentative signs of a turnaround in Europe. The second factor for the economic slowdown of South Asian countries is domestic and structural, namely the slowing pace of economic reforms that once were the key drivers of the region's dynamic economic performance and resilience. In India, for example, the previous Manmohan Singh government was expected to take reforms to the second phase, but allegations of corruption and the ensuing political paralysis slowed down the pace, and in some cases, reversed the reforms (Baru 2014). Accordingly, economic growth slowed down as investors lost confidence and there was a certain amount of political instability. Prime Minister Narendra Modi was elected in 2015 on a platform of economic reforms.

Also, before the partition of India and Pakistan, South Asia was among the most integrated regions of the world with high levels of intra-regional trade. Total trade volume among the countries of the region was estimated at around 20 per cent of total trade before the partition in 1947 (World Bank 2004). But now, despite a large number of institutions and initiatives that purportedly seek to promote economic cooperation, the South Asian region is among the least integrated regions of the world.

---

[2] The IMF has warned that to continue on the trend, India needs to revitalize the investment cycle and accelerate structural reforms (IMF 2015). Similarly, the ADB (2015) has flagged that 'Stalled parliamentary actions on structural reforms are a risk to an otherwise improving economic outlook'.

Objectives and Scope

Against the above background, the objective of this book is to argue that to jumpstart economic growth in their region, South Asian countries need to adopt a two-pronged strategy. First, South Asian countries need to complete the economic reform process that they had begun in the 1980s and the early 1990s. After having plucked the low-hanging fruits of 'first-generation' reforms, which focused mainly on macroeconomic areas of monetary, fiscal, and exchange rate management, and structural reforms (for example, industrial delicensing and trade, investment, and financial sector liberalization), South Asian countries need to focus on microeconomic reforms, comprising sectoral and second-generation reforms, mainly governance and institutional reforms, in order to support and sustain private sector–led economic growth.[3] Secondly, South Asian countries need to implement the second round of their 'Look East' policies (LEP2) to:

1. Link themselves to production networks[4] in East Asia,[5] their largest potential market for export (De 2010)
2. Develop production networks in manufacturing and services in their own region.

---

[3] 'Second-generation' reforms comprise continued reform of public institutions for improved governance at all levels (civil service, bureaucracy, and public administration); reform of institutions that create or maintain human capital (education and health); and improving the environment affecting the private sector (regulatory environment, flexibility in the labour market, legal and physical infrastructure, and clearly defined property rights). Second-generation reforms are frequently used in Latin America. Chibber (2006) uses a similar typology in discussing reforms in developing countries. In 1999, the IMF had organized a conference on the need for second-generation reforms.

[4] Several other terms have also been used to describe this phenomenon such as production fragmentation, supply chains, vertical specialization, and global value chains. These terms are used interchangeably in this book.

[5] ASEAN+3 countries which includes ASEAN, namely Brunei, Cambodia, Indonesia, Laos, Malaysia, Myanmar, Philippines, Singapore, Thailand, and Vietnam, and the '+3' such as China, Japan, and Republic of Korea.

As part of its economic reform program, India adopted an LEP in 1991 to promote closer ties with Southeast Asian countries (Rajendram 2014). Bangladesh followed suit in late 2002 (Islam and Khanam 2014) and Pakistan in 2003 with its 'Vision East Asia' initiative (Malik 2015). Other South Asian countries have not announced a formal LEP but have taken a number of policy actions to promote trade and investment and connectivity with East Asia. As discussed in Chapter 2, these policies have had a number of positive impacts.

This book draws on and builds upon existing studies on the subject. These include studies by Francois and Wignaraja (2009), Rana (2012a), and the Asian Development Bank and the Asian Development Bank Institute (ADB and ADBI 2015). While Rana (2012a) focuses on the historical perspectives of South Asia–East Asia linkages, the other two studies focus more on contemporary trade and investment issues between South Asia and East Asia (Francois and Wignaraja 2009) and South Asia and Southeast Asia (ADB and ADBI 2015). All of these studies, however, focus on the traditional type of trade where traded goods were produced entirely in one country and sold to another. This book's main focus is to examine how South Asian countries, besides the traditional type of trade, can enjoy the dynamic benefits associated with the newer trade theories of product fragmentation by joining production networks (Jones and Kierzkowski 1990; Kimura and Ando 2005). The East Asian region is dense with production networks. A natural question is, therefore, to ask how South Asia can develop production networks within its region and link these with networks in East Asia and benefit both from the static benefits of the traditional type of trade as well as from the network externalities of the product fragmentation process.[6]

---

[6] Using firm-level data from Malaysia and Thailand, which are important participants in East Asia's production network, Wignaraja, Kruger, and Tuazon (2013) have found that participation in production networks raises profits and is also associated with technological upgrading and higher R&D expenditure. Over time, production networks have also deepened and spread from electronics to other sectors such as automobiles, televisions, and cameras.

The book argues that round two of economic reforms and LEP2 will lead to a win-win situation for all countries in South Asia and East Asia as the policies will enhance trade and investment relationships and economic dynamism in the two regions. Economic reforms will directly increase economic growth in South Asia. Economic reforms are also a component of LEP2 and, hence, will have beneficial impacts on the trade and investment relationship between South Asia and East Asia which, in turn, will increase economic dynamism in both regions. South Asian countries will trade and invest more with neighbouring countries as inter-regional trade increases. Economic dynamism in South Asia will also result in new areas of comparative advantage impacting positively on South Asian trade and investment integration.

These arguments are consistent with and supported by the findings of Francois and Wignaraja (2009) and those by the ADB and ADBI (2015), which are summarized in the section on 'Potential and Impact of Enhancing Economic Linkages' in Chapter 2. The results of our perception survey presented in Chapter 6 also broadly support these conclusions. South Asia's integration with East Asia could, therefore, contribute to the re-emergence of a prosperous and integrated Asia, which had existed during the first 18 centuries of the post-Christian era (Rana 2012a).

Chapter-wise Findings

Chapter 1 focuses on the economic policy reforms in South Asia and identifies the unfinished agenda. After independence in 1947, both India and Pakistan, including East Pakistan (now Bangladesh), had adopted the Soviet-type import-substituting development model, which included high tariff barriers to trade and various forms of licensing systems to control competition and entry into industries. Smaller South Asian countries, such as Bhutan, Maldives, and Nepal, had also adopted a similar development strategy.

It was only in the 1980s and the 1990s that South Asian countries initiated their economic reform process. These reforms had placed the countries on a higher growth path. Researchers and analysts were focused on when these countries would catch up with East Asia. Presently, however, the pace of economic growth in South Asia has slowed down.

This chapter argues that one of the reasons for the slowdown in economic growth in South Asia has been the failure to complete the economic reforms program. The first round of economic reforms in South Asia focused on macroeconomic areas of monetary, fiscal, and exchange rate management, and structural reforms (for example, industrial delicensing, and trade, investment, and financial sector liberalization). Such reforms should have been followed by the more microeconomic reforms, which are sectoral reforms and second-generation reforms mainly to strengthen governance and institutions. Microeconomic reforms support the private sector-led economic growth from the first-generation reforms, which ran out of steam. This was because of—among other reasons—lack of law and order, and red tape and corruption in the public sector. By using various indicators of governance such as government effectiveness, rule of law, and control of corruption, this chapter argues that there is a significant 'governance gap' in South Asia which refers to how South Asia lags behind East Asia in terms of various governance indicators and how within South Asia some countries are ahead of others. The chapter proposes that in order to bolster economic growth, South Asian countries must implement additional reforms at the more microeconomic level.

The chapter also provides details on various unfinished policy reform agendas that should be adopted by each South Asian country. Implementation of microeconomic reforms, however, poses a difficult challenge as it requires a wider consensus and political support and has longer term focus.

Chapter 2 highlights that South Asian countries initiated their LEPs to enhance closer relations with East Asia as part of their economic reform program. While the three largest South Asian countries adopted LEPs formally, others adopted it informally. These policies, together with the first round of reforms, have had a number of positive effects. For example, trade between South Asia and East Asia has surged during the past decade and a half, albeit from a low base, and China has become India's largest trading partner. There is also a potential for larger trade and investment flows between South Asia and East Asia.

The chapter also reviews the traditional versus the newer theories of international trade associated with production networks and supply chains and their implications for trade policy. It argues that although the newer theories have both costs as well as benefits, the latter is believed to outweigh the former as there are significant dynamic network externalities in supply chain trade. It then makes the case for the LEP2 in South Asia.

Chapters 3 to 5 identify the production network participation gap or the 'PNP gap' between South Asia and East Asia and outline policies and actions that need to be implemented under the LEP2. Chapter 3 identifies the PNP gap between South Asia and East Asia using two different indicators—share of parts and components in total trade (Athukorala 2010) and the newly developed global value chains (GVC) participation index published by the United Nations Conference on Trade and Development (UNCTAD). The chapter also develops a simple empirical model to identify the key determinants of production network participation using the logit model with random effects.

This model helps us to identify the key components of the LEP2 that South Asian countries should implement to overcome the PNP gap with East Asia. These are:

1. Improving the business environment by completing the reform process begun in the 1980s and the early 1990s
2. Reducing logistics cost including 'at-the-border' costs through trade facilitation
3. Joining and participating in various ongoing regional trade and financial cooperation efforts in East Asia
4. Reducing communication and coordination costs in managing supply chains by improving ICT
5. Enhancing regional physical connectivity mainly through transport hardware and software.

Linking production hubs in various countries requires efficient service links including well-developed ICT infrastructure, so that production blocks in a supply chain can be managed efficiently. Chapter 4 has two objectives. The first is to review the level of ICT development in South Asia and East Asia, and the second is to recommend policies that South Asian countries could implement to close the 'digital divide' with East Asia and within their region. This chapter considers three dimensions of ICT development: access, availability and affordability, and ICT usage. Analysis from various indicators suggests that there is a significant digital divide between South Asia and East Asia and within the South Asian countries. The chapter then outlines policies that South Asian countries should implement to bridge the gap. These policies are grouped as national, regional, and Pan-Asian. At the national level, South Asian countries should improve coordination among relevant agencies and efficiently implement their ICT Master Plans and Broadband Plans. Stakeholder participation and political support are also essential to ensure success. South Asian countries also need to invest more in the ICT sector and open up the sector to both domestic and foreign investors. eGovernance also needs to be promoted. At the regional level, there is a need for a SAARC ICT Master Plan similar to the ASEAN ICT Master Plan. At the Pan-Asian level, South Asian countries should support and participate in the Asian Information Superhighway initiative of the United Nations Economic and Social Commission for Asia and the Pacific (UNESCAP).

Chapter 5 focuses on infrastructure connectivity issues that are required for providing efficient service links between production blocks in global production networks and supply chains. The chapter argues that although sea transport is expected to be the dominant form of connectivity in the foreseeable future, the case for reviving land connectivity in Asia has increased for a number of economic, security, and political reasons. These include:

1. Implementation of the Western Development Strategy or the so-called 'Go West' policy in China. More recently, China has also

launched the 'One Belt, One Road' policy to enhance connectivity with neighbouring countries

2. LEPs in South Asia, specially India and presently also in Myanmar, of which cross-border connectivity is an important component

3. Encouraging but gradual political and economic reforms in Myanmar, a node between South Asia and East Asia, which has provided a fillip for improving connectivity between South Asia and East Asia

4. Growing importance and potential of supply chain trade in the region where road and even air connectivity could be cost-effective for less bulky and high value-added parts and components

The chapter reviews the ongoing efforts to promote ASEAN–India connectivity, namely, the Mekong–India Economic Corridor (MIEC) and the trilateral highway connecting north-eastern states of India and Myanmar with Thailand, and the Bangladesh–China–India–Myanmar (BCIM) Economic Corridor. It also highlights bilateral and trilateral efforts to promote connectivity between India's north-eastern region and the neighbouring countries. The chapter asserts that these corridors would enhance Pan-Asian connectivity and present a win-win situation for all countries.

Chapter 6 presents the results of an online perception survey of Asian opinion leaders on economic integration between South Asia and East Asia. The objective of the survey was to assess the views of the stakeholders on the relative strengths of the key findings of the earlier chapters and to get their perspectives.

Asian opinion leaders were defined as representatives of the academia, government officials, business, and media. Among the questions asked were: What are the benefits and costs of economic integration between South Asia and East Asia? What are the respective roles of market-led and regional cooperation policies? What are the policies that South Asian countries should adopt under their LEP2 to link themselves with production networks in East Asia? What is the role of connectivity? What are the factors that have led to the revival of land connectivity or old South-western Silk Road in Asia? Should efforts to promote ASEAN–India connectivity be supported? Should the membership of East Asian institutions be expanded to cover South Asian countries or should South Asia establish its own institutions? Why is the level of economic integration in South Asia low and can South Asia–East Asia integration reinvigorate economic integration in South Asia?

The survey results present a fairly positive assessment of economic integration between South Asia and East Asia and its prospect. Many respondents, about three quarters of them, believed that the benefits of South Asia and East Asia integration would be faster and more resilient economic growth in the two regions leading to a win-win situation for both. Roughly four out of five respondents felt that integration between South Asia and East Asia should be market-led through improved connectivity and improved business environment. Less than two-thirds favoured regional cooperation policy to promote integration, namely South Asia lobbying to participate in various regional cooperation efforts in East Asia.

Over half of the respondents also felt that the case for a Pan-Asian free trade agreement (FTA) comprising all South Asian and East Asian countries was strong and that the South Asian countries should sign more trade and investment agreements with their East Asian counterparts. All South Asian countries should also seek to join the ongoing negotiations for the Regional Comprehensive Economic Partnership (RCEP).

Nearly four out of five respondents felt that India, the largest country in South Asia, should be represented in some capacity at the ASEAN+3 Economic Review and Policy Dialogue (ERPD) and the Chiang Mai Initiative Multilateralization (CMIM) and that this would help enhance Asia's voice in the G20. The survey also established the important role of improved connectivity in transport, energy, and communication in promoting South Asia–East Asia integration. Nearly three out of four respondents felt that improved connectivity should be the major modality for promoting integration. The survey found that the growing importance of supply chain trade and the Look East policies in South Asia were the major factors that had revived the case for land connectivity between South Asia and East Asia.

Many respondents felt that the case for ASEAN–India connectivity was strong. A large number of respondents also felt that trilateral cooperation between India–Nepal–China should be supported to improve Pan-Asian connectivity between South Asia, Central Asia, China, and ASEAN.

A large number of respondents (over 90 per cent) felt that political rivalries, border disputes, and suspicions in the region were the major reasons why South Asia, which was once a fairly well-integrated region, had become one of the least integrated regions of the world. Roughly, a similar number of respondents felt that closer economic linkages between the two regions of South and East Asia could lead to a revival of economic integration in South Asia.

A key recommendation of Chapter 3 is that India should be invited to participate in the ongoing macroeconomic policy coordination and monetary integration efforts in East Asia (ASEAN+3) to help enhance Asia's voice in the G20. These include the possible participation of India in the ASEAN+3 ERPD and the CMIM. The survey of stakeholders in Chapter 6 also supported this recommendation. Chapter 7 argues that the introduction of a regional monetary unit (RMU) or regional currency basket could facilitate regional surveillance in East Asia and facilitate macroeconomic policy coordination in the region. Given the present level of integration in East Asia, a single currency for East Asia is, however, still a long way off. The survey results presented in this chapter support these arguments and the stakeholders had a fairly positive assessment of the monetary integration process in East Asia and its prospects in the future. The respondents felt that ASEAN+3 Macroeconomic Research Office (AMRO) and CMIM could drive the process further.

Key Findings and Policy Recommendations

The key findings and policy recommendations of the book can be summarized as follows:

1. In order to jumpstart economic growth and promote economic integration in the region, South Asian countries need to implement round two of their economic reforms and the second round of their

Look East policies. The second round of economic reforms in South Asia should focus on the unfinished agenda of microeconomic reforms comprising sectoral reforms and the second-generation reforms, focusing mainly on governance and institutional reforms. South Asian countries also need to embark on LEP2 to:

- Link themselves to production networks in East Asia
- Develop production networks in manufacturing and services in their own region.

LEP2 will allow South Asian and East Asian countries to benefit mutually, not only from the static complementarities of the traditional trade theory but also from the dynamic complementarities of the new trade theory.

2. LEP2 in South Asia should comprise the following five, sometimes overlapping, policies:

- South Asian countries should complete the economic reform process begun in the 1980s and the early 1990s.
- South Asian countries should reduce logistics costs including 'at-the-border' costs through trade facilitation.
- South Asian countries should strive to deepen their trade and investment linkages and connection with East Asia. India, the largest economy in South Asia and a member of the G20, is already involved in negotiating the RCEP. It could also be invited to join various efforts to promote regional integration in East Asia. Other South Asian countries should join at an appropriate time.
- South Asian countries should improve their ICT systems to coordinate supply chains.
- South Asian countries should support ongoing efforts to enhance physical connectivity between the two regions as it would help to reduce trading costs.

3. Round two of economic reforms and LEP2 in South Asia will lead to a win-win situation for all countries in South Asia and East Asia as it will accelerate their integration and economic dynamism. It will also help to reinvigorate economic integration in South Asia which

is among the least integrated region in the world. It will, thereby, contribute to the re-emergence of a 'prosperous and integrated' Asia which had existed during the first 18 centuries of the post-Christian era (Rana 2012a).

4. Other key findings of the perception surveys are:

- Economic integration between South Asia and East Asia should be promoted using market-led approaches including improved connectivity which reduces trading costs.
- Projects under the ASEAN–India connectivity (namely, MIEC and the Trilateral Highway) and the BCIM Economic Corridor should be supported.
- The Yunnan–Myanmar–India–Nepal–Tibet–Yunnan Economic Corridor or the old South-western Silk Road should also be revived.
- In terms of institutional arrangements, the Bay of Bengal Initiative for Multi-Sectoral Technical and Economic Cooperation (BIMSTEC) should play a greater role in promoting connectivity between South Asia and East Asia. Cooperation between BIMSTEC, South Asia Subregional Economic Cooperation (SASEC), and Great Mekong Subregion (GMS), should also be promoted.
- With Maritime Asia becoming increasingly Continental Asia with expanding networks of roads, railways, and pipelines, membership of East Asian regional institutions should be expanded. Just as they did when the East Asia Summit was formed, ASEAN and ASEAN+3 should invite India to join the ASEAN+3 ERPD and to pledge funds to the CMIM. In addition to India, which is already involved in negotiating the RCEP, at some stage in the future, ASEAN and ASEAN+3 must also invite other South Asian countries to join the RCEP. India's membership in APEC must also be considered seriously.

1

POLICY REFORMS IN SOUTH ASIA
An Overview and the Unfinished Agenda

Introduction

After independence from Britain in 1947, both India and Pakistan, including East Pakistan, which is now Bangladesh, had adopted the Soviet-type import-substituting policies and erected high walls of protection on all sectors of the economy. This meant not only high tariffs but also various forms of licensing to control entry into industries. The resulting 'license raj'—rigid government controls over production and distribution of goods—in these countries had created inefficiencies, promoted public sector corruption, and constrained the rate of economic growth. The smaller South Asian countries—Bhutan, Maldives, and Nepal—had also adopted a similar development strategy. It was only two or three decades later in the 1980s and the early 1990s that South Asian countries started the economic reform process. While these reforms had placed the countries on a higher growth trajectory, researchers and analysts were focused on when these countries would catch up with East Asia (Rana 2011).

As discussed in the introduction, however, more recently, the pace of economic growth in South Asia has slowed down. This is for two reasons. The first reason is mainly due to the deteriorating global economic environment, especially after the global economic crisis of

2008–9. Even though economic recovery has begun in the industrial countries, it is still nascent and only tentative signs of a turnaround in Europe are visible. The second reason for the economic slowdown of South Asian countries is domestic and structural, namely the slowing pace of economic reforms that once were the key drivers of the region's dynamic economic performance and resilience.

This chapter focuses on the second reason for the recent economic slowdown in South Asia. McKinnon (1993) has argued that it is neither theoretically defensible nor practically feasible to implement all aspects of reform policies simultaneously. Inappropriate design and sequence can lead to the failure of a reform program. Economic history has recorded a number of such instances. An example is the Southern Cone Latin American case where efforts to reform the financial and trade sectors failed in the mid-1980s.

Following Rana (2011) and Rana and Hamid (1995), this chapter contends that South Asian countries did not sequence their reform programs properly. The first round of reforms in South Asia that began in the 1980s and the 1990s had focused on macroeconomic areas of monetary, fiscal, and exchange rate management, and structural reforms including industrial delicensing. A limited amount of trade, investment, and financial sector liberalization was also undertaken. This first round of reforms focused on unleashing market forces and increasing competition. They also sought to reduce the role of the government through industrial delicensing and placed limits on the ability of the government to run fiscal deficits and accumulate debt. These reforms contributed significantly to economic growth driven by the private sector. The first round of reforms should have been followed by the microeconomic reforms—sectoral and the second-generation reforms, to strengthen governance and institutions and make markets work better (Navia and Velasco 2003). But they were not and, as a result, private sector–led economic growth due to first-generation reforms ran out of steam partly because of the lack of law and order and because of red tape and corruption in the public sector. Keyfitz and Dorfman (1991) have identified 14 institutional requirements for sustained operation of private markets. These include law and order, security of persons and property, and trust. South Asian countries failed to achieve these institutional preconditions for markets to work. Panagariya (2014) has also argued that the abandonment of the reforms initiated by earlier governments is responsible for the recent slowdown in Indian economic growth.

Many studies have established the positive impacts of policy reforms on economic growth. A particularly interesting study is by Christiansen, Schindler, and Tressel (2009) of the IMF. They developed a model that can simultaneously assess the relationships between economic performance and three groups of economic policies. They find that while domestic financial reforms and trade reforms are robustly associated with economic growth, the relationship between capital account liberalization and growth is less robust.

The rest of the chapter is organized as follows. The next section briefly surveys the policy reforms implemented by various South Asian countries during the 1980s and 1990s and identifies the lack of action in the area of microeconomic reforms. Then, the chapter assesses the impacts of the first round of policy reforms on the economy. It explains that economic policies matter. The chapter also focuses on the governance gap in South Asia which refers to how South Asia lags behind East Asia in terms of various governance indicators and how, within the South Asian region, some countries are ahead of others in terms of these indicators.

The section on 'Long-term Economic Potential and the Need for Microeconomic Reforms' reviews studies by a number of analysts who argue that South Asian countries have the potential of achieving a sustained annual 8 to 10 per cent economic growth in the long term. In order to realize this potential, however, South Asian countries should, among others, take actions to implement microeconomic reforms. This poses a challenge because, unlike macroeconomic reforms, these reforms require a wider consensus and political support, and focus on the long term. Finally, the last section highlights that microeconomic reforms are the centrepiece of the new Narendra Modi government in India that is attempting to revive the manufacturing sector in the country. The unfinished policy reform agenda for individual South Asian countries is also presented in this chapter.

Survey of Policy Reforms in South Asia and Sequencing Issues

Among the South Asian countries, the process of policy reforms began the earliest in Sri Lanka in the early 1980s, supported by various facilities from the IMF. The measures involved stabilization packages together with structural measures in the areas of trade and financial sector reforms, including deregulation of interest rates. In India, the Narasimha Rao government that assumed power in mid-1991 reversed the previous inward-looking approach in response to a balance-of-payments crisis. Bangladesh started to liberalize its trade and industrial policy at about that time. Nepal and Pakistan began their economic reform program in the late 1990s (Devarajan and Nabi 2006)

In discussing issues related to the design and sequence of reforms, with reference to Rana (2011) and Rana and Hamid (1995), it is useful to distinguish between two categories. The first is macroeconomic reforms, which refer to monetary, fiscal, and exchange rate management, and structural reforms which include industrial delicensing, trade, investment, and financial sector reforms. The other category is microeconomic reforms which are sectoral such as agriculture and industrial sectors and second-generation reforms which include governance and institutional reforms.

South Asian countries have achieved considerable progress in the areas of macroeconomic and structural reforms including industrial deregulation, trade, exchange rate, and financial and fiscal sector reforms (Rana 2011). This was understandable because, in many cases, reforms were triggered by an economic crisis and foreign exchange crisis. Whereas, before reforms, a license was required to establish just about any type of business venture and to procure inputs including imported inputs. Such activities have been significantly deregulated in all South Asian countries after the reforms. Both tariff and non-tariff barriers have also been reduced significantly and the exchange rate, barring the existence of some regulations, is largely market-determined. Foreign investment is also being eagerly sought after and current account convertibility has been announced. The financial sector (including interest rates) has been deregulated to a large extent. Private banks and other types of financial institutions have been established and capital markets developed. In the area of fiscal reforms, Bangladesh, Sri Lanka, and Nepal have introduced the value-added tax (VAT) while other South Asian countries are in the process of introducing it. In an attempt to mobilize larger amounts of resources in the public sector, India and Pakistan have simplified the taxation system and expanded coverage. The public expenditure system has been streamlined in many countries.

Although the pace of microeconomic (sectoral, governance, and institutional) reforms has picked up in South Asia, it is still slow. These reforms are necessary to create the institutional framework required for private sector–led growth. After independence, India had inherited a small but efficient government from the British. It was ruled by the meritocratic Indian civil service and was well-governed. Subsequently, under the socialist model of development, the role of the state was greatly enlarged with the government being responsible for jobs, licenses, and ration cards. However, the capacity and competence of the civil service have not been strengthened despite the recommendations of many studies and committees. In 2004 and 2009, Prime Minister Manmohan Singh had an opportunity to strengthen governance and institutions but he did not do so (Chibber 2013). For example, the Second Administrative Committee had prepared 15 reports and various cabinet committees had approved most of the recommendations, but only 10 per cent of them were implemented (Maira 2012). A similar situation prevails in other South Asian countries as well, where private enterprises are being stifled because of red tape and corruption. There is despair over the delivery of even the simplest public service.

Corruption is the abuse of public trust. It is a form of stealing. It is also regressive, with the poor and the middle-class having to pay a higher share of their income as bribes, than the rich. Corruption, which has always been high in South Asia, has undergone a qualitative change since the reform of the 1990s. Earlier, giving out licenses and awarding government contracts were the primary sources of corruption. Post-reform, formulating policies that benefit the favored few and discretionary distribution of natural resources created an abundance of rent-seeking opportunities for politicians. Corruption money has also become a handy way of dealing with the fragmented and unstable political situation. A number of actions have been taken by South Asian countries to reduce corruption, but much more needs to be done.

A comparison of South Asia's and China's experience in implementing microeconomic reforms is instructive. Fifteen years after the initiation of reforms in 1978, China carried out sweeping reforms of the bureaucracy and public administration to ensure that a strengthened government emerged to meet new challenges and needs. This helped China strengthen the momentum of sustained growth, unlike in South Asia where governance and institutions continue to remain weak (Chibber 2013). In terms of the six indicators developed by the World Bank to monitor governance (see section on 'Governance Gap in South Asia), in 2015, China was perceived to be better than India in terms of control of corruption, regulatory quality, government effectiveness, and political stability. India was better in terms of voice and accountability, and rule of law.

Economic Impacts of Policy Reforms in South Asia

Initially, it was argued that, in India, a surge in economic growth had preceded the implementation of reforms and, hence, the latter could not be the cause for the former (DeLong 2003). However, such views have changed subsequently. The consensus view now is that economic policies do matter. Good policies can help lift rates of economic growth and lower poverty, while poor policies retard growth and stall poverty reduction (Chibber 2006; Panagariya 2014).

Data in Table I.1 of the introduction suggest that economic policies have had a positive impact in South Asia. The last two columns of the table show average GDP and per capita income growth rates in various South Asian countries 15 years before and after reform, assuming 1990 or 1991 as the year that reforms began. In most cases, post-reform average growth rates have been higher than the pre-reform ones. In India, average GDP growth rate was 6 per cent in the post-reform period as compared to 4.8 per cent in the pre-reform period. Post-reform per capita GDP growth rate in the country also averaged 4.2 per cent compared to 2.5 per cent in the pre-reform period. Similarly, in Bangladesh, pre-reform GDP growth rate averaged 3.9 per cent as compared to 5 per cent in the post-reform period. The corresponding figures were 4 per cent and 4.5 per cent for Nepal and 4.6 per cent and 4.8 per cent, respectively, for Sri Lanka. The only country where average GDP and per capita income growth rate declined during the post-reform period was Pakistan and this was mainly because of problems associated with political instability in the country.

Governance Gap in South Asia

Governance gap in South Asia can be illustrated by using the Worldwide Governance Indicators (WGIs) published by the World Bank which compiles indicators to assess six broad dimensions of governance—voice and accountability, political stability and absence of violence/terrorism, government effectiveness, regulatory quality, rule of law, and control of corruption.[1] In addition, we compute a summary of overall governance indicator (OGI) to assess trends as the simple average of the six indicators in the World Bank database.

Figure 1.1 shows that in 2002, OGI was higher in East Asia than in South Asia. During the period between 2002 and 2015, the OGI increased in East Asia but fell in South Asia (until 2013). The governance gap between South Asia and East Asia has, therefore, widened. The only subregion that had a lower OGI indicator than South Asia was CLMV (Cambodia, Laos, Myanmar, and Vietnam). In recent years, however, the gap has narrowed suggesting that CLMV could soon catch up with South Asia in terms of OGI.

Figure 1.2 shows that during the period 2002–15, OGI deteriorated in South Asia because five out of the six governance indicators fell. The only governance indicator that improved in South Asia during this period was the voice and accountability indicator. Jha and Zhuang

---

[1] WGI are composite governance indicators based on 30 underlying data sources (including surveys and perceptions).

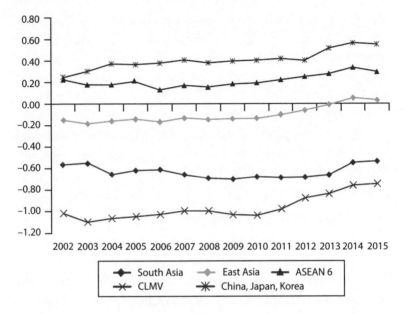

Figure 1.1   OGI by Subregions (2002–15)
Source: Calculated by authors based on data on World Governance Indicators.
Note: Indicator ranges from −2.5 to +2.5 in most cases with higher value correspond-
ing to better governance. Subregional score is the simple average of the country scores.

(2014) have, however, found that the voice and accountability and the
political stability indicators are the ones that are the least correlated with
economic growth. After 2012 or 2013, all six indicators have improved in
South Asia although several indicators are still below the 2002 level (for
example, government effectiveness and regulatory quality indicators).

OGI indicators for individual South Asian countries are shown in
Figure 1.3.[2] During the period between 2002 and 2015, OGI had
declined in Maldives and Pakistan. It had remained about the same
in India. The OGI had, however, improved somewhat in Bangladesh
and Nepal (after 2005), in Bhutan (after 2007), and in Sri Lanka (after
2008) when peace was restored in the country. After 2012 and 2013,
OGI indicators have improved in all South Asian countries.

---

[2] Individual time series are provided in Appendix A1.1 for those with
further interest in the subject.

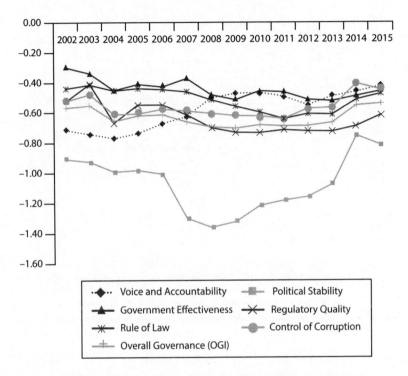

Figure 1.2 Governance Indicators for South Asian Countries (2002–15)
Source: Calculated by authors based on data on World Governance Indicators.
Note: Indicator ranges from −2.5 to +2.5 in most cases with higher value
corresponding to better governance. Subregional score is the simple average
of the country scores.

Table 1.1 shows the ranking of South Asian countries by OGI in
2002 and 2015. The data show that there exists a considerable governance gap in South Asia. In 2015, while Bhutan, Sri Lanka, and India
had the highest OGI in South Asia, Bangladesh, Nepal, Pakistan, and
Afghanistan had the lowest. The ranking of Maldives fell considerably
from 2002 to 2015.

Governance gap often results in gaps in the provision of public
services. Figure 1.4 shows that South Asia trails East Asia, Southeast
Asia, and Central Asia in terms of infrastructural quality, health, and
higher education. It is only in primary education where South Asia
ranks better than Central Asia.

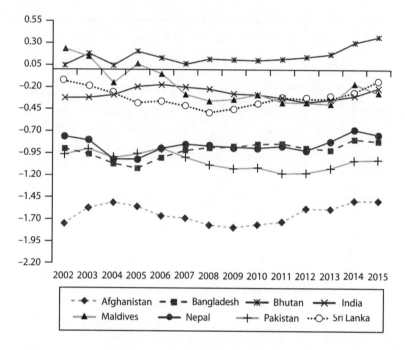

Figure 1.3   OGI for South Asian Countries (2002–15)
Source: Calculated by authors based on data on World Governance Indicators.
Note: Indicator ranges from −2.5 to +2.5 in most cases with higher value
corresponding to better governance. Subregional score is the simple average
of the country scores.

Table 1.1   Ranking of South Asian Countries by OGI

Ranking	2002	2015
1	Maldives	Bhutan
2	Bhutan	Sri Lanka
3	Sri Lanka	India
4	India	Maldives
5	Nepal	Nepal
6	Bangladesh	Bangladesh
7	Pakistan	Pakistan
8	Afghanistan	Afghanistan

Source: Calculated by authors based on data on World Governance Indicators,
World Bank.

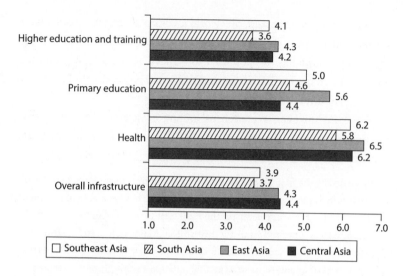

Figure 1.4 Quality of Public Services by Asian Subregion (2013)
Source: Estimated by ADB based on data from World Economic Forum, Global
Competitiveness Report.
Note: 1 = worst, 7 = best. Subregional score is the simple average of the country scores.

Long-term Economic Potential and the Need for Microeconomic Reforms

According to many economic forecasters, in the long run, most South
Asian countries are expected to register higher economic growth. This
is particularly true for India. Examples are the much-quoted Goldman
Sachs report which forecasts that India has the potential to grow by
8 per cent per annum until 2050 and at that time three of the four
largest economies in the world will be in Asia and in this order: China,
the United States, India, and Japan (Wilson and Purushothaman 2003).
The 2007 Goldman Sachs report even forecast that India will overtake
the US faster than expected and be the second-largest economy in the
world by 2050 after China (Poddar and Yi 2007).

An ADB report (2009) has suggested that India has the potential to
grow by 9.5 per cent per annum during the next 30 years and move
from a poor, developing economy status to an advanced economy in a
generation. By that time, Asia's share of world GDP would have also

exceeded 50 per cent and the world's centre of gravity would have shifted, once again, to Asia. More recently, Panagariya (2014) has argued that India has the potential to achieve an 8 per cent economic growth rate in the medium term and this could be accelerated to 10 per cent per annum with deeper reforms.

There is, however, a consensus among economic forecasters that for India to realize this growth potential, it must fully complete its economic reform process.[3] As the ADB report (2009) has noted

> Propelled by the first generation of macroeconomic reforms launched around 1990, which plucked the low-hanging fruit, India has been able to jumpstart growth. But it is still reliant on the basic institutional structures, practices, and mindsets inherited from the British Raj. Major policy and institutional reforms seemingly are undertaken only in times of crisis and under duress, not as part of a long-term strategy that anticipates and promotes changes.

In other words, India, and to a large extent, other South Asian countries need to implement additional reforms, at the microeconomic level, that is sectoral and second-generation reforms, focusing on governance and institutional changes to make markets work better. Unlike macroeconomic reforms, however, successful implementation of microeconomic reforms, particularly second-generation reforms, requires a wider consensus and political support in the concerned countries. As the ADB (2009) report notes, 'The dilemma is that such reforms generate benefits only in the long term, making them hard for policymakers

---

[3] Economic reforms alone will not be sufficient. The ADB report (2009) mentions two other requirements. First, as its fortunes become more closely linked with the world, India will have to bear the responsibility of preserving the global economic commons—such as climate change, free trade, and stable international capital movements. India will have to play a fair and constructive role in various forums such as the World Trade Organization (WTO), G20, and the UN. Second, five of the seven countries that border India are on the Foreign Policy 2008 list of failed states. India needs to promote greater stability in the region through regional cooperation. It has the size and clout to lead regional cooperation efforts in South Asia.

with short time horizons to set as priorities. Yet without them, policy measures to support sustained economic growth will become less and less effective'.

Modi Government in India and the Unfinished Reform Agenda in South Asia

In India, there has been a realization that the software and IT-enabled services (SITS) sector alone cannot provide employment to millions of labourers expected to be released from the agricultural sector as India moves up the development ladder. The development of the SITS sector in India was accidental.[4] It does not have strong linkages to the rest of the economy and accounts for only about 10 per cent of the Indian GDP (Konana et al. 2014). In all East Asian countries including China, fast growth in the manufacturing sector has led to economic transformation, modernization, and creation of jobs. This process has not started yet in India where, while the share of the service sector to GDP has increased from about 50 per cent in 1990–1 to about 65 per cent in 2011–12, the share of manufacturing has remained stagnant at around 15 per cent.

In September 2014, Prime Minister Narendra Modi launched a 'Make in India' campaign with a view to reversing this trend. Both foreign as well as domestic investors are to be encouraged and a number of initiatives have been launched. These include Skills India (the human resource component), Digital India (the communications component), and Smart Cities (development of 100 urban centres). The targets (Government of India 2014) are to:

1. Increase manufacturing sector growth to 12–14 per cent per annum over the medium term
2. Increase the share of manufacturing in GDP to 25 per cent by 2022
3. Create 100 million jobs in the sector by 2022

---

[4] Shortage of skilled labour in the US provided opportunity for Indian software companies to showcase their relatively skilled and cheap labour force.

Microeconomic reforms to improve the business environment underpin the 'Make in India' campaign.

The performance of labour-intensive manufacturing in India such as apparel, footwear, light consumer goods, and processing and assembling activities has been poor compared to East Asia. A handful of manufacturing industries that have done well in India—automobiles and auto parts, chemicals, engineering goods, and petroleum refining—are all capital-intensive with very few workers employed per unit of capital investment. The only way to create good jobs for the vast and rapidly rising workforce is to create the enabling environment for the growth of labour-intensive manufacturing. The focus in India is, however, to be in more sustainable new industries including solar technology, LED lighting, small cars, medical appliances, and weapons—rather than trying to follow China's success with consumer electronics in its drive to become a manufacturing powerhouse.

As Panagariya (2014) has argued, reviving the manufacturing sector in India is challenging and requires actions on many different fronts mainly in the microeconomic areas:[5]

1. End the paralysis at the level of central government
2. Forge a partnership with states
3. Reassure investors, both foreign and domestic
4. Restore health of the banks
5. Revive the agriculture sector
6. Accelerate infrastructure development
7. Enhance labour market flexibility
8. Improve land acquisition policies
9. Cut administrative red tape and reduce corruption
10. Implement effective privatization policies

---

[5] A number of first-generation reforms such as the introduction of efficient goods and service tax and realigning corporate income taxes with those in East Asia are also required. Stability of tax regimes, renouncing retrospective changes, and greater transparency are also required. The problem of high non-performing loans in several banks also needs to be addressed.

A detailed set of policy reforms required in India to support its drive to increase the manufacturing sector—both macroeconomic and structural microeconomic but mainly the latter—is presented in Appendix A1.2.

Prime Minister Narendra Modi's government has been implementing these reforms in a gradual and politically sustainable manner, especially because the government does not have a majority in the Upper House. During his first year in office, the prime minister implemented a number of economic reform measures (Box 1.1) but investor confidence has yet to turn around in a sustained manner. As in China, for sensitive reforms, an experimental approach has been adopted. A case in point is the liberalization of the labour market in Rajasthan where companies with up to 300 workers can fire workers easily. Several other states (Gujarat and Andhra Pradesh) have also partially liberalized their labour market. This is because a big-bang approach would be too disruptive in a large country like India (Rana and Hamid 1995).

The Modi government has made an important breakthrough in introducing a national sales tax, the Goods and Service Tax (GST), to replace overlapping federal and state taxes. The GST will transform Asia's third-largest economy into a single market, increase tax revenues, and facilitate business across borders. The GST was implemented in July 2017.

The major unfinished reform agenda for other South Asian countries are presented in Appendix A1.2. These matrices are based on a survey of economic reports of various international institutions (ADB, World Bank, and IMF) and other sources. The agenda is extensive and includes, among others, rural infrastructure, credit and incentives to the agricultural sector, restructuring private enterprises in most countries, improving tax administration in Nepal and Pakistan, implementing various standards and codes and best practices for the financial sector, improving labour market flexibility, and upgrading governance at all levels.

Box 1.1   Recent Reform Measures in India

- Auction of Natural Resources: The government has decided to auction all natural resources and telecom spectrum to stem corruption in awarding contracts.
- Energy Subsidies: The government took advantage of oil price declines to eliminate costly diesel subsidies providing a boast to the financial sector.
- Foreign Direct Investment (FDI): A series of laws have been enacted to increase the limits on FDI in sectors from insurance and pensions to defences, leaving India with one of the most open FDI regimes in emerging markets.
- Infrastructure Development: The government claims that road construction has increased from 2 kilometres a day under the previous administration to 12–14 kilometres a day and may reach 30 kilometres in two years. The government also claims that there is adequate power generation but transmission bottlenecks are still a concern.
- Taxation: Prime Minister Modi has promised to end 'tax terrorism' where authorities imposed 'retrospective' rules.
- Labour Market Reforms: These reforms are being implemented by India's states. Several states such as Rajasthan have partially liberalized labour laws.
- Social Reforms: Prime Minister Modi has been active on economic policy but his approach to social issues such as education and health has been less active.
- Urban Sector Reforms: Create 100 urban centres offering adequate water and electrical supplies, good sanitation and cleanliness, efficient public transport, safety for women, and green building.

Source: 'Narendra Modi: One Direction,' *Financial Times*, 17 May 2015.

APPENDIX A1.1

Table A1.1 Governance Indicators for South Asian Countries (2002–15)

Afghanistan

	2002	2003	2004	2005	2006	2007	2008	2009	2010	2011	2012	2013	2014	2015
Voice and Accountability	-1.57	-1.28	-1.25	-1.18	-1.19	-1.12	-1.24	-1.46	-1.48	-1.41	-1.32	-1.29	-1.18	-1.15
Political Stability	-2.21	-2.26	-2.30	-2.09	-2.23	-2.40	-2.69	-2.70	-2.55	-2.48	-2.42	-2.50	-2.42	-2.50
Government Effectiveness	-1.64	-1.18	-0.88	-1.23	-1.49	-1.40	-1.48	-1.50	-1.47	-1.46	-1.40	-1.40	-1.34	-1.34
Regulatory Quality	-1.87	-1.49	-1.50	-1.65	-1.67	-1.68	-1.60	-1.67	-1.53	-1.54	-1.21	-1.19	-1.13	-1.01
Rule of Law	-1.77	-1.67	-1.71	-1.72	-1.96	-1.92	-1.95	-1.91	-1.90	-1.93	-1.72	-1.67	-1.53	-1.59
Control of Corruption	-1.43	-1.55	-1.42	-1.46	-1.44	-1.59	-1.64	-1.51	-1.62	-1.55	-1.41	-1.43	-1.33	-1.34
Overall Governance (OGI)	-1.75	-1.57	-1.51	-1.55	-1.66	-1.69	-1.76	-1.79	-1.76	-1.73	-1.58	-1.58	-1.49	-1.49

Source: Calculated by authors based on data on World Governance Indicators.

Note: Political stability includes absence of violence and terrorism.

Bangladesh

	2002	2003	2004	2005	2006	2007	2008	2009	2010	2011	2012	2013	2014	2015
Voice and Accountability	-0.52	-0.63	-0.68	-0.60	-0.48	-0.54	-0.47	-0.30	-0.28	-0.32	-0.42	-0.42	-0.47	-0.49
Political Stability	-1.08	-1.14	-1.38	-1.84	-1.48	-1.50	-1.48	-1.54	-1.40	-1.39	-1.35	-1.63	-0.92	-1.15
Government Effectiveness	-0.70	-0.71	-0.78	-0.86	-0.77	-0.68	-0.71	-0.79	-0.75	-0.76	-0.83	-0.80	-0.77	-0.73
Regulatory Quality	-1.01	-0.92	-1.10	-1.03	-0.96	-0.91	-0.89	-0.85	-0.83	-0.80	-0.96	-0.91	-0.94	-0.93
Rule of Law	-0.90	-1.02	-1.00	-0.97	-0.89	-0.83	-0.76	-0.77	-0.79	-0.71	-0.91	-0.82	-0.72	-0.70
Control of Corruption	-1.18	-1.33	-1.49	-1.41	-1.42	-1.05	-1.02	-1.03	-1.02	-1.05	-0.87	-0.89	-0.91	-0.88
Overall Governance (OGI)	-0.90	-0.96	-1.07	-1.12	-1.00	-0.92	-0.89	-0.88	-0.85	-0.84	-0.89	-0.91	-0.79	-0.81

Source: Calculated by authors based on data on World Governance Indicators.
Note: Political stability includes absence of violence and terrorism.

Bhutan

	2002	2003	2004	2005	2006	2007	2008	2009	2010	2011	2012	2013	2014	2015
Voice and Accountability	-1.23	-1.19	-0.92	-1.03	-1.01	-0.84	-0.56	-0.51	-0.46	-0.46	-0.32	-0.18	-0.14	-0.06
Political Stability	0.60	0.91	1.17	1.30	1.31	0.62	0.75	0.82	0.77	0.86	0.81	0.80	1.08	1.10
Government Effectiveness	0.73	0.38	-0.14	0.28	0.18	0.19	0.22	0.48	0.57	0.62	0.48	0.40	0.27	0.41
Regulatory Quality	-0.47	-0.01	-0.81	-0.43	-0.60	-0.73	-0.83	-1.10	-1.19	-1.18	-1.12	-1.08	-1.01	-0.71
Rule of Law	0.09	0.23	0.36	0.36	0.26	0.37	0.37	0.18	0.12	0.14	0.19	0.26	0.35	0.51
Control of Corruption	0.58	0.75	0.62	0.75	0.66	0.74	0.77	0.81	0.82	0.74	0.82	0.84	1.27	0.98
Overall Governance (OGI)	0.05	0.18	0.05	0.21	0.13	0.06	0.12	0.11	0.10	0.12	0.14	0.18	0.30	0.37

Source: Calculated by authors based on data on World Governance Indicators.
Note: Political stability includes absence of violence and terrorism.

India

	2002	2003	2004	2005	2006	2007	2008	2009	2010	2011	2012	2013	2014	2015
Voice and Accountability	0.36	0.39	0.38	0.39	0.42	0.43	0.44	0.45	0.43	0.39	0.35	0.42	0.39	0.39
Political Stability	-1.24	-1.53	-1.22	-0.99	-1.06	-1.15	-1.10	-1.33	-1.23	-1.29	-1.25	-1.18	-0.98	-0.92
Government Effectiveness	-0.13	-0.07	-0.10	-0.08	-0.05	0.11	-0.03	-0.01	0.02	-0.01	-0.18	-0.17	-0.20	0.10
Regulatory Quality	-0.38	-0.36	-0.40	-0.24	-0.23	-0.27	-0.36	-0.30	-0.37	-0.33	-0.47	-0.46	-0.45	-0.39
Rule of Law	-0.04	0.10	0.04	0.16	0.19	0.11	0.09	0.02	-0.04	-0.11	-0.10	-0.08	-0.09	-0.06
Control of Corruption	-0.50	-0.44	-0.41	-0.40	-0.30	-0.42	-0.36	-0.48	-0.51	-0.57	-0.57	-0.56	-0.46	-0.38
Overall Governance (OGI)	-0.32	-0.32	-0.29	-0.19	-0.17	-0.20	-0.22	-0.27	-0.29	-0.32	-0.37	-0.34	-0.30	-0.21

Source: Calculated by authors based on data on World Governance Indicators.
Note: Political stability includes absence of violence and terrorism.

Maldives

	2002	2003	2004	2005	2006	2007	2008	2009	2010	2011	2012	2013	2014	2015
Voice and Accountability	-0.53	-0.92	-1.12	-0.99	-1.00	-0.91	-0.31	-0.08	-0.10	-0.21	-0.52	-0.44	-0.33	-0.50
Political Stability	1.03	1.02	0.54	0.83	0.80	0.09	-0.14	-0.22	-0.13	-0.21	-0.28	0.22	0.69	0.48
Government Effectiveness	0.28	0.01	-0.11	0.16	0.04	0.00	-0.27	-0.45	-0.21	-0.31	-0.16	-0.31	-0.37	-0.38
Regulatory Quality	0.74	0.57	-0.10	0.44	0.29	-0.02	-0.39	-0.41	-0.40	-0.40	-0.35	-0.45	-0.36	-0.42
Rule of Law	0.07	0.15	0.08	0.23	0.12	-0.02	-0.16	-0.17	-0.33	-0.57	-0.50	-0.71	-0.49	-0.52
Control of Corruption	-0.16	0.05	-0.17	-0.30	-0.53	-0.83	-0.87	-0.68	-0.53	-0.52	-0.44	-0.66	-0.11	-0.27
Overall Governance (OGI)	0.24	0.15	-0.15	0.06	-0.05	-0.28	-0.36	-0.34	-0.28	-0.37	-0.37	-0.39	-0.16	-0.27

Source: Calculated by authors based on data on World Governance Indicators.
Note: Political stability includes absence of violence and terrorism.

Nepal

	2002	2003	2004	2005	2006	2007	2008	2009	2010	2011	2012	2013	2014	2015
Voice and Accountability	−0.85	−0.92	−1.15	−1.19	−0.91	−0.59	−0.54	−0.47	−0.48	−0.50	−0.70	−0.56	−0.48	−0.43
Political Stability	−1.79	−1.95	−2.12	−2.11	−1.92	−1.92	−1.84	−1.62	−1.60	−1.42	−1.38	−1.11	−0.72	−0.93
Government Effectiveness	−0.49	−0.57	−0.75	−0.84	−0.78	−0.65	−0.76	−0.94	−0.86	−0.88	−0.99	−0.93	−0.83	−1.04
Regulatory Quality	−0.58	−0.42	−0.53	−0.50	−0.50	−0.55	−0.62	−0.70	−0.74	−0.72	−0.81	−0.85	−0.85	−0.79
Rule of Law	−0.53	−0.62	−0.76	−0.84	−0.63	−0.64	−0.72	−0.90	−1.01	−0.95	−0.79	−0.75	−0.68	−0.70
Control of Corruption	−0.32	−0.34	−0.81	−0.63	−0.63	−0.71	−0.72	−0.65	−0.65	−0.74	−0.83	−0.67	−0.54	−0.55
Overall Governance (OGI)	−0.76	−0.80	−1.02	−1.02	−0.90	−0.85	−0.87	−0.88	−0.89	−0.87	−0.92	−0.81	−0.68	−0.74

Source: Calculated by authors based on data on World Governance Indicators.

Note: Political stability includes absence of violence and terrorism.

Pakistan

	2002	2003	2004	2005	2006	2007	2008	2009	2010	2011	2012	2013	2014	2015
Voice and Accountability	−1.22	−1.26	−1.23	−1.06	−0.90	−0.97	−0.87	−0.90	−0.84	−0.85	−0.87	−0.83	−0.76	−0.76
Political Stability	−1.70	−1.58	−1.56	−1.76	−2.04	−2.43	−2.57	−2.63	−2.67	−2.81	−2.68	−2.60	−2.40	−2.54
Government Effectiveness	−0.39	−0.39	−0.45	−0.42	−0.37	−0.46	−0.70	−0.78	−0.76	−0.81	−0.79	−0.79	−0.75	−0.66
Regulatory Quality	−0.79	−0.73	−0.88	−0.61	−0.45	−0.50	−0.57	−0.55	−0.58	−0.63	−0.73	−0.70	−0.69	−0.62
Rule of Law	−0.75	−0.73	−0.83	−0.88	−0.84	−0.88	−0.98	−0.84	−0.74	−0.91	−0.91	−0.87	−0.78	−0.79
Control of Corruption	−0.92	−0.73	−1.06	−1.04	−0.76	−0.74	−0.80	−1.04	−1.07	−1.05	−1.06	−0.93	−0.81	−0.76
Overall Governance (OGI)	−0.97	−0.90	−1.00	−0.96	−0.89	−1.00	−1.08	−1.12	−1.11	−1.18	−1.17	−1.12	−1.03	−1.02

Source: Calculated by authors based on data on World Governance Indicators.

Note: Political stability includes absence of violence and terrorism.

Sri Lanka

	2002	2003	2004	2005	2006	2007	2008	2009	2010	2011	2012	2013	2014	2015
Voice and Accountability	−0.15	−0.12	−0.19	−0.21	−0.30	−0.43	−0.46	−0.49	−0.52	−0.56	−0.60	−0.62	−0.73	−0.37
Political Stability	−0.85	−0.88	−1.06	−1.19	−1.43	−1.74	−1.80	−1.35	−0.92	−0.70	−0.71	−0.59	−0.33	−0.03
Government Effectiveness	−0.06	−0.20	−0.40	−0.29	−0.18	−0.09	−0.12	−0.12	−0.18	−0.10	−0.24	−0.16	0.09	0.01
Regulatory Quality	0.18	0.10	−0.04	−0.35	−0.25	−0.26	−0.35	−0.26	−0.20	−0.11	−0.12	−0.15	−0.08	−0.05
Rule of Law	0.32	0.24	0.20	0.15	0.19	0.14	0.00	−0.07	−0.08	−0.07	−0.11	−0.25	−0.15	0.07
Control of Corruption	−0.24	−0.26	−0.14	−0.37	−0.18	−0.10	−0.19	−0.37	−0.40	−0.37	−0.24	−0.22	−0.34	−0.37
Overall Governance (OGI)	−0.13	−0.19	−0.27	−0.38	−0.36	−0.41	−0.49	−0.44	−0.38	−0.32	−0.33	−0.33	−0.26	−0.12

Source: Calculated by authors based on data on World Governance Indicators.

Note: Political stability includes absence of violence and terrorism.

APPENDIX A1.2
Unfinished Reform Agenda in South Asian Countries

Table A1.2a   Unfinished Reform Agenda: Afghanistan

I. Macroeconomic and Structural Reforms	
Fiscal Reforms and Public Sector Management	• Need to gradually achieve fiscal sustainability to reduce the reliance on donor support through revenue mobilization, better expenditure management, and service delivery. • Introduce the VAT, and consider other new sources of tax revenues (for example, Excise Tax). • Need to expand public development expenditures on essential infrastructure and service delivery.
Financial Sector Reforms	• Strengthen the banking sector by improving regulation and enforcement. • Promote wider use of mobile banking services and microfinance lending; promote bank penetration in rural areas • Increase financial literacy among the public and ensure adequate financial consumer protection. • Banks should move from traditional relationship-based lending to market-oriented lending.

II.A. Microeconomic Reforms: Sectoral	
Agriculture Sector Reforms and Land Issues	• Need to increase investments in irrigation and extension services. • Need to focus on subsectors with the greatest potential, irrigated wheat, livestock, and horticulture. • Need to improve efforts to build and improve downstream agro-processing activities.
Industrial Policy and Public Sector Reforms	• Need to tap the potential of extractive industries sector through legislative reforms and financing.
Infrastructure Development	• Need to engage proactively to establish the country's role as a transit route linking energy-rich Central Asian countries with energy-hungry South Asian countries. • Need to engage more actively with downstream riparian countries to secure necessary water resources. • Improve grid connectivity in the rural areas to reduce the urban–rural gap in access to power supply. • Need to prevent further power plant development project delays. • Needs a new railway strategy to improve operations and maintenance capacity. • Needs urgent action to improve operation and maintenance of roads; Restructuring and improvement of urban transportation remains a priority.
II.B. Microeconomic Reforms: Governance and Institutional	
Public Administration and Civil Service Reforms	• Need to clarify the subnational–national governance framework, including removing overlapping institutional mandates. • Need to improve the capacity of core civil service and reduce reliance on parallel civil service. • Enhance the role of provincial line departments and administrations in both planning and budget execution. • Establish institutions at the village level for better district policy coordination.
Labour Market Reforms	• Promote the payment of equal wages to women workers and provide equal opportunities to women in employment. • Strictly enforce labour laws that prohibit child labour and forced labour practices. • Develop individualized small business startup programs with market study, micro-credit, and training components.

(Cont'd)

Table A1.2a (*Cont'd*)

Corruption Control	• Need to strengthen public financial management.
Legal Reforms/ Property Rights	• Enact Anti-Money Laundering (AML) legislation consistent with the Financial Action Task Force (FATF) recommendation and adopt a national strategy that will include money laundering and terrorist financing risk assessments and measures to investigate and confiscate the proceeds of crime. • Implement measures to enhance the transparency of non-profit organizations.
Regulatory Reforms	• Need to strengthen the central bank's financial supervision department. • Strengthen prudential regulations and lending practices in the banking sector.

Sources: Data from Afghanistan Government (2013); IMF (2014a); The Asia Foundation (2011); World Bank (2014a); World Bank (2014b).

Table A1.2b   Unfinished Reform Agenda: Bangladesh

I. Macroeconomic and Structural Reforms	
Fiscal Reforms and Public Sector Management	• Raise fuel and electricity prices to lower subsidy cost. • Implement tax measures that reduce exemptions and exclusions, improve tax administration by simplifying laws and procedures, and reduce scope for evasion by introducing advanced auditing and enforcement techniques. • Encourage voluntary compliance by simplifying and automating tax payment system and by curbing the discretionary power of tax officials.
Monetary Policy Reforms	• Adopt stronger risk management and controls, and place ceilings on credit growth by state-owned banks based on their performance and financial soundness.
Financial Sector Reforms	• Develop a liquid bond market to expand sources for private sector financing.
International Trade	• Tariffs need to be cut, and the dispersion in rates reduced to enhance competitiveness. • Trade infrastructure and logistics, including port services and automation, need to be improved to lower transaction costs and facilitate faster clearance of goods.

II.A. Microeconomic Reforms: Sectoral	
Agriculture Sector Reforms and Land Issues	• Improve rural and 'farm-to-market' roads. • Support further productivity improvements in the agriculture sector through improved farm technology. • Enhance regional water cooperation with countries in the region.
Infrastructure Development	• Improve electricity and transport-related infrastructure and logistics. • Improve regional transport connectivity with surrounding countries.

II.B. Microeconomic Reforms: Governance and Institutional	
Public Administration and Civil Service Reforms	• Projects under public–private partnerships need to be expedited by developing capacity in line agencies to design, bid, and award such contracts.
Labour Market Reforms	• For the garments industry, develop skilled candidates for middle and senior management, needed both to improve labour relations and to raise production efficiency through better quality control, labelling, and shipment. • Improve labour safety standards, wages, and working conditions.
Legal Reforms/ Property Rights	• Implement a cohesive land-titling project since large share of land parcels are owned with inadequate documentation. • Enhance the capacity of the Land Office.
Regulatory Reforms	• Improve oversight over fire and building safety standards to prevent industrial accidents especially for the garments industry.

Sources: Data from ADB (2014b); Rahman (2014); World Bank (2014c).

Table A1.2c Unfinished Reform Agenda: Bhutan

I. Macroeconomic and Structural Reforms	
Financial Sector Reforms	• Develop a credit information system for more efficient provision of credit. • Introduce targeted micro-credit programs.
International Trade	• Improve trade-related transport logistics such as harmonization of documents and procedures.

(*Cont'd*)

Table A1.2c   (*Cont'd*)

II.A. Microeconomic Reforms: Sectoral	
Agriculture Sector Reforms and Land Issues	• Provide crop insurance schemes to help farmers manage shocks due to price fluctuations and calamities. • Agribusiness, which is an emerging sector in the country, needs to be developed further and the government should put in place policies and incentives to encourage and support farmers.
Industrial Policy and Public Sector Reforms	• Encourage private sector development to create more jobs outside the agricultural sector.
Infrastructure Development	• Improve rural road access throughout the country. • Encourage private investment in hydropower sector using public/private partnerships and subcontracting.

Sources: Data from ADB (2014b); Bhutan (2014); World Bank (2014d).

Table A1.2d   Unfinished Reform Agenda: India

I. Macroeconomic and Structural Reforms	
Fiscal Reforms and Public Sector Management	• Improve and streamline the GST and simplify the direct tax system. • Cut subsidies to the middle class more aggressively including eliminating petrol and diesel subsidies. • Pass the Insurance Laws Amendment Bill which seeks to raise the foreign direct investment (FDI) cap in the sector to 49 per cent. • Reduce corporate income tax rates • Multiple taxes, including taxes on intra-state transactions, need to be removed.
Monetary Policy Reforms	• Strengthen the Reserve Bank's independence. • Promote consolidation of the banking sector • Address the health of public sector banks which suffer from high level of non-performing loans.
Financial Sector Reforms	• Consumer protection system should be created together with the creation of a financial redress agency with presence in every district. • Institutionalize micro-prudential regulations. • Create a resolution corporation that identifies distressed financial firms and closes them down. • Create a database covering the Indian financial sector for systemic risk management.
International Trade	• Enhance trade linkages with other countries, especially in East Asia.

II.A. Microeconomic Reforms: Sectoral

Agriculture Sector Reforms and Land Issues	• Privatize the Food Corporation of India to curb corruption and leakages in India's food grain distribution system. • Amend the Agriculture Produce Marketing Committee Act by delisting fruits and vegetables which would allow farmers to sell to anyone.
Industrial Policy and Public Sector Reforms	• Reform bankruptcy laws which discourage firms to enter the formal sector. • Privatize the railways sector by establishing a number of companies. • Privatize public sector enterprises especially those involved in manufacturing.
Infrastructure Development	• Improve coordination between various government agencies to accelerate India's road building program. • Privatize Air India which absorbs a substantial amount of subsidy. • Relax the floor-space index and allow taller buildings that can help improve the urban environment. • Improve gateway infrastructure by improving capacity of ports and rail and road connectivity to ports. • Introduce 'best practices' in custom procedures.

II.B. Microeconomic Reforms: Governance and Institutional

Public Administration and Civil Service Reforms	• Implement reforms that enhance the quality and productivity in the civil service. • Reform the Indian Police Service to increase its autonomy and accountability. • Improve centre-state relations by decentralizing functions such provision of public goods to states and at the same time improving relations between the central government and the states.
Labour Market Reforms	• Create a 'resource pool' to retrain retrenched workers and teach them new skills. • Rationalize labour laws (presently numbering more than 50) and reduce it to four or five laws that cover all labour-related issues such as minimum wage, social security, and so on.
Corruption Control	• Bar persons charged with heinous crimes from running for office. • Fully implement the provisions of the Lokpal and Lokayuktas Act.

(Cont'd)

Table A1.2d (*Cont'd*)

Legal Reforms/ Property Rights	• Law Commission should be given additional resources to revise, repeal, and update old laws. • Approve and implement the Judicial Standards and Accountability Bill which aims to improve the quality and integrity of the judiciary. • Need to increase budget and human capacity of the judiciary to make the judicial system more efficient. • Repeal the Land Acquisition Law to make it easier for companies to acquire land especially for infrastructure projects.
Regulatory Reforms	• Insulate utilities (specially electricity companies) from interference by state governments.

Sources: Data from ADB (2014b); Bhagwati and Panagariya (2013); Debroy et al. (2014); World Bank (2014e).

Table A1.2e Unfinished Reform Agenda: Maldives

I. Macroeconomic and Structural Reforms	
Fiscal Reforms and Public Sector Management	• Improve the effectiveness of targeted subsidy programs, for example , in the electricity sector. • Need to consolidate and rationalize the tax structure.
International Trade	• Potential sectors with key comparative advantages include transport, energy, education, health, financial services and Information and Communication Technology (ICT).
II.B. Microeconomic Reforms: Governance and Institutional	
Public Administration and Civil Service Reforms	• Reduce the size of the civil service.
Labour Market Reforms	• Generate jobs and diversify the economy away from tourism into other sectors. • Develop specialized skill for diversification of the economy.

Sources: Data from United Nations Development Programme (2014); World Bank (2014f).

Table A1.2f Unfinished Reform Agenda: Nepal

I. Macroeconomic and Structural Reforms

Fiscal Reforms and Public Sector Management	• Fiscal policy needs to support growth through higher public spending in key areas such as: power generation/distribution, transportation, and so on. • Expand or create more fiscal space to finance additional social spending and investment by, for example, reducing implicit subsidies to the Nepal Oil Corporation and reducing its losses.
Monetary Policy	• Need to control the volatility and excess liquidity in the banking system through sterilization measures. • Reconsider the proposed cap on interest rate margins to improve access to credit. • Closely monitor the evolution of bank balance sheets and new loans to reduce financial sector vulnerability.
Financial Sector Reforms	• Need to improve access to credit by small- and medium-scale enterprises. • Need to restructure public sector banks. • Adopt the planned Financial Sector Development Strategy.
International Trade	• Need to improve terms of trade through targeted interventions, revamping of export subsidies, and enhancing trade finance. • Need to overcome supply-side constraints, especially high transit costs due to being landlocked. • Improve implementation of bilateral transit treaty which facilitates the export of goods from Nepal to India.
Exchange Rate	• Need to continually evaluate the peg to the Indian rupee.

II.A. Microeconomic Reforms: Sectoral

Agriculture Sector Reforms and Land Issues	• Enhance agricultural productivity by:
	  i. Focusing on irrigation infrastructure development and its management.
	  ii. Rationalizing and streamlining input subsidies.
	• Promote development of agribusiness by:
	  i. Enhancing the role of the private/cooperative sector in input supply.
	  ii. Developing agricultural value chains and strengthening the Agribusiness Promotion Unit under the Ministry of Agricultural Development.

(Cont'd)

Table A1.2f   (*Cont'd*)

	• Support crop diversification in remote areas by:
	  i. Developing area-specific plans for technological upgradation in remote regions.
	  ii. Identifying and supporting production of non-traditional crops for the Indian market.
	• Modernize land policy and administration by reviewing existing land laws and regulations.
	• Enhance the government's strategic policy framework for the agriculture sector.

Industrial Policy and Public Sector Reforms	• Need to establish a more robust competition authority.
Infrastructure Development	• Initiate electricity tariff reform for eventual full cost recovery. • Develop a road map for power sector development. • Address Kathmandu's growing urban transport challenges. • Revive the proposed fast track road between Kathmandu and the Terai plains.

II.B. Microeconomic Reforms: Governance and Institutional

Public Administration and Civil Service Reforms	• Strengthen the office of the auditor general. • Develop a new framework to adapt the civil service to the new federal structure. • Strengthen health insurance and contributory pension schemes to civil servants and implement an effective promotion and transfer policy. • Improve procurement and contracting in terms of both competition among contractors and enhancing technical capacity for proper procurement planning.
Labour Market Reforms	• Need to improve the efficiency of labour market institutions to ensure fair enforcement of labour standards. • Need to focus on employment-based infrastructure investments which could lead to employment creation, reduce inequality and, enhance rural productivity.
Corruption Control	• Anti-corruption agency (CIAA) must develop comprehensive whistle-blower protection legislation. • Improve awareness about the Right to Information Act and also the capacity for its implementation.

Legal Reforms/ Property Rights	• Need to implement the legal framework for anti-money laundering and terrorism finance. • Enhance the capacity of the Department of Money Laundering Investigation and the special court to handle anti-money laundering cases. • Alleviate the regulatory burden on firms by simplifying bureaucratic procedures and making laws and regulations transparent—especially in the areas of licensing and taxes. • Introduce community-based land reforms to redistribute surplus land to the landless and land-poor households.
Regulatory Reforms	• Improve the credit information bureau and implement the long-overdue secured transactions framework. • Update the country's investment legislation and investment procedures to increase transparency.

Sources: Data from International Labour Organization (2013); IMF (2014b); Shanti (2014); Transparency International (2010); World Bank (2014g); World Bank (2014h); World Trade Organization (2012).

Table A1.2g   Unfinished Reform Agenda: Pakistan

I. Macroeconomic and Structural Reforms	
Fiscal Reforms and Public Sector Management	• Need to strengthen tax administration by expanding the income tax net, and strengthening the administration and transparency of other taxes (such as sales taxes, custom taxes, and excise taxes).
Monetary Policy	• Adjust policy interest rate to ensure positive real interest rates. • Re-evaluate the level of minimum capital requirement for the financial sector.
Financial Sector Reforms	• Need to reduce non-performing loans (NPLs) by speeding up recovery processes, providing favourable tax treatment for write-offs, and supporting markets for distressed debt. • Enact amendments to the State Bank of Pakistan law to strengthen its autonomy and enhanced governance structure. • The Deposit Protection Fund Act and the Securities Bill Act need to be finalized and implemented.

(Cont'd)

Table A1.2g (*Cont'd*)

International Trade	• Simplify tariff rates and eliminate the statutory regulatory orders that establish special tariff rates. • Improve trade relations with Pakistan's commercial partners, especially those in South Asia. • Consider establishing special economic zones.
Exchange Rate	• Fine-tune the exchange rate policy to gear towards rebuilding international reserves. • Need to allow greater flexibility of the exchange rate.

II.A. Microeconomic Reforms: Sectoral

Agriculture Sector Reforms and Land Issues	• Need to narrow the substantial yield gap between high-value crops and major cereals as that would boost agricultural productivity. • Need to increase spending on public agricultural research and human resource capacity. • Need to resolve the problem of inefficient water use by setting up a more efficient water allocation system to increase farmers' access to water.
Industrial Policy and Public Sector Reforms	• Finalize the implementation of the plans to import liquefied natural gas to improve energy supply. • Need to maintain strong commitment to privatization plans of public sector enterprises • Need to build the institutional capacity of the Water and Power Development Authority (WAPDA). • Encourage the conversion of power plants from oil-based to coal-based plants.
Infrastructure Development	• Enhance investment in basic infrastructure services. • Improve connectivity between cities and as well as mobility within cities. • Integrate land use planning with transportation and infrastructure to proactively manage urban growth and enhance liveability. • Need to improve the maintenance of and new investment in the transport system. • Initiate performance contracts to tackle losses, raise payment compliance, and improve energy efficiency and service delivery in public sector energy companies.

II.B. Microeconomic Reforms: Governance and Institutional

Public Administration and Civil Service Reforms	• Improve the efficiency of the civil service at all levels (federal, provincial and local). • Improve inter-governmental coordination to make decentralization work: give greater autonomy to local government for resource mobilization. • Promote greater use of government services online.

Labour Market Reforms	• Introduce education reforms through better governance and collaboration with private sector to ensure that necessary skills are taught. • Need to design a structured set of national regulations to guide inspection policy towards 'best practice' standards. • Need to increase investment in rural development coupled with livelihood programs to provide more employment opportunities to the rural population. • Provide poor women with access to resources and services to increase rural productivity and non-farm rural employment.
Corruption Control	• Cease attempts to replace the National Accountability Bureau with a new commission, which has a more limited scope and jurisdiction. • Strengthen the Right to Information Bill to meet international standards and raise public awareness. • Develop a comprehensive whistle-blower protection legislation.
Legal Reforms/ Property Rights	• Need to ease business regulations and procedures across a wide range of areas, both at the central and the provincial level. • Modernize land entitlements and transactions and ensure transparency. • Effectively implement the anti-money laundering framework. • Refine land regulations, bye-laws, and land disposition to increase land supply.

Sources: Data from IMF (2014c); Refaqat. et al. (2014); Transparency International (2010); World Bank (2014i).

Table A1.2h Unfinished Reform Agenda: Sri Lanka

I. Macroeconomic and Structural Reforms	
Financial Sector Reforms	• Amend the Securities and Exchange Commission Law to build a more vibrant capital market. • Improve access to credit by small- and medium-scale enterprises.
International Trade	• Introduce more competition in sectors such as airport services, cargo handling, and port services where the government has a monopoly
Exchange Rate	• Adjust the exchange rate to improve the competitiveness of the country's exports.

(Cont'd)

Table A1.2h   (*Cont'd*)

II.A. Microeconomic Reforms: Sectoral	
Agriculture Sector Reforms and Land Issues	• Provide incentives for tea replanting and improving labour productivity in the sector.
Industrial Policy and Public Sector Reforms	• Rationalize the incentive structure in the industrial sector to help enhance resource allocation and efficiency. • Upgrade the manufacturing and services base, so that employment generation shifts away from the current low-productivity sectors such as construction, tourism, and retail trade.
Infrastructure Development	• Upgrade rural access roads and rehabilitate national roads. • Diversify the fuel mix in the energy sector and lessen reliance on oil-based energy generation source.
II.B. Microeconomic Reforms: Governance and Institutional	
Public Administration and Civil Service Reforms	• Depoliticize the use of the 'Urgent Bill' provision of the Constitution which allows the government to pass controversial laws under an expedited process reserved for emergencies.
Labour Market Reforms	• Provide systems and incentives to give the labour force the types of skills needed for a knowledge economy. • Consider gradual increases in the retirement age of formal-sector employees • Increase female labour force participation and address the high youth and female unemployment and its causes. • Extend pension coverage for workers in the informal sector, where the majority of the most vulnerable workers are employed.
Corruption Control	• Improve transparency and accountability mechanisms especially in state-owned enterprises to reduce opportunities for corruption.
Regulatory Reforms	• Set up an independent Food Authority by statute dedicated to food control administration.

Sources: Data from ADB (2014b); Aturupane et al. (2014); Transparency International (2012, 2014); World Bank (2012, 2014j); World Bank (2012).

2

ECONOMIC RELATIONS BETWEEN SOUTH ASIA AND EAST ASIA
Trends, Potential, and Impacts

Together with its economic reform program, in 1991, India initiated its 'Look East' Policy (LEP) to enhance its economic relations with Southeast Asian countries. Since then, the focus and objectives of LEP have broadened to cover all East Asian countries and building economic, institutional, and defence links with the region. In 2015, the Modi government upgraded its LEP to an 'Act East' policy. This was in order to intensify its outreach to key partners to boost India's economic growth, to balance externally against China, and to expand its global role (Rajendram 2014). Bangladesh also adopted an LEP in late 2002 (Islam and Khanam 2014), followed by Pakistan, which adopted its 'Vision East Asia' in 2003 (Malik 2015). Other South Asian countries have not formally adopted an LEP but have taken a number of actions to boost trade, investment, and connectivity with East Asia (Table 2.1).

India has been an active participant in various consultative meetings and dialogues initiated by ASEAN, such as the ASEAN Regional Forum, East Asia Summit, and the Mekong–Ganga Cooperation, and holds summit-level dialogues with ASEAN. India, Bangladesh, and Sri Lanka are also members of the Asia-Pacific Trade Agreement. India, Bangladesh, Sri Lanka, Nepal, and Bhutan are members of the BIMSTEC. India is also a member of the Mekong–Ganga cooperation.

Table 2.1   Policy Actions by South Asian Countries to Promote Economic
Relations with East Asia: Some Highlights

1975	• Bangkok Agreement was signed by Bangladesh, India, Laos, Korea, Sri Lanka, and China.
1985	• SAARC was established with Bangladesh, Bhutan, India, Maldives, Nepal, Pakistan, and Sri Lanka as members. Afghanistan joined in 2007.
1991	• India adopted the Look East Policy to strengthen economic relationships with East Asian countries.
1992	• ASEAN Free Trade Area (AFTA) signed. • India became a sectoral dialogue partner of ASEAN.
1995	• India became a full dialogue partner of ASEAN.
1996	• India was admitted to the ASEAN Regional Forum.
1997	• Bay of Bengal Initiative for Multi-Sectoral Technical and Economic Cooperation (BIMSTEC) was established. Present members include Bangladesh, Bhutan, India, Myanmar, Nepal, Sri Lanka, and Thailand.
2000	• Mekong–Ganga Cooperation was established with India, Thailand, Myanmar, Cambodia, Laos, and Vietnam in November.
2002	• India–ASEAN partnership was upgraded to summit-level dialogue. • Bangladesh introduced Look East policy.
2003	• A Framework Agreement on Comprehensive Economic Cooperation (CECA) between India and ASEAN was signed, incorporating free trade agreement. • Pakistan developed its Vision East Asia policy.
2004	• Long-Term Partnership for Peace, Progress and Shared Prosperity was signed by India and ASEAN. • BIMSTEC FTA Framework Agreement was signed.
2005	• East Asia Summit was established and India became a member. • India-Singapore CECA became effective in August. • The Bangkok Agreement was renamed as the Asia-Pacific Trade Agreement (APTA).
2006	• China became an observer of SAARC.
2007	• China–Pakistan FTA became effective in June.
2008	• Pakistan–Malaysia Closer Economic Partnership became effective in January.
2010	• Comprehensive Asia Development Plan was submitted by Economic Research Institute for ASEAN and East Asia to East Asia Summit which proposed the Mekong–India Economic corridor and the Trilateral Highway projects. • Master Plan on ASEAN Connectivity was approved.

- ASEAN–India Comprehensive Economic Cooperation Agreement (in goods trade) became effective in January and a comprehensive pact on services and investment was finalized in December 2012.
- India–Korea Comprehensive Economic Partnership Agreement became effective in January.

2011
- Malaysia–India Comprehensive Economic Cooperation Agreement became effective in July.
- Japan–India Comprehensive Economic Cooperation Agreement became effective in August.

2012
- Negotiation on Regional Comprehensive Economic Partnership started in November.
- 20th Commemorative ASEAN–India Summit was held in December.

2013
- Pakistan–Indonesia FTA became effective in September.
- Ministerial-Level Forum for Bangladesh–China–India–Myanmar (BCIM) Economic Corridor initiated.

2014
- Bangladesh and China signed a memorandum of understanding (MOU) to set up China Economic and Industrial Zone in Chittagong.

2015
- The second phase of China–Pakistan Free Trade Agreement was negotiated in October.
- China–Pakistan Economic Corridor and BCIM Economic Corridor are officially classified as 'closely' related to the Belt and Road Initiative of China.
- The first investment project under China's Silk Road Fund is the $1.65 billion Karot hydropower project in Pakistan.
- India's 'Look East' Policy was upgraded to 'Act East' Policy.
- India and Singapore updated their relationship to a strategic partnership.
- ASEAN Economic Community came into effect.

2016
- Asia Infrastructure Investment Bank (AIIB) was launched in January. Founding members from South Asia include Bangladesh, India, Maldives, Nepal, Pakistan, and Sri Lanka.

FTAs under Negotiation

- BIMSTEC Free Trade Agreement
- Regional Comprehensive Economic Partnership
- India–Indonesia Comprehensive Economic Cooperation Arrangement
- Pakistan–Singapore Free Trade Agreement
- India–Thailand Free Trade Agreement
- China– Sri Lanka Free Trade Agreement
- China–Maldives Free Trade Agreement
- Pakistan–Thailand Free Trade Agreement

Source: Compiled by the authors.

As part of its LEP, India has signed FTAs, including Comprehensive Economic Cooperation and Comprehensive Economic Partnership Agreements, with ASEAN as a whole and two members, Singapore and Malaysia. India has also signed FTAs with Japan and Korea. FTAs with Thailand and Indonesia and the RCEP are in the pipeline. Pakistan has signed FTAs with China, Malaysia, and Indonesia and those with Singapore and Thailand are in the pipeline. In contrast to India and Pakistan, other South Asian countries appear to be more cautious in signing FTAs. Sri Lanka and Maldives are negotiating FTAs with China.

In the area of connectivity and infrastructure development, however, South Asian countries are more active. All eight SAARC members, aside from Afghanistan and Bhutan, are founding members of the AIIB. Also, the China–Pakistan Economic Corridor and the BCIM Economic Corridor have been reported to be 'closely' related to China's Belt and Road Initiative. The Karot hydropower project in Pakistan is likely to be the first project to be financed by China's Silk Road Fund.

Economic reforms and LEPs implemented both formally and informally by the South Asian countries have continued to enhance economic linkages between South Asia and East Asia. Trade between South Asia and East Asia has surged during the past decade and a half, albeit from a low base, and China has become India's largest trading partner. Investment flows from East Asia to South Asia are also increasing.

This chapter argues that South Asian countries need to embark on the second round of economic reforms and LEP2 to:

1. Link themselves to production networks in East Asia
2. Develop production networks in manufacturing and services within their region.

Such policies would allow both regions to benefit mutually, not only from static complementarities of the Ricardo and Heckscher–Ohlin type (or twentieth-century trade, as Baldwin [2013] prefers) but also from dynamic complementarities based on augmented product fragmentation and new economic geography theories pioneered by Jones and Kierzkowski (1990) and Kimura and Ando (2005).[1] As in East Asia, economic integration between the two regions would increase and so would economic growth and welfare. Moreover, South Asian integration would increase and LEP2 would also poise South Asia to benefit from the gradual but encouraging opening up of Myanmar, which is a node for South Asia–East Asia relations and connectivity. Benefits from joining production networks (or twenty-first-century trade) stem from network externalities, which means that each individual country's gain increases with the size of the network (Baldwin 2013).

LEP2 will be a win-win situation for all countries in South Asia and East Asia as the policies are likely to enhance their integration and economic dynamism. It will also help to reinvigorate economic integration in South Asia, which is among the least integrated regions of the world. The details will be discussed in the third section of this chapter.

Before World War II, South Asia was a well-integrated part of the British Empire. Then in 1947, Pakistan and India became independent. At that time, more than half of Pakistan's imports came from India and nearly two-thirds of its exports went to India. Similar trade relations existed between India and Sri Lanka, where immigrants from South India had settled much earlier. Total trade volumes among the countries of the region were estimated at around 20 per cent of total trade before the partition in 1947 (World Bank 2004). After the separation of Pakistan, tensions between the two countries increased. As bickering over water rights, territory, and currency valuation increased, trade between Pakistan and India diminished. In the 1950s and 1960s, all the countries in South Asia pursued import substitution development strategies while eschewing export promotion. The level of intra-regional trade fell to about 4 per cent by the end of the 1950s and decreased further to 2 per cent by 1967 (Rana 2012a).

---

[1] Using firm-level data from Malaysia and Thailand, which are important participants in East Asia's production network, Wignaraja, Kruger, and Tuazon (2013) have found that participation in production networks raises profits and is also associated with technological upgrades and higher R&D expenditure. Over time, production networks have also deepened and spread from electronics to other sectors such as automobiles, televisions, and cameras.

The level of intra-regional trade in South Asia began to increase only after the countries in the region abandoned import substitution policies and began to adopt trade liberalization measures in the 1990s. In recent years, the level of intra-regional trade has increased to around 5 per cent of total trade, but South Asia is still among the least integrated regions of the world (Rana 2012a).

The reason for the low level of intra-regional trade in South Asia is not the lack of official institutional arrangements to promote regional cooperation. Just like ASEAN, South Asia has SAARC. In the area of trade, the SAARC has the South Asian Preferential Trading Agreement (SAPTA), which subsequently became the South Asian Free Trade Agreement (SAFTA). For money and finance, they have the Network of Central Bank Governors and Finance Secretaries of the SAARC Region (SAARCFINANCE). The South Asian Growth Quadrangle and SASEC are concerned with connectivity.

There are many reasons for the low level of integration in South Asia. The most obvious ones are the hostility between India and Pakistan and other countries, and India's failure to promote greater stability in the region through regional cooperation (Rana 2012). India prefers bilateral negotiations rather than multilateral ones. This political impasse has no easy solution and the recent 'step-by-step' improvements in India–Pakistan relations could reverse quickly. While East Asian countries have pushed ahead with the regional cooperation agenda despite political conflicts, conflicts in South Asia have been serious stumbling blocks and have suffocated integration efforts. Since a direct approach to promoting integration through regional cooperation policies in South Asia has not worked well, this chapter makes the case for an indirect approach. The indirect approach comprises implementing the second round of LEP2 by South Asia.

In the above context, this chapter is organized as follows. The next section reviews trends in economic linkages between South Asia and East Asia. The last section assesses the potential for and impacts of economic linkages between the two subregions using both the static complementary measures and the more dynamic measures focusing on the potential for vertical integration under the 'augmented product fragmentation and new economic geography' theories.

Economic Linkages between South Asia and East Asia

South Asia's total merchandise trade (exports plus imports) to East Asia has grown exponentially in absolute terms albeit from a low base (Figure 2.1). It increased about twenty-fold during the period 1990 to 2015, from $12.7 billion to $227.5 billion. The annual growth rate was relatively moderate until 2002 but it has surged since. The exception was in 2009 when it dipped because of the global economic crisis and again in 2012 and 2015 when the global economic environment was not favourable. As expected, the two largest components of this trade are the bilateral trade between the two 'giant' economies of India and China, and the trade between India and ASEAN. The former has overtaken the latter since 2009.

There are, however, a number of issues that should be considered:

1. India accounts for the largest share of South Asia–East Asia trade, with Pakistan a distant second. Other countries trade much less with East Asia (Table 2.2).
2. All South Asian countries have a trade imbalance with East Asia, with India's imbalance being the largest (Table 2.2).

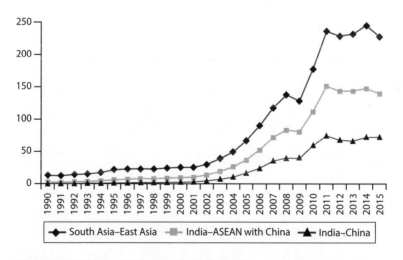

Figure 2.1   Total Trade between South Asia and East Asia ($ billion) (1990–2015)
Source: International Monetary Fund, Direction of Trade Statistics.

Table 2.2 Total Trade and Trade Balance of South Asian countries with East Asia, $ Mn

	Total Trade					Trade Balance				
	1990	2000	2005	2010	2015	1990	2000	2005	2010	2015
Afghanistan	292	199	294	667	689	(287)	(182)	(280)	(658)	(663)
Bangladesh	1454	3345	4958	12189	18888	(1144)	(3008)	(4433)	(10761)	(15212)
India	6379	14567	48934	138225	170477	(1184)	(3103)	(8110)	(40249)	(81279)
Maldives	112	199	365	605	762	(81)	(177)	(259)	(533)	(661)
Nepal	316	411	464	1145	1222	(288)	(384)	(443)	(1096)	(1138)
Pakistan	3023	3719	8253	18589	30535	(1056)	(1567)	(5999)	(12760)	(23164)
Sri Lanka	1116	2796	3120	5685	4919	(742)	(1934)	(2402)	(3642)	(3804)
South Asia	12693	25236	66388	177105	227492	(4782)	(10355)	(21925)	(69699)	(125921)

Source: International Monetary Fund, Direction of Trade Statistics.
Note: Data are not available for Bhutan.

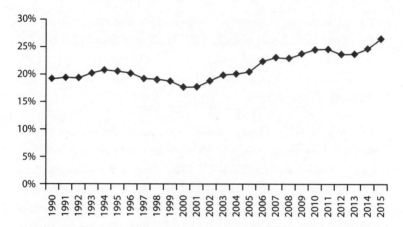

Figure 2.2 Total Trade between South Asia and East Asia (as a Percentage of South Asia's Total Trade with the World) (1990–2015)
Source: International Monetary Fund, Direction of Trade Statistics.

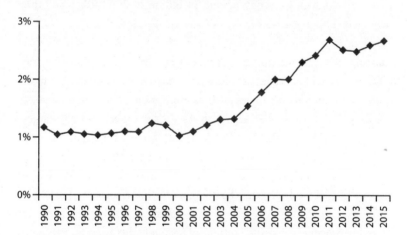

Figure 2.3 Total Trade between South Asia and East Asia (As a Percentage of East Asia's Total Trade with the World) (1990–2015)
Source: International Monetary Fund, Direction of Trade Statistics.

3. East Asia is more important to South Asia than vice versa (Figures 2.2 and 2.3).
4. While South Asia's total trade with the European Union (EU) and the United States have shown a declining trend and intra-South Asian trade has stagnated, South Asia's total trade with East Asia

has shown an increasing trend, especially in the case of India and Pakistan (Table 2.3). Similarly, East Asia's total trade with the EU and US has also declined, while it has not changed very much with South Asia. Intra-East Asian trade has, however, increased quite significantly (Table 2.3).

In terms of FDI, although inflows into South Asia (especially to India) have been increasing, in 2015, they were only about one-fifth of the inflows into East Asia (Table 2.4). The absence of comparable data on FDI by source country limits an analysis of investment relationships between South Asia and East Asia. Those available from FDI Markets on greenfield investments[2] suggests that FDI flows between South Asia and East Asia have nearly doubled from $5.0 billion in 2003 to $8.3 billion in 2013, but from a low base. Annual flows of FDI from South Asia to East Asia were only about $4 billion in 2003–13, while they were $10 billion the other way (Wignaraja, forthcoming)

Data from national sources suggest that East Asian countries are starting to become important sources of FDI for South Asian countries (Table 2.5). China, Malaysia, Singapore, and Thailand are joining traditional high-income countries such as Hong Kong, Korea and Japan, as 'source' countries for FDI in South Asia. China is the seventh-largest source of FDI for Pakistan, the thirteenth-largest for Sri Lanka, and the fourteenth-largest for Bangladesh. Similarly, Malaysia is the second-largest source of FDI for Sri Lanka. Singapore is the second-largest source of FDI for India, the third-largest for Bangladesh and the fifth-largest for Sri Lanka. A total of 1,500 Indian companies are currently based in Singapore and the number of airline flights from Singapore to various Indian cities has increased greatly. The automobile industry in India is benefitting from FDI from Korea and Japan while the electronics industry is benefitting from FDI from Korea, Taiwan, and Singapore. Infrastructure in India and other South Asian countries is also profiting from FDI from China, Malaysia, and Singapore.

---

[2] Greenfield investments are defined as cross-border investments in a new physical project or expansion of an existing investment that creates new jobs and capital investment.

Table 2.3 Direction of Total Trade (Exports plus Imports) of South Asian and East Asian Countries (Per cent)

	South Asia			East Asia			EU			US			ROW		
	1990	2000	2015	1990	2000	2015	1990	2000	2015	1990	2000	2015	1990	2000	2015
Afghanistan	14	30	50	48	26	10	25	15	6	2	2	8	11	27	26
Bangladesh	6	8	10	27	23	27	24	21	24	13	14	7	30	34	32
India	2	2	3	15	16	26	32	23	14	13	13	9	39	46	48
Maldives	13	22	15	59	43	38	17	11	14	7	9	3	5	15	30
Nepal	12	39	62	40	18	18	28	12	6	8	10	2	13	21	12
Pakistan	3	4	7	23	19	34	31	21	13	13	15	6	31	42	40
Sri Lanka	6	7	22	25	23	20	21	21	19	15	20	13	33	29	26
South Asia	3	4	5	19	18	26	30	22	14	13	14	9	35	42	46
China	1	1	3	21	33	26	14	15	15	10	16	14	53	35	42
Japan	1	1	1	21	31	42	19	15	11	28	25	15	31	28	31
Korea	1	1	2	29	37	43	14	12	11	26	20	12	31	30	32
Brunei	0	0	5	82	74	74	6	7	9	7	12	1	5	7	11
Cambodia	5	0	1	69	36	61	17	13	15	0	30	10	9	21	13
Indonesia	1	3	6	52	51	56	16	14	9	12	12	8	19	21	21
Laos	0	1	2	86	73	89	9	14	3	1	1	1	4	12	5
Malaysia	2	2	4	50	49	56	16	13	10	17	19	9	16	17	21
Myanmar	6	5	5	59	62	84	13	9	4	3	9	1	20	14	6
Philippines	1	0	1	33	40	54	15	14	11	27	25	13	25	22	21
Singapore	2	2	3	40	47	50	15	13	10	18	16	9	25	22	28
Thailand	2	2	3	43	45	53	19	14	10	16	17	9	21	23	25
Vietnam	0	1	3	28	56	57	11	14	11	0	4	11	61	25	18
East Asia	1	1	2	29	37	38	17	14	12	22	20	13	31	27	35

Source: Data from International Monetary Fund, Direction of Trade Statistics.
Note: Data are not available for Bhutan; ROW = Rest of the world.

Table 2.4 World FDI Inflows into South Asia and East Asia ($ Mn)

	1990	1995	2000	2005	2010	2015
Afghanistan	0.0	-0.1	0.2	271.0	211.3	58.0
Bangladesh	3.2	92.3	578.6	845.3	913.3	2235.4
Bhutan	1.6	0.1	N.A.	6.2	25.8	12.1
India	236.7	2,151.0	3,358.0	7,621.8	21,125.4	44208.0
Maldives	5.6	7.2	22.3	73.2	216.5	323.9
Nepal	5.9	N.A.	-0.5	2.5	86.7	51.4
Pakistan	278.3	492.1	309.0	2,201.0	2,022.0	864.7
Sri Lanka	43.4	65.0	173.0	272.0	477.6	681.2
South Asia	574.8	2,807.6	4,670.5	11,292.9	25,078.7	48,434.7
China	3,487.1	37,520.5	40,714.8	72,406.0	114,734.0	135,610.0
Japan	1,806.0	41.4	8,322.7	2,775.4	-1,250.8	-2,250.0
Korea	788.5	1,775.8	9,283.4	6,308.5	10,110.1	5,042.0
Brunei	7.0	582.8	549.6	289.5	625.7	173.2
Cambodia	N.A.	150.7	148.5	381.2	782.6	1,701.0
Indonesia	1,092.0	4,419.0	-4,550.0	8,336.0	13,770.6	15,508.2
Laos	6.0	95.1	33.9	27.7	278.8	1,219.8
Malaysia	2,611.0	5,815.0	3,787.6	4,065.3	9,060.0	11,121.5
Myanmar	225.1	317.6	208.0	234.9	1,284.6	2,824.0
Philippines	550.0	1,459.0	2,240.0	1,854.0	1,298.0	5,234.0
Singapore	5,574.7	11,942.8	15,515.3	18,090.3	53,622.7	65,262.4
Thailand	2,575.0	2,070.0	3,410.1	8,066.6	9,146.8	10,844.6
Vietnam	180.0	1,780.4	1,298.0	1,954.0	8,000.0	11,800.0
East Asia	22,177.6	74,183.5	151,469.7	165,749.5	304,170.7	264,090.7

Source: Data from UNCTAD and FDI Indicators Online.

Note: N.A. means that data are not available.

Table 2.5 FDI Inflows from East Asia ($ Mn)

	India (2014)		Pakistan (2013)		Bangladesh (2014)		Sri Lanka (2010)	
	Flow	Rank	Flow	Rank	Flow	Rank	Flow	Rank
China	219.9	18	109.8	7	46.7	14	4.1	13
Japan	2,320.1	4	33.1	17	99.6	8	13.5	10
Korea	138.3	19	35.8	14	140.4	4	N.A.	N.A.
Indonesia	10.6	40	N.A.	N.A.	1.6	37	N.A.	N.A.
Malaysia	96.0	21	25.1	18	59.2	12	72.7	2
Philippines	90.2	22	93.6	8	0.02	54	N.A.	N.A.
Singapore	7,568.4	2	9.5	25	140.6	3	42.4	5
Taiwan	22.5	33	N.A.	N.A.	48.3	13	N.A.	N.A.
Thailand	18.1	34	6.1	28	11.1	25	N.A.	N.A.
Vietnam	0.1	80	N.A.	N.A.	N.A.	N.A.	N.A.	N.A.
Total	189,605.2		2,665.3		2,058.9		516.3	

Source: Data from India: Ministry of Finance, 2014; Pakistan: Board of Investment, 2013; Sri Lanka: Board of Investment, 2010; Bangladesh: Board of Investment, 2014.

Note: N.A. means that data are not available.

Potential and Impacts of Enhancing Economic Linkages

A number of studies have suggested that both the potential and the impacts of enhancing linkages between South Asia and East Asia are large. First, one commonly used method for such an analysis is the calculation of revealed comparative advantage (RCA), a Ricardian comparative advantage concept, which measures the relative advantage or disadvantage a country has in a certain class of goods and services. It is the proportion of a country's exports of the category under consideration divided by the proportion of world exports of that category. A country is said to have a revealed comparative advantage if the value of RCA is greater than one. Our RCA calculations presented in Appendix A2.1 show that while there are considerable overlaps there is also substantial potential for enhancing trade between the two regions. The data show that South Asia has comparative advantages in mainly primary goods, labour-intensive manufacture, and IT services, while East Asia has the comparative advantage across a much wider range of products. These include primary goods like crude rubber and fish; labour-intensive manufacture such as textiles, travel goods, and footwear; and more capital- and knowledge-intensive items such as office machines and telecommunications equipment.

Also, beyond the static analysis above, there is substantial potential for South Asia to link itself to production networks in East Asia and the world. India could also develop production networks in South Asia in agro-processing and services. Multinational-led production networks (product fragmentation and vertical specialization) were key contributors to the regional integration and dynamism of East Asia. Recent evidence of rising FDI from East Asia to South Asia, as discussed above, and increasing real wages in the coastal provinces of China suggest the potential of linking the two regions. South Asian countries have some production sharing with East Asia in apparel and textiles (for example, Bangladesh, Sri Lanka, and India), in automobiles (for example, India), electrical and telecom parts (for example, Sri Lanka), but a lot more needs to be done.

Production networks are not a new concept in East Asia. Production networks of the 1960s, 1970s, and the 1980s in East Asia were based on Akamatsu's 'flying geese' theory which involved economic growth of the region in stages. Entire industries relocated between countries as comparative advantage changed (Figure 2.4).[3] At that time, production networks were triangular: Japan and the newly industrialized economies (NIEs) exported parts for electrical appliances, office and telecommunication equipment, and textiles to third generation countries (Indonesia, Malaysia, the Philippines, and Thailand) which, in turn, completed the processing stage and exported the final goods to the US and Europe. Since the early 1990s, more sophisticated and complex production networks have emerged under the second phase of the flying geese theory which involve the transshipment of parts and components—back-and-forth trade in parts and components across boundaries.

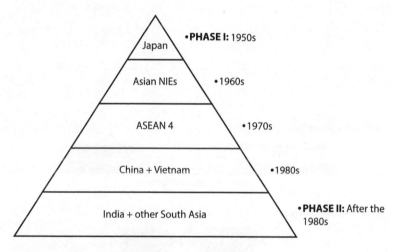

Figure 2.4 Flying Geese Theory—Phases I and II
Source: Authors.

---

[3] The 'flying geese' theory focused on five stages of industrial development: A product would be first introduced through import, then import substitution would occur, followed by export orientation, eventually the industry would mature and real wages would rise, and the industry would relocate either abroad as FDI or perish.

Jones and Kierzkowski (1990) and Kimura and Ando (2005) have pioneered the 'augmented fragmentation and new economic geography' theory to explain these developments. Unlike in the traditional factor endowment theory trade where goods are produced in their entirety in a particular country, the newer theories of trade involve slicing and dicing a product into parts and components and relocating them to various countries or production blocks (PBs) and bringing them together to produce the final product through efficient service links. Figure 2.5 shows the production process before and after fragmentation. Formation of production networks and supply chains has been driven by rapid advances in production technology, a decrease in communication costs (to coordinate and manage) supply chains, and transport costs.

Benefits of joining production networks can be significant. First, production networks provide countries an opportunity to industrialize at a faster rate than otherwise. Many of today's industrialized countries have developed by building entire supply chains within their territories with all the challenges, cost, and time. The emergence

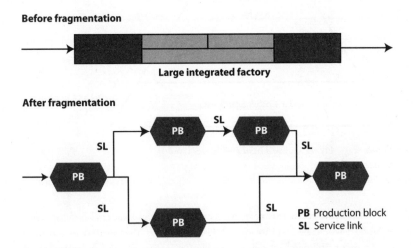

Figure 2.5   Fragmentation Theory—Production Blocks and Service Links
Source: Economic Research Institute for ASEAN and East Asia (2010).

of production networks, however, allows countries to industrialize much more rapidly by joining global production networks rather than building an entire supply chain at home. First, fragmentation enables countries to participate in world markets by eliminating the need to master all components in the production of a final good. Second, participation in production networks increases productivity since it facilitates access to intermediate products from abroad which are cheaper and of a better quality. Participation in such trade can also be an important way for developing countries to build productive capacity, through 'technology borrowing' rather than 'technology transfer' (Baldwin 2012). Third, production networks are associated with other benefits such as learning and knowledge spillovers. Learning from interaction with global actors might cover benefits such as improving production processes and attaining consistent and high-quality technology. Fourth, production networks allow access to markets and distribution networks developed by brand holders (Humphrey and Schmitz 2000).

While the potential benefits from joining production networks are large, there are also costs and risks. The growth contribution of production networks can be limited if countries capture only small shares of value-added in a chain. Also technology dissemination, skill building, and upgrading are not automatic. Developing countries could also be vulnerable to external shocks (ADB 2014a). Despite the risks, however, UNCTAD (2013a) has found a positive correlation between supply chain trade, economic growth, and per capita income. Our regression analysis in Chapter 3 has also found a positive correlation between participation in global value chains and the logistic performance index, a key determinant of participation in the supply chain.

Supply chain trade differs markedly from traditional trade in final goods. In supply chain trade, firms must set up production facilities in many countries and connect these factories—moving personnel, capital, and technology between many locations. It is not only final goods that cross national boarders but also intermediate goods, services, technology, and skilled labour. A much wider set of policies or the so-called twenty-first-century trade policies must be adopted to promote supply chain trade. These include development of ICT, protection of intellectual property rights, harmonization of standards, trade facilitation, transportation, and logistics. One practical implication of supply chain trade is that although average tariffs may be fairly low, 'fairly low' may still be too high when parts and components cross national borders multiple times. Another implication is that domestic policies become a more important barrier to international trade than in the past.

By using an augmented gravity model, De (2010) has found that East Asia holds the greatest potential for growth for South Asia. India's trade potential is the highest with the Asia-Pacific region, followed by the European Union and the North American Free Trade Agreement (NAFTA), and then by South Asia. The estimates of the gravity model suggested that trade with developing East Asia had the potential to increase by 32 per cent per annum by 2014 (or an incremental $360 billion in exports by 2014 compared to an actual of $126 billion in 2008). This is twice the potential increase in trade with the EU and thrice as large as with NAFTA.

Using a computable general equilibrium (CGE) modelling, Francois and Wignaraja (2009) have found that a broader South Asia–East Asia integration would provide larger income gains to South Asia than South Asian integration alone (Table 2.6). South Asian countries as a group would gain $22.4 billion or 2 per cent relative to 2017 baseline income (in constant 2001 prices) from a South Asia–East Asia FTA. This estimated gain is much higher than income gains to South Asia from a South Asian free trade agreement under the SAFTA ($3.7 billion or 0.3 per cent of the baseline income). Interestingly, their results also show that if only India were to participate in an FTA with East Asia, other South Asian countries (such as Bangladesh, Pakistan, and Sri Lanka) would lose. If, however, other South Asian countries would 'Look East' together with India, all countries in both the regions would benefit from a broader South Asia–East Asia FTA. Benefit to India would also increase from $17.8 billion to $18.2 billion. The positive income effects of a broader South Asia–East Asia FTA could enhance economic integration in South Asia as complementarities increase.

Table 2.6 Income Effects of Alternative FTA Scenarios

	South Asia FTA		East Asia FTA		East Asia and India FTA		South Asia and East Asia FTA	
	Value ($ Mn)	Per cent	Value ($ Mn)	Per cent	Value ($ Mn)	Per cent	Value ($ Mn)	Per cent
Bangladesh	351	0.31	(297)	(0.26)	(355)	(0.31)	1,874	1.66
India	1,138	0.14	(2,371)	(0.30)	17,779	2.23	18,240	2.29
Pakistan	625	0.42	(824)	(0.55)	(862)	(0.58)	298	0.20
Sri Lanka	335	1.08	(117)	(0.38)	(123)	(0.40)	631	2.03
Others	1,246	3.37	(12)	(0.03)	(240)	(0.65)	1,380	3.73
South Asia	3,695	0.33	(3,620)	(0.32)	16,199	1.44	22,423	1.99
East Asia	(540)	(0.01)	226,855	2.17	239,097	2.29	241,485	2.31
ROW	361	0.00	(9,316)	(0.03)	(3,934)	(0.01)	(3,001)	(0.01)
World	3,516	0.01	213,919	0.45	251,363	0.52	260,907	0.54

Source: Francois and Wignaraja (2009).

Note: ROW is rest of the world; changes are computed relative to projected 2017 baseline at constant 2001 price; Data in brackets are negative values.

A recent study by the ADB and ADBI (2015) has found that although integration between South and Southeast Asia[4] has been increasing, the present level of trade continues to be below the potential. By using an advanced computable general equilibrium model, it also finds that the potential benefit of reduction of trading costs, either by reducing policy variables such as tariffs and non-tariff barriers to trade or improving 'hard' and 'soft' infrastructure (including transport links and trade facilitation), would be large, especially to South Asia. If the two regions succeed in reducing inter-regional tariffs and reducing non-tariff barriers by 50 per cent and decreasing South Asian–Southeast Asian trade costs by 15 per cent, welfare in South Asia and Southeast Asia would rise by 8.9 per cent and 6.4 per cent, respectively, by 2030 relative to the baseline. The gains would be driven by rising exports and competitiveness, particularly in South Asia. South Asia does much better in the context of a cross-regional FTA than merely an intra-regional FTA. The results suggest a two-track approach to economic integration in South Asia, that is, intra-regional integration together with linkages of South Asian countries with Southeast Asia.

[4] Defined as the ASEAN countries.

APPENDIX A2.1
Technical Appendix

This technical appendix assesses the relative comparative advantages of South Asian and East Asian countries by using three indices:

1. Composition of exports
2. Revealed comparative advantages
3. Bilateral trade intensities.

Data in Table A2.1 show that the top five exports of South Asian and East Asian countries differ quite significantly. While South Asia's top five exports comprise mainly primary goods (including minerals) and labour-intensive manufactured products (for example, textiles and apparels),[1] East Asia's top five exports comprise mineral fuels; electrical machinery, and equipment and parts; vehicles (Thailand); and chemicals.

A mapping of RCAs of South Asia and East Asia is presented in Table A2.2 at the HS1 two-digit level (see Table A2.4 for the formula). Only RCAs that are greater than or equal to one (that is, above-average RCAs) are presented in order to identify overlaps in above-average RCAs. The most significant overlaps are in Section I (Vegetable Products) and Section XI (Textiles). But data show that broadly South Asian countries have comparative advantages in Section I (Animal Products), Section V (Mineral Products), and Section VIII (Hides,

[1] India's top five exports also include vehicles, machinery, and mechanical appliances.

Skins, and Leather). Similarly, East Asian countries have comparative advantage in Section IV (Foodstuffs), Section V (Chemical Products), Section VI (Plastics and Rubber Products), Section IX (Wood and Wood Products), Section X (Pulp and Pulp Products), and Section XV (Metal and Metal Products).

Bilateral trade intensities are more accurate measures of comparative advantage. They capture the propensity of countries to trade more or less with partners than would be expected on the basis of their corresponding shares of world trade (see Table A2.4 for formula). An index value of greater than one indicates a less-than-expected intensity to trade. For the sake of brevity, index values of 'greater than one' and 'less than one' are described as above-average and below-average, respectively. Data in Table A2.3 show that bilateral trade intensities of South Asian countries with other South Asian countries tend to be above-average than with the East Asian countries. The exceptions are Bangladesh which has above-average intensity with eight East Asian countries; India, Pakistan, and Sri Lanka which have above-average intensities with five East Asian countries; and Maldives which has above-average intensities with four East Asian countries. The situation is similar with East Asian countries, which tend to have above-average intensities with other East Asian countries. This finding suggests that countries desire to trade more with neighbouring countries in the region than with those outside the region. But, of course, as shown in Table A2.3, there are many exceptions to this finding.

Table A2.1 Composition of Exports (Top Five Exports) of South Asian and East Asian Countries

SOUTH ASIA

Rank	1st	2nd	3rd	4th	5th
Afghanistan (2012)	Commodities not specified according to kind	Edible fruit and nuts; peel of citrus fruit or melons	Carpets and other textile floor coverings	Coffee, tea, maté, and spices	Oil seeds and oleaginous fruits
Bangladesh (2007)	Articles of apparel and clothing accessories, knitted or crocheted	Articles of apparel and clothing accessories, not knitted or crocheted	Fish and crustaceans, molluscs and other aquatic invertebrates	Other vegetable textile fibres; paper yarn and woven fabric of paper yarn	Other made-up textile articles; sets; worn clothing and worn textile articles; rags
Bhutan (2011)	Iron and steel	Electrical machinery and equipment and parts thereof; sound recorders and reproducers, television image and sound recorders and reproducers, and parts and accessories of such articles	Salt; sulphur; earths and stone; plastering materials, lime and cement	Copper and articles thereof	Inorganic chemicals; organic or inorganic compounds of precious metals, of rare-earth metals, of radioactive elements or of isotopes

(Cont'd)

Table A2.1 (Cont'd)

Rank	1st	2nd	3rd	4th	5th
India (2012)	Mineral fuels, mineral oils, and products of their distillation; bituminous substances; mineral waxes	Natural or cultured pearls, precious or semi-precious stones, precious metals, metals clad with precious metal, and articles thereof; imitation jewellery	Organic chemicals	Vehicles other than railway or tramway rolling-stock, and parts and accessories thereof	Nuclear reactors, boilers, machinery, and mechanical appliances; parts thereof
Nepal (2011)	Iron and steel	Carpets and other textile floor coverings	Articles of apparel and clothing accessories, not knitted or crocheted	Man-made filaments; strip and the like of man-made textile materials	Man-made staple fibres
Pakistan (2012)	Cotton	Other made-up textile articles; sets; worn clothing and worn textile articles; rags	Cereals	Articles of apparel and clothing accessories, knitted or crocheted	Articles of apparel and clothing accessories, not knitted or crocheted
Sri Lanka (2012)	Articles of apparel and clothing accessories, knitted or crocheted	Articles of apparel and clothing accessories, not knitted or crocheted	Coffee, tea, maté, and spices	Rubber and articles thereof	Natural or cultured pearls, precious or semi-precious stones, precious metals, metals clad with precious metal, and articles thereof; imitation jewellery; coins

EAST ASIA

Rank	1st	2nd	3rd	4th	5th
Brunei (2012)	Mineral fuels, mineral oils and products of their distillation; bituminous substances; mineral waxes	Organic chemicals	Nuclear reactors, boilers, machinery, and mechanical appliances; parts thereof	Electrical machinery and equipment and parts thereof; sound recorders and reproducers and reproducers, television image and sound recorders and reproducers, and parts and accessories of such articles	Optical, photographic, cinematographic, measuring, checking, precision, medical, or surgical instruments and apparatus; parts and accessories thereof
Cambodia (2012)	Articles of apparel and clothing accessories, knitted or crocheted	Printed books, newspapers, pictures, and other products of the printing industry; manuscripts, typescripts, and plans	Footwear, gaiters, and the like; parts of such articles	Vehicles other than railway or tramway rolling-stock, and parts and accessories thereof	Articles of apparel and clothing accessories, not knitted or crocheted

(Cont'd)

Table A2.1 (Cont'd)

Rank	1st	2nd	3rd	4th	5th
China (2012)	Electrical machinery and equipment and parts thereof; sound recorders and reproducers, television image and sound recorders and reproducers, and parts and accessories of such articles	Nuclear reactors, boilers, machinery, and mechanical appliances; parts thereof	Articles of apparel and clothing accessories, knitted or crocheted	Furniture; bedding, mattresses, mattress supports, cushions, and similar stuffed furnishings; lamps and lighting fittings, not elsewhere specified or included; illuminated signs, illuminated nameplates and the like; prefabricated buildings	Optical, photographic, cinematographic, measuring, checking, precision, medical, or surgical instruments and apparatus; parts and accessories thereof
Indonesia (2012)	Mineral fuels, mineral oils and products of their distillation; bituminous substances; mineral waxes	Animal or vegetable fats and oils and their cleavage products; prepared edible fats; animal or vegetable waxes	Electrical machinery and equipment and parts thereof; sound recorders and reproducers, television image and sound recorders and reproducers, and parts and accessories of such articles	Rubber and articles thereof	Nuclear reactors, boilers, machinery, and mechanical appliances; parts thereof

Japan (2012)	Vehicles other than railway or tramway rolling-stock, and parts and accessories thereof	Nuclear reactors, boilers, machinery, and mechanical appliances; parts thereof	Electrical machinery and equipment and parts thereof; sound recorders and reproducers, television image and sound recorders and reproducers, and parts and accessories of such articles	Optical, photographic, cinematographic, measuring, checking, precision, medical, or surgical instruments and apparatus; parts and accessories thereof	Iron and steel
Malaysia (2012)	Electrical machinery and equipment and parts thereof; sound recorders and reproducers, television image and sound recorders and reproducers, and parts and accessories of such articles	Mineral fuels, mineral oils, and products of their distillation; bituminous substances; mineral waxes	Nuclear reactors, boilers, machinery, and mechanical appliances; parts thereof	Animal or vegetable fats and oils and their cleavage products; prepared edible fats; animal or vegetable waxes	Rubber and articles thereof

(Cont'd)

Table A2.1 (Cont'd)

Rank	1st	2nd	3rd	4th	5th
Myanmar (2010)	Mineral fuels, mineral oils, and products of their distillation; bituminous substances; mineral waxes	Natural or cultured pearls, precious or semi-precious stones, precious metals, metals clad with precious metal, and articles thereof; imitation jewellery; coins	Edible vegetables and certain roots and tubers	Wood and articles of wood; wood charcoal	Articles of apparel and clothing accessories, not knitted or crocheted
Philippines (2012)	Electrical machinery and equipment and parts thereof, sound recorders and reproducers, television image and sound recorders and reproducers, and parts and accessories of such articles	Machinery and mechanical appliances; parts thereof	Wood and articles of wood; wood charcoal	Optical, photographic, cinematographic, measuring, checking, precision, medical, or surgical instruments and apparatus; parts and accessories thereof	Vehicles other than railway or tramway rolling stock

Singapore (2012)	Electrical machinery and equipment and parts thereof; sound recorders and reproducers, television image and sound recorders and reproducers, and parts and accessories of such articles	Mineral fuels, mineral oils, and products of their distillation; bituminous substances; mineral waxes	Nuclear reactors, boilers, machinery, and mechanical appliances; parts thereof	Commodities not specified according to kind	Organic chemicals
Korea (2012)	Electrical machinery and equipment and parts thereof; sound recorders and reproducers, television image and sound recorders and reproducers, and parts and accessories of such articles	Vehicles other than railway or tramway rolling-stock, and parts and accessories thereof	Nuclear reactors, boilers, machinery, and mechanical appliances; parts thereof	Mineral fuels, mineral oils, and products of their distillation; bituminous substances; mineral waxes	Ships, boats, and floating structures

(Cont'd)

Table A2.1 (*Cont'd*)

Rank	1st	2nd	3rd	4th	5th
Thailand (2012)	Nuclear reactors, boilers, machinery, and mechanical appliances; parts thereof	Electrical machinery and equipment and parts thereof; sound recorders and reproducers, television image and sound recorders and reproducers, and parts and accessories of such articles	Vehicles other than railway or tramway rolling-stock, and parts and accessories thereof	Rubber and articles thereof	Mineral fuels, mineral oils, and products of their distillation; bituminous substances; mineral waxes
Vietnam (2011)	Electrical machinery and equipment and parts thereof; sound recorders and reproducers, television image and sound recorders and reproducers, and parts and accessories of such articles	Mineral fuels, mineral oils, and products of their distillation; bituminous substances; mineral waxes	Articles of apparel and clothing accessories, not knitted or crocheted	Footwear, gaiters, and the like; parts of such articles	Articles of apparel and clothing accessories, knitted or crocheted

Source: Authors' calculations from Comtrade 2012.

Table A2.2   Above-Average RCAs[2] for South Asian and East Asian Countries, 2012, HS Sections I–XXI

	South Asia					East Asia									
	AF	IN	MV	PK	SL	CN	HK	ID	JP	KH	KR	MY	PH	SG	TH
Section I: Animal Products, Animals															
H1-01 Live animals															
H1-02 Meat and edible meat offal		1.5		1.2											
H1-03 Fish, crustaceans, molluscs, aquatic invertebrates, n.e.s.		2.1		1.9	4.1	1.0		2.7					1.5		2.3
H1-04 Dairy products, eggs, honey, edible animal products, n.e.s.															
H1-05 Product of animal origin, n.e.s.	4.2			4.3		1.8									
Section II: Vegetable Products															
H1-06 Live trees, plants, bulbs, roots, cut flowers, and so on.															
H1-07 Edible vegetables and certain roots and tubers				1.9		1.0									1.8

(*Cont'd*)

[2] See Table A2.4 for formula.

Table A2.2 (*Cont'd*)

	South Asia					East Asia									
	AF	IN	MV	PK	SL	CN	HK	ID	JP	KH	KR	MY	PH	SG	TH
H1-08 Edible fruits, nuts, peel of citrus fruits, melons				2.6	2.0								3.8		1.0
H1-09 Coffee, tea, maté, and spices	53.9	4.0		1.1	74.8			4.7							
H1-10 Cereals		4.2		11.4						2.5					2.8
H1-11 Milling products, malt, starches, inulin, wheat gluten				10.4	9.2										5.0
H1-12 Oil seed, oleaginous fruits, grain, seed, fruits, and so on, n.e.s.	8.3	1.1													
H1-13 Lac, gums, resins, vegetable saps and extracts, n.e.s.		30.3		10.2									4.0		
H1-14 Vegetable plaiting materials, vegetable products, n.e.s.	5.3		6.0	37.4	1.1		3.9				5.2	1.4	1.0		
Section III: Oils and Fats															
H1-15 Animal, vegetable fats and oils, cleavage products, and so on.			0.0	1.4				17.4				13.3	3.4		

Section IV: Foodstuffs

Code	Description								
H1-16	Meat, fish and seafood food preparations, n.e.s.		30.7	1.6	1.6		2.9		11.8
H1-17	Sugars and sugar confectionary	2.5	3.3				1.3		6.1
H1-18	Cocoa and cocoa preparation				2.3	2.2			2.2

Section IV: Foodstuffs

Code	Description								
H1-19	Cereal, flour, starch, milk preparations, and products					1.5		1.1	1.4
H1-20	Vegetable, fruit, nut, etc., food preparations			1.7	1.1		3.1		2.5
H1-21	Miscellaneous edible preparations			1.8	1.1	1.4			2.2
H1-22	Beverages, spirits, and vinegar		1.2					1.1	
H1-23	Residues, wastes of food industry, animal fodder	2		2.1					1.2

(Cont'd)

Table A2.2 (Cont'd)

| | South Asia | | | | | East Asia | | | | | | | | | |
	AF	IN	MV	PK	SL	CN	HK	ID	JP	KH	KR	MY	PH	SG	TH
H1-24 Tobacco and manufactured tobacco substitutes		1.4			3.9			1.8		1.3		1	1.9		1.7
Section V: Mineral Products and Fuels															
H1-25 Salt, sulphur, earth, stone, plaster, lime, and cement		2.4		11.6											
H1-26 Ores, slag, and ash								2					1.6		
H1-27 Mineral fuels, oils, distillation products, and so on.		1.4						2.5				1.5		1.4	
Section VI: Chemical Products															
H1-28 Inorganic chemicals, precious metal compound, isotopes						1									
H1-29 Organic chemicals		1.8							1.2		1.7			2.2	1.1
H1-30 Pharmaceutical products		1.2													
H1-31 Fertilizers									1.4						
H1-32 Tanning dyeing extracts, tannins, derivatives, pigments, and so on.		1.5													

Code	Description										
H1-33	Essential oils, perfumes, cosmetics, toiletries									1.4	1.9
H1-34	Soaps, lubricants, waxes, candles, modelling pastes					1.7		1.2	1.3	1	
H1-35	Albuminoids, modified starches, glues, enzymes					1					
H1-36	Explosives, pyrotechnics, matches, pyrophores, and so on.	1.2	4.2	1.6					2.0		
H1-37	Photographic or cinematographic goods					5.6					
H1-38	Miscellaneous chemical products										
Section VII: Plastic and Rubber Products											
H1-39	Plastics and articles thereof				1.0	1.2	1.7	1.0	1.0	1.1	1.7

(Cont'd)

Table A2.2 (Cont'd)

		South Asia					East Asia									
		AF	IN	MV	PK	SL	CN	HK	ID	JP	KH	KR	MY	PH	SG	TH
H1-40	Rubber and articles thereof					8.2			4.3	1.4	1.7	1.3	3.1			5.9
Section VIII: Hides, Skins and Leathers																
H1-41	Raw hides and skin(other than fur skins) and leather		2.4		11.8			3.2				1.1				1.4
H1-42	Articles of leather, animal gut, harness, travel goods		1.9		7.3		3.7	3.7								
H1-43	Fur skins and artificial fur, manufactures thereof						2.0	4.5								
Section IX: Wood and Wood Products																
H1-44	Wood and articles of wood, wood charcoal								2.6				2.8	6.2		1.3
H1-45	Cork and articles of cork					1.2	6.0		3.0							
H1-46	Manufactures of plaiting material, basketwork, and so on.													6.2		

Section X: Pulp and Paper Products

Code	Description						
H1-47	Pulp of wood, fibrous cellulosic material, waste, etc.	1.0		2.9			
H1-48	Paper and paperboard, articles of pulp, paper, and board			2.0			
H1-49	Printed books, newspapers, pictures, and so on.	1.7	1.3		109.3	2.2	

Section XI: Textiles

Code	Description						
H1-50	Silk	3.4	4.9	1.1		1.1	
H1-51	Wool, animal hair, horsehair, yarn, and fabric thereof	1.7	1.4				
H1-52	Cotton	7.8	55.6	1.1	1.9	1.8	1.0
H1-53	Vegetable textile fibres n.e.s, paper yarn, woven fabric	6.2	1.3	68.6	2.9	1.0	1.4

(Cont'd)

Table A2.2 (Cont'd)

	South Asia					East Asia									
	AF	IN	MV	PK	SL	CN	HK	ID	JP	KH	KR	MY	PH	SG	TH
H1-54	Man-made filaments		3.2				2.8		3.0	1.3		2.5				1.3
H1-55	Man-made staple fibres		3.2		8.6	1.6	2.4		5.6	1.2		1.6	1.3			2.9
H1-56	Wadding, felt, non-wovens, yarns, twine, cordage, and so on					2.1	1.4			1.0		1.1				1.3
H1-57	Carpets and other textile floor coverings	192.6	5.3		5.6		1.3									
H1-58	Special woven or tufted fabric, lace, tapestry, and so on		1.2		1.5	4.4	3.2	2.7				1.3		1.0		1.2
H1-59	Impregnated, coated, or laminated textile fabric						2.5			1.0		1.8				
H1-60	Knitted or crocheted fabric					2.0	3.3	3.0				4.5				
H1-61	Articles of apparel, accessories, knit or crochet		1.6		7.1	18.2	3.7	2.0	1.6		44.9			1.4		
H1-62	Articles of apparel, accessories, not knit or crochet		2.6		7.0	19.6	3.0	2.0	2.0		2.8			1.5		

Section XIII: Stone and Glass Products

Code	Description	Values
H1-63	Other made textile articles, sets, worn clothing, and so on.	4.1 40.3 1.5 3.5 1.0
Section XIII: Stone and Glass Products		
H1-68	Stone, plaster, cement, asbestos, mica, etc. articles	1.5 1.0 1.6 1.2
H1-69	Ceramic Products	1.5 3.2 3.2
H1-70	Glass and glassware	1.8 1.0 1.9 1.1 1.2
Section XIV: Gemstones		
H1-71	Pearls, precious stones, metals, coins, and so on.	4.2 1.9 1.3 4.4 1.6
Section XV: Metals and Metal Products		
H1-72	Iron and steel	1.1 2.0 1.9
H1-73	Articles of iron or steel	1.6 1.6 1.1 1.3
H1-74	Copper and articles thereof	1.0 1.2 1.2 1.7 1.1
H1-75	Nickel and articles thereof	3.2
H1-76	Aluminium and articles thereof	1.0 1.0

(Cont'd)

Table A2.2 (Cont'd)

	South Asia					East Asia									
	AF	IN	MV	PK	SL	CN	HK	ID	JP	KH	KR	MY	PH	SG	TH
H1-78	Lead and articles thereof			1.9	2.1						1.9	2.0		1.0	
H1-79	Zinc and articles thereof	2.1									2.2	1.6			
H1-80	Tin and articles thereof							24.2				8.2	17.7	4.9	4.3
H1-81	Other base metals, cements, articles thereof					1.6			2.0						
H1-82	Tools, implements, cutlery, etc. of base metal			1.0		1.7			1.5		1.0			1.0	
H1-83	Miscellaneous articles of base metal					1.9									1.0
Section XVI: Machinery, Electrical, and Electronic Goods															
H1-84	Nuclear reactors, boilers, machinery, and so on.					1.5	1.2		1.6				1.2	1.1	1.4
H1-85	Electrical, electronic equipment					1.9	3.3		1.3		1.7	2.1	3.1	2.3	1.0

Section XVII: Transport Equipment

Item	Description									
H1-86	Railway, tramway locomotives, rolling-stock, equipment		1.3	2.3						
H1-87	Vehicles other than railway, tramway				2.6	1.6				1.3
H1-88	Aircraft, spacecraft, and parts thereof								1.4	
H1-89	Ships, boats, and other floating structures	1.6	1.1	2.1	3.1	7.6		2.3		

Section XVIII: Instruments (Optical, Photographic, Medical, Musical)

Item	Description									
H1-90	Optical, photo, technical, medical, etc., apparatus		1.0	1.0	2.0	2.1	1.0	1.2	1.2	
H1-91	Clocks and watches and parts thereof			6.1				1.0	1.3	
H1-92	Musical instruments, parts and accessories		2.2	7.5	2.3					

Section XIX: Arms and Ammunition

Item	Description									
H1-93	Arms and ammunition, parts and accessories thereof					1.2		1.3		

(Cont'd)

Table A2.2 *(Cont'd)*

	South Asia					East Asia									
	AF	IN	MV	PK	SL	CN	HK	ID	JP	KH	KR	MY	PH	SG	TH
Section XX: Miscellaneous															
H1-94 Furniture, lighting signs, prefabricated buildings						3.2						1.2			
H1-95 Toys, games, sports requisites				1.7	1.1	3.2	4.4								
H1-96 Miscellaneous manufactured articles					1.9	3.1	1.6		1.4						
Section XXI: Art and Antiques															
H1-97 Works of art, collectors pieces and antiques															
H1-99 Commodities not elsewhere specified	19.0		26.0						1.3					2.4	

Source: Authors' Calculation from Comtrade 2012.

AF= Afghanistan; CN= China; HK= Hong Kong; ID= Indonesia; IN= India; JP= Japan; KH= Cambodia; KR= Korea; MV= Maldives; MY= Malaysia; PH= Philippines; PK= Pakistan; SG= Singapore; SL= Sri Lanka; TH= Thailand; n.e.s. = not elsewhere specified

Table A2.3 Bilateral Trade Intensities for South Asian and East Asian Countries 2012

	South Asia							East Asia												
	AF	BD	IN	MV	NP	PK	SL	CN	JP	KR	BR	KH	ID	LA	MY	MM	PH	SG	TH	VN
Afghanistan	0.00	1.00	3.28	0.00	0.00	116.23	0.22	0.50	0.24	0.55	0.05	3.48	0.61	0.00	0.20	0.00	0.10	0.06	1.23	0.00
Bangladesh	0.88	0.00	4.50	0.25	4.68	4.19	1.75	1.38	0.64	1.03	1.47	0.08	1.93	0.10	2.36	1.93	0.19	1.75	1.12	0.00
India	3.44	4.63	0.00	4.37	26.32	1.58	8.12	0.86	0.52	0.88	2.30	0.28	2.20	0.82	1.57	3.59	0.44	1.51	0.91	0.89
Maldives	0.00	0.30	3.99	0.00	0.03	1.64	63.06	0.48	0.22	0.09	0.00	0.00	1.59	0.00	5.56	0.00	0.46	8.49	5.48	0.00
Nepal	0.00	5.36	24.75	0.04	0.00	0.16	0.18	2.82	0.20	0.11	0.03	0.03	0.14	0.00	0.45	0.00	0.10	0.76	0.73	0.00
Pakistan	120.31	4.77	1.45	1.75	0.15	0.00	7.35	1.56	0.61	0.74	0.06	0.43	2.11	0.02	2.42	1.30	0.49	0.59	1.00	0.86
Sri Lanka	0.21	1.38	7.40	58.75	0.17	6.38	0.00	1.05	0.55	0.47	0.02	0.24	1.47	0.00	2.59	0.20	0.30	2.66	1.46	0.00
China	0.52	1.11	0.86	0.51	2.96	1.65	0.47	0.00	1.93	1.96	0.90	1.34	1.30	1.76	1.35	2.88	1.10	1.03	1.31	1.81
Japan	0.25	0.67	0.54	0.22	0.20	0.64	0.63	1.89	0.00	2.13	6.77	0.60	3.07	0.60	2.46	1.76	3.18	1.19	3.40	2.46
Korea	0.56	0.96	0.77	0.10	0.11	0.72	0.48	2.23	2.06	0.00	3.54	1.13	2.40	0.67	1.30	2.41	2.20	1.81	0.98	3.22
Brunei	0.04	1.32	2.25	0.00	0.02	0.06	0.02	0.79	6.99	3.73	0.00	0.05	2.50	0.00	3.35	0.04	1.05	4.03	2.54	5.38
Cambodia	3.62	0.08	0.25	0.00	0.03	0.39	0.24	1.22	0.61	1.09	0.05	0.00	1.29	0.46	1.44	0.00	0.27	3.18	13.63	24.15
Indonesia	0.56	1.77	2.20	1.48	0.12	1.97	1.60	1.48	2.69	2.39	2.20	1.24	0.00	0.26	3.87	1.71	2.71	6.92	3.49	1.79
Laos	0.00	0.12	0.87	0.00	0.00	0.02	0.00	1.81	0.63	0.67	0.00	0.49	0.29	0.00	0.13	0.00	0.02	0.18	41.24	15.86
Malaysia	0.16	2.20	1.27	4.68	0.37	2.06	2.18	1.72	2.11	1.15	3.08	1.19	4.33	0.11	0.00	2.63	2.17	8.06	3.76	2.50

(Cont'd)

Table A2.3   (Cont'd)

| | South Asia | | | | | | | East Asia | | | | | | | | | | | | |
	AF	BD	IN	MV	NP	PK	SL	CN	JP	KR	BR	KH	ID	LA	MY	MM	PH	SG	TH	VN
Myanmar	0.00	2.22	3.62	0.00	0.00	1.41	0.24	2.73	1.74	2.38	0.04	0.00	1.85	0.00	3.17	0.00	0.62	2.71	21.60	1.55
Philippines	0.06	0.17	0.44	0.31	0.06	0.31	0.19	2.01	2.68	2.28	0.67	0.19	2.51	0.01	2.49	0.39	0.00	3.33	3.38	2.72
Singapore	0.08	1.82	1.71	11.36	1.00	0.81	3.48	1.08	1.14	1.82	5.89	4.17	6.78	0.23	8.05	3.68	4.88	0.00	2.34	2.44
Thailand	1.29	1.08	0.90	5.47	0.76	1.07	1.55	1.42	3.15	1.00	2.61	14.91	3.73	41.33	4.45	21.22	4.08	2.56	0.00	3.05
Vietnam	0.00	0.85	1.03	0.00	0.00	0.72	0.38	1.88	2.21	2.91	4.47	22.19	1.84	12.92	3.07	1.31	1.96	2.30	2.91	0.00

AF= Afghanistan; CN= China; HK= Hong Kong; ID= Indonesia; IN= India; JP= Japan; KH= Cambodia; KR= Korea; MV= Maldives; MY= Malaysia; PH= Philippines; PK= Pakistan; SG= Singapore; SL= Sri Lanka; TH= Thailand

Source: Authors' calculations from International Monetary Fund, Direction of Trade Statistics.

Table A2.4   Index Formulas

Revealed Comparative Advantage (RCA) Index

$$RCA_{ij} = (X_{ij}/X_i)/(X_{wj}/X_w)$$

where RCA_{ij} is country i's revealed comparative advantage (RCA) in product j, X_{ij} is country i's exports of product j, X_i is country i's total exports, X_{wj} is the world exports of product j, and X_w is the world total export.

Bilateral Trade Intensity Index

Intensity of Country i's bilateral trade with Country j

$$T_{ij} = [(X_{ij}+M_{ij})/(X_i+M_i)]/\{[(X_{wj}+M_{wj})-(X_{ij}+M_{ij})]/[(X_w+M_w)-(X_i+M_i)]\}$$

where

T_{ij} = Total trade intensity index of Country i with Country j

X_{ij} = Exports of Country i to j

M_{ij} = Imports of Country i from j

X_i = Total exports of Country i

M_i = Total imports of Country i

X_{wj} = Total world exports to Country j

M_{wj} = Total world imports from Country j

X_w = Total world exports

M_w = Total world imports

3

POLICIES TO INCREASE PRODUCTION
NETWORK PARTICIPATION RATES

Thanks to substantial declines in transportation and communication costs in addition to ever-expanding globalization, outsourcing—contracting out production of intermediate materials and services at arm's length (Jones and Kierzkowski 2001)—has diffused deeply into the East Asian region since the mid-1980s. The ADB (2014a) estimates that Asia's share of GVC trade grew by more than 10 per cent from 36.9 per cent in 1995 to 48.0 per cent in 2008, and the spike was driven mainly by rising production networks in China and developing Southeast Asia. Two factors account for the exceptionally important intra-firm and arm's-length relationships in East Asia (Ando and Kimura 2005). First, East Asia involves a relatively large number of countries at different levels of development, with large market size and abundant natural and human capital resources. Cross-country differences in factor prices and other locational advantages have made production fragmentation and vertical specialization along the value chain economically viable. Second and more importantly, until recently the East Asian production networks were, to a large extent, policy-driven. From the 1970s and the 1980s, most East Asian countries including China employed import-substitution industrialization. Through this, the governments ushered in selective FDI, particularly from the Asian forerunners (that is, Japan, Korea, and Taiwan) to nurture potential infant manufacturing industries like automotive and electronics industries. These industries were handpicked due to the nature of high value-added and potential backward and forward linkages with other industries through diffusions of knowledge and technology. As the industries started to take off, industrialization strategies were transitioned toward export-orientation whereby export-processing zone and export promotion policies have allowed domestic industries to competitively take part in the East Asian production networks (Ando 2010; Kimura and Obashi 2011).

In contrast to the East Asian countries, South Asian countries are relatively less well-linked to GVC. This reflects the fact that economic policy reforms in South Asia began only in the 1990s, about two or three decades after the East Asian countries and these countries are yet to implement second-generation reforms to improve the business environment (see Chapter 1).

This chapter identifies the production network participation gap or PNP gap between South Asia and East Asia and outlines the components of a second round of Look East policies that South Asian countries need to implement to overcome the gap. This chapter also develops a simple empirical framework to identify the key determinants of production network participation using the fractional logit model with random effects. The estimation results substantiate the hypotheses that South Asian countries could boost participation in production networks by improving logistics (including ICT development, trade facilitation at the border, infrastructure development, domestic business environment, and by deepening regional economic integration).

The rest of the chapter is organized as follows. The next section identifies the PNP gap between South Asia and East Asia by using two different indicators—the share of parts and components in total trade (Athukorala 2010) and the newly developed GVC participation index published by UNCTAD. The section on 'Determinants of PNP Participation' develops a logit model to analyse the determinants of production network participation and discusses the empirical results. The next section outlines the major policies that South Asian countries should implement to enhance their participation in global production networks.

Significance of Production Networks in South Asia and East Asia

Two standard approaches are used in the literature to analyse the importance of production networks at a country level:

1. A country's share of world trade in parts and components (P&C) using Athukorala's approach (2010)
2. GVC participation index published by UNCTAD.

The former defines the notion of production networks as trade in parts and components and is commonly utilized in the existing studies such as Ando and Kimura (2005), Ando (2006), Athukorala and Yamashita (2006), Athukorala and Menon (2010), and, more recently, Chongvilaivan and Thangavelu (2012) and Wignaraja et al. (2013). However, 'parts and components' industry classifications are rather ad hoc, and the measurement is often hampered by limited information on trade in parts and components. An alternative indicator is based on GVC participation. This examines sources of value added in trade and is, thus, more intuitive than parts and components shares. GVC participation is defined as 'the portion of a country's exports that is part of a multi-stage trade process, by adding to the foreign value added used in a country's own exports and also the value added supplied to other countries' exports' (UNCTAD 2013b). The first portion, the foreign value-added used in a country's own exports, is concerned with production activities contracted out at arm's length to foreign providers and captures the 'upstream component'. The second portion, in contrast, gauges a country's own exports that are further processed by foreign counterparts and is known as the 'downstream component'. Given this definition, GVC participation can be used to examine the extent to which industries in a country rely on internationally integrated production networks.

Figure 3.1 and Table 3.1 present the PNP rates for the eight SAARC member countries and 13 East Asian countries during the period 2002 to 2011. While Figure 3.1 shows the average PNP rate for the countries during the entire period, Table 3.2 shows the annual trend. Both the figure and the table show that there is a sizeable PNP gap between South Asia and East Asia. Figure 3.1 shows that the average PNP rate for East Asia was 53.5 per cent during the period 2002–11 while it was 41.4 per cent in South Asia. During this period, the average PNP rate was the highest in Singapore (72.7 per cent), followed by Malaysia (65.5 per cent), Philippines (64.3 per cent), Korea (61.4 per cent), Vietnam (58.3 per cent), and Thailand (54.2 per cent). Average PNP rates were lower in South Asian countries—Bhutan (53.8 per cent),

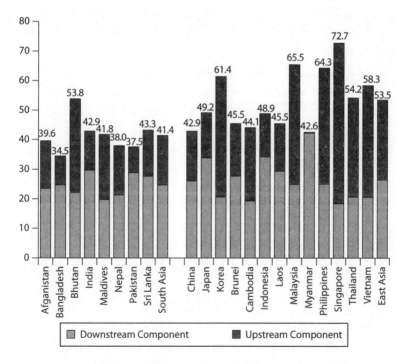

Figure 3.1 Production Network Participation Rate (Per cent) (2002–11)
Source: UNCTAD-Eora GVC Database.
Note: The upstream component is the share of foreign value added in a country's exports; The downstream component is the share of value-added supplied to other countries' exports in a country's total exports.

Table 3.1 Global Value Chain Participation Rates in South Asia and East Asia (Per cent) (2002–11)

	2002	2003	2004	2005	2006	2007	2008	2009	2010	2011
Afghanistan	33.89	33.27	34.26	37.07	39.97	39.82	41.13	43.14	46.82	46.38
Bangladesh	28.51	29.81	31.75	33.69	35.85	37.13	38.95	34.27	36.26	38.41
Bhutan	52.92	52.98	55.86	56.63	57.95	55.30	55.64	50.13	50.34	50.67
India	39.52	40.66	42.63	43.70	44.51	44.28	45.45	40.67	42.86	44.85
Maldives	26.78	27.80	31.65	42.92	48.63	48.17	49.22	44.25	48.22	50.59
Nepal	32.87	32.54	35.32	38.13	40.36	40.54	42.51	37.20	39.90	40.16
Pakistan	33.97	34.54	35.87	37.11	38.37	38.82	39.84	35.47	39.34	42.13
Sri Lanka	39.34	39.88	42.29	43.20	45.09	46.11	46.98	41.03	43.42	45.49
South Asia	35.98	36.43	38.70	41.56	43.84	43.77	44.96	40.77	43.40	44.83
China	39.90	42.07	44.43	44.19	45.04	44.71	44.80	39.86	41.73	42.48
Japan	44.28	45.11	47.57	49.28	51.40	52.15	53.17	47.85	49.68	51.30
Korea	55.52	56.73	58.84	60.21	62.32	63.19	66.29	61.83	63.65	65.11
Brunei	39.50	40.02	43.61	44.20	47.50	49.64	51.51	45.31	46.56	47.25
Cambodia	37.16	38.60	40.69	43.39	46.80	48.39	49.63	43.46	46.11	47.14
Indonesia	45.59	45.50	48.50	49.49	50.42	51.38	52.87	46.63	48.54	49.78
Laos	41.35	41.37	43.26	46.64	48.80	49.44	50.95	43.44	44.34	45.38
Malaysia	64.15	64.39	65.88	66.16	67.20	67.55	66.93	63.00	64.47	64.94
Myanmar	45.56	44.45	44.73	43.75	44.68	43.69	43.99	37.64	38.32	39.21
Philippines	63.83	64.93	65.51	65.78	66.08	65.81	65.67	60.83	61.89	62.13
Singapore	75.10	72.80	73.44	73.80	74.00	72.84	73.64	69.71	70.74	71.33
Thailand	54.32	53.63	54.66	53.76	53.64	54.22	54.71	52.83	54.28	55.54
Vietnam	52.23	53.37	54.53	54.61	56.96	58.70	59.73	56.37	67.54	69.37
East Asia	50.65	51.00	52.74	53.48	54.99	55.52	56.45	51.44	53.68	54.69

Source: Data from UNCTAD-Eora GVC Database (unpublished data provided to the authors for research purposes).

Table 3.2 Shares of the World Production Network Exports (2001–13)
(Per cent Averaged over Subperiods)

	2001–4	2005–8	2009–13
Bangladesh	0.26	0.28	0.49
India	0.45	0.60	0.84
Pakistan	0.11	0.10	0.12
Sri Lanka	0.12	0.11	0.12
Rest of South Asia	0.01	0.00	0.00
South Asia	0.95	1.10	1.58
China	12.54	19.20	24.99
Japan	11.12	9.61	7.90
Korea	4.16	4.89	4.85
Brunei	0.02	0.01	0.00
Cambodia	0.08	0.09	0.15
Indonesia	0.77	0.74	0.77
Laos	0.01	0.01	0.01
Malaysia	3.20	3.00	2.70
Myanmar	0.03	0.01	0.02
Philippines	1.46	1.32	0.95
Singapore	2.18	1.89	1.67
Thailand	1.50	1.80	2.00
Vietnam	0.31	0.45	1.08
East Asia	38.65	43.97	47.68

Source: Wignaraja (2016).

Sri Lanka (43.3 per cent), and India (42.9 per cent, roughly the same as in Myanmar). Within SAARC, Afghanistan, Bangladesh, Nepal, and Pakistan are at the bottom of PNP rates with less than 40 per cent of total exports.

Table 3.1 shows that while the PNP rate increased in both South Asia as well as East Asia during the period 2002 to 2011 (except in 2009), it increased faster in the former region. Hence, the PNP gap between the two regions has narrowed to some extent, from 14.67 per cent in 2002 to 9.86 per cent in 2012, although it continues to remain large.

In Figure 3.1, we can also observe that in East Asia, the upstream component of PNP rates accounts for a larger share than the downstream component. This means that the East Asian countries' leverage on the global production networks is principally by utilizing imported intermediate products, as opposed to supplying parts and components to foreign producers. It is the other way around in South Asia, suggesting that SAARC member countries join global production networks by exporting parts and components for further processing.

Table 3.2 provides data on trends in world production network trade since 2001 for East Asia and South Asia. These were computed using the Athukorala (2010) method. The data highlight the growing role of East Asia in world production network trade over the 2000s. Between 2001–4 and 2009–13, East Asia's share of the world production network trade rose significantly from 39 per cent to 48 per cent. South Asia's share of the world production network trade also rose but only from 1 per cent to 1.6 per cent. The PNP gap between East and South Asia has therefore widened. Within East Asia, China (25 per cent), followed by Japan (8 per cent), and Korea (5 per cent) accounted for the largest share of the world production network trade, while in South Asia, India (0.8 per cent) and Bangladesh (0.5 per cent) accounted for the largest shares. Also, while East Asia flourished on trade in P&C for the manufactured sector, India focused on the services, due mainly to its expertise in technologies, reasonable number of technical innovators, an existing strong business process outsourcing (BPO) market, and supportive government policy (Thangavelu and Chongvilaivan 2013).

Summing up, unlike East Asia, South Asia has not been successful in linking itself to global production networks. The reason is that South Asia is lagging behind in terms of well-established logistics (including ICT development, trade facilitation, and infrastructure development) in which low service link costs make geographically dispersed production nodes along the vertically linked value chain possible for leveraging on economic complementarities and gains from vertical specialization. The environment for doing business is also not very good in South Asia. Finally, unlike in East Asia, South Asian countries are not well-linked with each other in terms of trade and capital flows.

As highlighted in ADBI (2014), the underdevelopment of logistics in South Asia poses serious concerns that the region will not be able to realize the full potential of the supply chain trade. Figure 3.2 highlights this point by demonstrating a fitted plot between GVC participation rates and logistic performance indices (values) among South Asian and

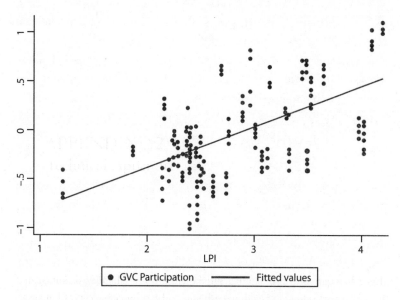

Figure 3.2   A Fitted Plot of GVC Participation versus Logistics Performance Index in South Asia and East Asia
Source: Authors' calculation based on the World Bank's World Development Indicators (WDI) and UNCTAD-Eora GVC Databases.
Note: The values of GVC Participation rates are logit-transformed.

East Asian countries. The relationship appears to slope positively, suggesting that logistics performance is a key driver of participation in global production networks in the region.

Determinants of PNP Participation

While the East Asian countries, especially developing ones, have participated actively in global value chains, it is discernably less so in South Asia. A natural question arises: What are the policies that South Asian countries should adopt to link themselves to global production networks? We developed a simple econometric model to answer this question by analysing the determinants of PNP participation in South Asia and East Asia.

Our empirical framework builds on the model of trade in parts and components, incorporating the variables that capture service link costs, as in Golub, Jones, and Kierzkowski (2007). We use UNCTAD's

GVC participation rates as the dependent variable. As hypothesized above, logistics development in different forms, business environment, and regional economic ties may be the catalysts of GVC participation. Therefore, these three are the independent variables in our model. Our model takes the following form:

$$GVCP_{it} = \alpha_0 + \beta_1 GDPP_{it} + \beta_2 FDI_{it} + \beta_3 LPI_{it} + \beta_4 SAARC_i$$
$$+ \beta_5 ASEAN_i + \beta_6 IMPSTV_i + \beta_7 CHINA_i + \beta_8 INDIA_i \qquad (1)$$
$$+ \beta_9 GFC_t + \mu_i + v_t + \varepsilon_{it}$$

where ε_{it} is the stochastic error term. $GVCP_{it}$ is the GVC participation rate. GDP per capita ($GDPP_{it}$), expressed in a logarithmic form, enters the specification to control for a country's stage of economic development (Athukorala 2010; Athukorala and Menon 2010). FDI_{it} stands for the stock of FDI inflows per capita expressed in logarithmic form. It aims to capture how the business environment conducive to foreign investors influences GVC participation.[1]

Central to our analysis are the logistics performance indicators (LPI) and the dummies of regional economic groupings. LPI_{it} is the value of LPI expressed in a logarithmic form. $SAARC_i$ and $ASEAN_i$ are the dummies of SAARC and ASEAN groupings.[2] They take value of unity if they are the members of the groupings; and nil otherwise. $IMPSTV_i$ is the dummy of major developing ASEAN member countries including Indonesia, Malaysia, the Philippines, Singapore, Thailand, and Vietnam. As discussed above, these countries are major players of the East Asian production networks. $CHINA_i$ and $INDIA_i$ are the dummies for China and India, respectively, to account for their large, emerging economies. GFC_i is the time dummy of the global financial crisis in 2008–9 when international demands and trade severely plunged, thereby affecting GVC participation. μ_i and v_t are unobservable country- and time-specific characteristics.

---

[1] A more appropriate proxy of the degrees to which business environments are conducive to foreign investors are the World Bank's 'ease of doing business' indicators. However, for most countries in the dataset, the surveys are available only from 2010 onwards.

[2] Since the samples include eight South Asian countries, ten ASEAN countries, and Plus Three countries, the dummy of East Asia needs to be dropped from the specification due to perfect collinearity.

Three econometrics issues are addressed. First, since the dependent variable ranges from zero to one, model (1) is estimated by using the fractional logit method (Maddala 1983; Papke and Wooldridge 1996) for efficiency. Second, as is well known, the estimation can be subject to omitted variable biases. In order to address this issue, random effects estimates were obtained using the generalized least squares (GLS) methods. We also performed the Breusch–Pagan Lagrangian multiplier test for random effects (Breusch and Pagan 1979). As is well known, if the statistic rejects the null hypothesis of no random effects, the test is in favour of the random effects estimation as opposed to the fixed effects estimation with the standard ordinary least squares method. Lastly, due to variation in country size, the stochastic error term could be subject to the heteroskedasticity problem. We, therefore, opted for the heteroskedasticity–robust estimators.

As defined above, GVC participation comprises two components—upstream and downstream components. The former pertains to the foreign value added used in a country's own exports while the latter reflects a country's own exports that are further processed by foreign counterparts. It is, therefore, of interest to investigate how the determinants of GVC participation influence the upstream and downstream components. Hence, we estimated, two different forms of equation using UNCTAD's database for 12 East Asian countries (except for Myanmar) and 8 South Asian countries during 2002 to 2011.

$$
\begin{aligned}
UGVCP_{it} = \alpha_0 &+ \beta_1 GDPP_{it} + \beta_2 FDI_{it} + \beta_3 LPI_{it} + \beta_4 SAARC_i \\
&+ \beta_5 ASEAN_i + \beta_6 IMPSTV_i + \beta_7 CHINA_i + \beta_8 INDIA_i \quad (2)\\
&+ \beta_9 GFC_t + \mu_i + v_t + \varepsilon_{it}
\end{aligned}
$$

and

$$
\begin{aligned}
DGVCP_{it} = \alpha_0 &+ \beta_1 GDPP_{it} + \beta_2 FDI_{it} + \beta_3 LPI_{it} + \beta_4 SAARC_i \\
&+ \beta_5 ASEAN_i + \beta_6 IMPSTV_i + \beta_7 CHINA_i \quad (3)\\
&+ \beta_8 INDIA_i + \beta_9 GFC_t + \mu_i + v_t + \varepsilon_{it}
\end{aligned}
$$

where $UGVCP_{it}$ and $DGVCP_{it}$ are the upstream and downstream components of GVC participation, respectively.

Tables 3.3 and 3.4 provide the summary of statistics and correlation matrix of control variables, respectively. Out of 200 observations, 185

Table 3.3 Summary of Statistics

Variable	No. of Obs.	Mean	S.D.	Min	Max
$GVCP_{it}$	210	48.88	10.76	26.78	75.1
$UGVCP_{it}$	210	23.13	13.57	0.15	59.98
$DGVCP_{it}$	210	25.74	6.20	9.94	44.88
$GDPP_{it}$	200	7.61	1.52	5.45	10.52
FDI_{it}	205	20.82	2.53	13.81	26.52
LPI_{it}	200	1.01	0.25	0.19	1.43

Source: Authors' calculation.
Note: $GDPP_{it}$, FDI_{it} and LPI_{it} are expressed in a logarithmic form.

observations or 92.5 per cent enter the econometric models, due to missing observations. Although correlation of some variables such as $GDPP_{it}$ and LPI_{it} appears to be rather high around 0.7–0.8, dropping these variables does not affect the main findings and, thus, the relatively high correlation can be deemed as acceptable.

Table 3.5 presents the fractional logit results based on the random effects GLS estimation. The first column is pertinent to the estimation of the GVC participation equation (1) while the second and third columns break down GVC participation into the upstream and downstream components as in equations (2) and (3), respectively. The Wald Chi-square tests are statistically significant at 1 per cent across all estimations and point to satisfactory goodness of fit. Additionally, the Breusch–Pagan tests are statistically significant at 1 per cent, in favor of random effects as opposed to fixed effects and standard ordinary least squares estimations.

The main findings of our econometric analysis are as follows:

1. GVC participation, both upstream and downstream, is positively correlated with the level of a country's economic development. As shown in Table 3.5, the coefficient of $GDPP_{it}$ is positive and statistically significant at 1 per cent across all equations. This is not surprising and is consistent with the casual observation that more advanced countries in South Asia and East Asia like China, India, Indonesia, Malaysia, Singapore, and Thailand tend to participate more actively in global production networks than the lower-income countries. It should, however, be noted that the causality between GDP per capita and

Table 3.4 Correlation Matrix

	$GDPP_{it}$	FDI_{it}	LPI_{it}	$SAARC_i$	$ASEAN_i$	$IMPSTV_i$	$CHINA_i$	$INDIA_i$	GFC_t
$GDPP_{it}$	1								
FDI_{it}	0.46	1							
LPI_{it}	0.76	0.70	1						
$SAARC_i$	-0.44	-0.50	-0.60	1					
$ASEAN_i$	0.04	0.18	0.26	-0.73	1				
$IMPSTV_i$	0.25	0.36	0.42	-0.58	0.79	1			
$CHINA_i$	0.02	0.42	0.19	-0.20	-0.21	-0.16	1		
$INDIA_i$	-0.13	0.23	0.10	0.28	-0.20	-0.16	-0.06	1	
GFC_t	0.03	0.04	0.06	0.01	-0.01	-0.003	-0.003	-0.003	1

Source: Authors' calculation.

Table 3.5 Random Effects GLS Estimation of the GVC Participation Equations

Variable	GVC Participation	Upstream Component	Downstream Component
$GDPP_{it}$	.2420*** (.0596)	.2372** (.0988)	.1376** (.0655)
FDI_{it}	.0247** (.0117)	.0235 (.0161)	.0201* (.0114)
LPI_{it}	.1894 (.1440)	.9352** (.1877)	−.3884*** (.1352)
$SAARC_i$	.4660* (.2763)	.7944 (.5365)	.1985 (.3294)
$ASEAN_i$	.7087** (.3331)	1.110* (.6546)	.2958 (.4000)
$IMPSTV_i$	.0950 (.2311)	.0191 (.4767)	−.2122 (.2851)
$China_i$	.0701 (.3606)	.0923 (.7358)	.2170 (.4423)
$India_i$	−.1058 (.2900)	−.6344 (.6046)	.3350 (.3593)
GFC_t	.0016 (.0270)	−.0261 (.0346)	.0315 (.0251)
Constant	−3.062*** (.5474)	−5.239*** (.9137)	−2.358*** (.5994)
No. of Obs.	185	185	185
Wald Chi-squared	82.79***	70.44***	23.73***
Breusch-Pagan Test	271.31***	415.01***	397.68***

Source: Authors' calculation.
Note: * Statistically significant at 10 per cent; ** statistically significant at 5 per cent; *** statistically significant at 1 per cent; Robust standard errors in parentheses.

GVC participation can run the other way, that is, GVC participation serving as a catalyst of economic development. Causality issues are not the focus of this chapter and should be explored in further research.

2. Inward FDI is a key driver of GVC participation. This implies that countries with business environment conducive to foreign investors tend to participate more in GVC trade (Golub et al. 2007). However, the positive effects of FDI are statistically significant only in the downstream, not the upstream, component. As shown in Table 3.5, the coefficients of FDI_{it} are positive and statistically significant at 1 and 10 per cent in the first and third columns, respectively, while that in the upstream component equation in the second column, albeit positive, appears to be statistically insignificant. An explanation for this finding has been put forward by Chongvilaivan (2012) and Fujita and Hamaguchi (2012), whereby inward FDI flows from high-income countries fuel participation in global production networks by developing Asian countries. Intuitively, in the context of

developing Asia, inward FDI from advanced countries, especially the European Union, Japan, and the US, is to operate production facilities in low-wage countries and supply parts and components for other downstream production activities overseas through exports (see, for instance, Hiratsuka 2011). This pattern of the FDI–GVC participation nexus is widely discerned in major industries in East Asia, especially electronics and automotive industries. As countries' exports go to downstream activities in other countries, inward FDI is a complement to the downstream component of GVC participation.

3. Interestingly, logistics performance influences the upstream and downstream components of GVC participation in opposite ways. This results in the statistically insignificant effect on overall GVC participation. As shown in Table 3.5, the coefficient of LPI_{it} in the upstream component column is positive and statistically significant at 1 per cent. This implies that, in line with Zeddies (2011), improved logistics performance advocates a country's GVC participation in the upstream activities. This may be explained by the fact that development of logistics infrastructure allows businesses and operators to tap imported parts and components, thereby substantiating the upstream component of GVC participation. On the other hand, logistics performance is negatively correlated with GVC participation in the downstream activities as the coefficient of LPI_{it} in the downstream component column turns out to be negative and statistically insignificant. One possible explanation of the negative relationship is that a country with superior logistics infrastructure tends to be the location for final assembly as opposed to the location for sourcing parts and components.

4. The regional economic integration platforms, SAARC and ASEAN, serve as a driver of GVC participation. Specifically, the coefficient of $SAARC_i$ in the GVC participation column appears to be positive and statistically significant at 10 per cent although the effects on the upstream and downstream components, individually, are not statistically significant. In comparison with SAARC, ASEAN gives a bigger push to GVC participation. This could be because the level of economic integration is deeper in ASEAN than in SAARC. The

positive coefficient of $ASEAN_i$ in the GVC participation column is more pronounced than that of $SAARC_i$ and statistically significant at 5 per cent. In addition, while the effects on the downstream component remain insignificant, the coefficient of $ASEAN_i$ is positive and statistically significant at 10 per cent. This implies that ASEAN member countries are more deeply engaged in the upstream component of GVC participation.

5. The dummies for ASEAN-6 ($IMPSTV_i$), China, and India are not statistically significant across all specifications. This suggests that after controlling for various factors discussed above, these country-specific effects are negligible. Likewise, the coefficient of GFC_t is statistically insignificant across all estimations. This means GVC participation by countries in South Asia and East Asia was unaffected by the plunge in global trade during the global economic crisis in 2008–9.

The Second Round of Look East Policies

As explained in Chapter 2, in order to further enhance economic linkages between South Asia and East Asia, the former group of countries should implement the second round of Look East policies to

1. Link themselves with global production networks, especially those in East Asia, their largest potential market
2. Develop production networks in manufacturing and services within their region.

The econometric analysis in the previous section suggests that such policies should, broadly comprise: improving the business environment by completing the reform process begun in the 1980s and the early 1990s, improving logistics costs including 'at the border' through trade facilitation, especially for the upstream component of GVC participation, and joining and participation in various ongoing regional trade and financial cooperation efforts. Although not included in the model, two related policies are able to reduce communication and coordination costs in the management of supply chains by improving ICT, and enhancing regional physical connectivity through transport hardware to reduce logistic costs.

Accordingly, LEP2 that should be implemented by South Asian countries should comprise five, sometimes overlapping, policies. The first component of LEP2 should be to complete the reform process begun in the 1980s and the early 1990s. South Asia has made significant progress in reducing tariff barriers to external trade. But there is still room to reduce these barriers further as they are higher in South Asia than in other Asian regions and even low tariffs are a significant deterrent to supply chain trade as parts and components cross national boundaries several times (Figure 3.3). With reduction in tariffs, however, non-tariff barriers including governance, regulatory barriers, transport, and standards have become more important determinants of competitiveness in South Asia.

South Asian countries need to accelerate the implementation of microeconomic reforms including second-generation reforms. These comprise continued reforms of the agricultural and industrial sectors; public institutions for improved governance at all levels (civil service, bureaucracy, and public administration); institutions that create or maintain human

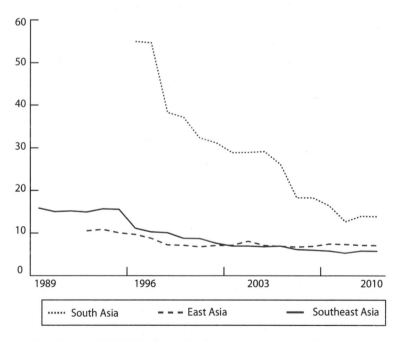

Figure 3.3 MFN Tariff Trends in Asia (Weighted using Imports)
Source: Reproduced with permission from ADB (2012).

capital (education and health); and improving the environment affecting the private sector (regulatory environment, flexibility in the labour market, legal and physical infrastructure, and clearly-defined property rights). These reforms are required to mobilize domestic private sector investment as well as to reduce behind-the-border costs for trade and FDI. In India, for example, manufacturing comprises only 15 per cent of the GDP, the same as in the 1960s because it is constrained by entrenched bureaucracy, poor infrastructure, restrictive labour laws, and absence of property rights. Unlike in China, therefore, this sector has not been able to absorb too much labour force. This is now starting to change and the Indian model of IT-enabled service-led growth is slowly starting to give way to the more traditional development model where both industry and services drive economic growth and create jobs. But the journey is long. Unlike macroeconomic reforms, however, successful implementation of second-generation reforms require a wider consensus in the countries and a long-term orientation.

The need for second-generation reforms in South Asia is highlighted by various indicators from the World Bank and the ADB. According to the World Bank's Doing Business Survey 2015, in terms of overall 'ease of doing business' rankings, South Asia, on average, ranks lower than East Asia and Latin America. As shown in Table 3.6, in most South Asian countries, the overall ranking deteriorated in 2015 compared to 2005.[3] Poor performance of South Asia reflects mainly the difficulties in enforcing contracts, trading across borders, getting electricity, dealing with construction permits, and in paying taxes. India's ranking in 2015 was 130—slightly better than that of Laos—which was mainly due to difficulties in enforcing contracts, dealing with construction permits, and paying taxes.

As shown in Table 3.7, the ADB provides a further breakdown of trading costs. These suggest that the real costs to export and import are, on an average, higher in South Asia than in East Asia and Latin America. Again, it is only Africa that performs worse than South Asia

---

[3] The number of countries ranked in the 2015 survey has increased compared to the 2006 survey from 155 to 189. The methodology has also changed for various sub-indices over the years.

Table 3.6 Ease of Doing Business Indicators (2015)

	Ease of Doing Business Rank		Starting a Business	Dealing with Construction Permits	Getting Electricity	Registering Property	Getting Credit	Protecting Minority Investors	Paying Taxes	Trading Across Borders	Enforcing Contracts	Resolving Insolvency
	2015	2016										
Afghanistan	183	122	42	186	159	186	101	189	163	175	180	159
Bangladesh	176	65	122	138	187	185	157	70	151	173	189	151
Bhutan	73	104	94	97	54	51	82	114	19	26	47	169
India	130	116	155	185	26	138	44	13	172	143	172	136
Maldives	135	31	65	62	145	172	133	123	134	147	105	135
Nepal	107	55	109	123	131	72	139	63	142	69	152	89
Pakistan	144	60	141	150	170	169	82	27	156	172	157	85
Sri Lanka	110	75	74	88	86	155	118	42	158	90	163	75
South Asia	134	N.A.	95	118	122	127	97	78	124	137	148	125
China	90	91	127	177	97	42	62	123	131	96	5	53
Japan	29	10	89	60	15	49	82	53	70	49	48	2
Korea	5	27	11	31	1	39	44	13	23	32	1	4
Brunei	101	N.A.	84	37	21	134	62	102	89	142	93	57
Cambodia	135	133	180	183	136	120	7	114	124	102	178	72
Indonesia	114	115	151	116	49	118	62	70	104	108	166	76
Laos	148	147	160	47	155	65	75	165	146	120	88	169
Malaysia	18	21	112	13	8	40	20	3	61	60	42	46
Myanmar	177	N.A.	146	66	149	143	175	179	119	159	188	164

(Cont'd)

Table 3.6 (*Cont'd*)

Philippines	95	113	171	85	22	112	118	137	115	95	136	56
Singapore	1	2	6	10	10	19	20	1	8	41	2	29
Thailand	26	20	78	42	37	68	82	27	109	56	51	23
Vietnam	78	99	121	24	96	59	32	87	167	93	69	125
East Asia	78	N.A.	113	83	66	82	70	84	92	62	82	70
Latin America	107	N.A.	113	105	84	118	89	107	130	100	104	106
OECD	25	N.A.	46	48	37	44	57	43	42	24	45	23

Source: World data from World Bank (2015k); World Bank (2006).

Table 3.7 Trading Costs by Subregion (2012)

	Real Cost to Export (Man days)	Real Cost to Import (Man days)	Time to Export (Days)	Time to Import (Days)	Documents to Export (Number)	Documents to Import (Number)
Asia	9.9	12	16.4	14.8	5.7	6.4
East Asia	7.2	7.6	16	14.1	5.7	4.7
Southeast Asia	9.4	11.7	13.2	13.2	4.9	5.9
Central Asia	41.4	64.8	56.5	59.9	8.6	10.2
South Asia	34.5	35.6	20.4	17.2	7.8	8.7
High-income countries	6.0	6.4	8.9	8.6	4.0	4.7
Latin America	25.1	28.5	20.7	15.2	6.2	6.3
Africa	114.7	152.3	38.3	29.5	9.1	8.2

Source: Data from ADB (2012).
Note: Asia does not include the Pacific and Oceania. Nominal costs to export/import per country were deflated by gross domestic product per work (in constant 1990 purchasing power parity $) per country and weighted based on each country's contribution to total regional/subregional export and import 2011 values; Organization for Economic Co-operation and Development (OECD) excluding Japan and Korea.

and the only Asian subregion that fares worse than South Asia is Central Asia. The number of documents required for exporting and importing in South Asia are about twice of those in high-income countries. The same is true for time to export and import.

ADB (2012) also provides data that permit a comparison of the quality of infrastructure across various Asian subregions as shown in Table 3.8. They show that, as expected, the overall quality of all types of infrastructure, including roads, rail, ports, air, and electricity, has improved in 2012 across all Asian subregions compared to 2008. The most significant increases have been made in road infrastructure,

Table 3.8 Infrastructure Quality Index-Share of G7 Average by Subregion (Per cent) (2012)

	Overall Infrastructure	Infrastructure Type				
		Road	Rail	Port	Air	Electricity
Asia	76 (+9)	71 (+6)	69 (+2)	75 (+3)	80 (+1)	67 (+3)
East Asia	90 (+9)	87 (+5)	98 (+9)	92 (+3)	89 (+1)	90 (+7)
Southeast Asia	80 (+6)	79 (+5)	58 (−1)	83 (+3)	86 (−2)	73 (0)
Central Asia	71 (+10)	59 (+5)	64 (−3)	55 (−4)	71 (−1)	63 (+7)
South Asia	61 (+10)	60 (+6)	55 (+3)	70 (+7)	72 (0)	41 (−3)

Source: Data from ADB (2012).
Note: Asia does not include the Pacific and Oceania; G7 includes Canada, France, Germany, Italy, Japan, the United Kingdom, and the United States; Values are regional/subregional averages. Figures show the ratio between the indices of the individual countries/regions and the G7 average. Figures in parentheses show the increase/decrease in index points from 2008.

followed by electricity and ports. However, the quality of railway and air infrastructure has not improved much. The data show that the overall quality of infrastructure is the worst in South Asia, followed by Central Asia, and that infrastructure quality is the best in East Asia followed by Southeast Asia. The quality of infrastructure in South Asia averages about 60 per cent of the G7 level, while the corresponding figure was 90 per cent in East Asia. Overall, the quality of infrastructure in Asia is, on average, three-quarters that of the G7.

The second component of LEP2 should be to reduce logistic costs including at-the-border costs through trade facilitation. Logistic services involve the process of planning, implementing, and controlling the efficient and cost-effective flow and storage of raw materials, inventory, and finished goods from a point of origin to the point of consumption. With production fragmented across countries, efficient logistics is a key determinant of a country's competitiveness and ability to attract production blocks. Trade facilitation at the border is also important.

To improve trade facilitation at the border, delays in customs inspection need to be minimized, while cargo handling and transfer, and processing of documents need to be modernized. Customs procedures need to be modernized by:

1. Aligning the customs code to international standards
2. Simplifying and harmonizing procedures
3. Making tariff structures consistent with the international harmonized tariff classification
4. Adopting and implementing the WTO Customs Valuation Agreement

South Asian countries have made some progress in implementing many of these procedures but much more remains to be done.

Overall weaknesses in trade facilitation and connectivity are captured by the logistics performance index calculated by the World Bank using perception-based indicators. As shown in Table 3.9, these use surveys of operators and the index ranges from one (lowest) to five (highest). The index focuses on several variables: customs performance, infrastructure, international shipments, logistics competence, tracking and tracing, and timeliness. These indices show that, on average, South Asia is not only behind the OECD but also behind East Asia and Latin America. It is only ahead of Africa. South Asia scores particularly low on the infrastructure component of the index. South Asia has, therefore, a long way to go in terms of improving trade facilitation and logistics.

The third component of South Asia's LEP2 should seek to deepen further economic linkages with East Asia. Countries that have formally or informally adopted Look East policies should strive to improve them to enhance trade and investment linkages and connectivity with East Asia. India, the largest country in South Asia and a member of G20, has already been invited to negotiate the RCEP. Eventually, other South Asian countries could also follow to join the RCEP (Francois and Wignaraja 2009). India should actively lobby and negotiate its participation in ongoing macroeconomic and monetary integration efforts in East Asia. A few years back, the former Thai Minister of Finance Chalongphob Sussangkarn (2010) had proposed that India, Australia, and New Zealand be made associate members and contributing partners—short of full membership—of the Chiang Mai Initiative Multilateralization, a $240 billion bailout fund among ASEAN+3 countries. This proposal should be explored further. Expanded membership

Table 3.9 Logistic Performance Index (2016)

Country	LPI Rank	LPI Score	Customs	Infrastructure	International Shipments	Logistics Competence	Tracking/ Tracing	Timeliness
Afghanistan	150	2.1	2.2	1.8	2.4	2.2	1.8	2.6
Bangladesh	87	2.7	2.6	2.5	2.7	2.7	2.6	2.9
Bhutan	135	2.3	2.2	2.0	2.5	2.3	2.2	2.7
India	35	3.4	3.2	3.3	3.4	3.4	3.5	3.7
Maldives	104	2.5	2.4	2.6	2.3	2.4	2.5	2.9
Nepal	124	2.4	1.9	2.3	2.5	2.1	2.5	2.9
Pakistan	68	2.9	2.7	2.7	2.9	2.8	2.9	3.5
South Asia	N.A.	2.6	2.4	2.5	2.7	2.6	2.6	3.0
China	27	3.7	3.3	3.8	3.7	3.6	3.7	3.9
Japan	12	4.0	3.9	4.1	3.7	4.0	4.0	4.2
Korea	24	3.7	3.5	3.8	3.6	3.7	3.8	4.0
Brunei	70	2.9	2.8	2.8	3.0	2.6	2.9	3.2
Cambodia	73	2.8	2.6	2.4	3.1	2.6	2.7	3.3
Indonesia	63	3.0	2.7	2.7	2.9	3.0	3.2	3.5
Laos	152	2.1	1.9	1.8	2.2	2.1	1.8	2.7
Malaysia	32	3.4	3.2	3.5	3.5	3.3	3.5	3.7
Myanmar	113	2.5	2.4	2.3	2.2	2.4	2.6	2.9
Philippines	71	2.9	2.6	2.6	3.0	2.7	2.9	3.4
Singapore	5	4.1	4.2	4.2	4.0	4.1	4.1	4.4

Thailand	45	3.3	3.1	3.4	3.1	3.1	3.2	3.6
Vietnam	64	3.0	2.8	3.1	2.7	2.9	2.8	3.5
East Asia	N.A.	3.2	3.0	3.2	3.1	3.1	3.2	3.6
Latin America and Caribbean	N.A.	2.7	2.5	2.7	2.5	2.6	2.7	3.1
Sub-Saharan Africa	N.A.	2.5	2.4	2.5	2.3	2.4	2.4	2.8
High Income: OECD	N.A.	3.8	3.6	3.6	3.7	3.7	3.8	4.1

Source: Data from World Bank (2016).

of the CMIM and the ERPD would strengthen Asia's voice at the G20 high table (Rana 2012b). Joint policy coordination meetings of the expanded ASEAN+3 would provide a robust regional agenda for the ASEAN chair to table at the G20 Summits.

The fourth component of LEP2 in South Asia should be to improve ICT to reduce communication coordination costs of supply chains. Data in Chapter 4 show that although South Asian countries outperform several East Asian countries, especially the low-income Cambodia, Laos, and Myanmar, they lag behind other East Asian countries in ICT development.

The fifth and final component is improving regional physical infrastructure connectivity. The dominant mode for freight transport between South Asia and East Asia is ocean transport, which accounts for about 80 per cent of the total, as there is no land transport services that are operational at the present time and also because ocean transport is the most cost-effective way of moving bulky items (Rana 2012b). Rapid growth in trade has been accommodated through the introduction of larger container ships. However, expansion and diversification of feeder services and bottlenecks, primarily in public ports, are issues that remain to be addressed.

More recently, the need for land connectivity, both road and rail, has increased for several reasons.

1. Wages are rising sharply in the coastal region of China and industries are being relocated inwards.
2. The recent cautious political and economic reforms in Myanmar have provided a fillip to various transportation projects in the region.
3. Service links between production blocks in supply chains are time-sensitive and land transportation may be viable especially between neighbouring countries.

In the case of high-value items (for example, perishable goods), even airfreight could be viable. At the request of the East Asia Summit, the Economic Research Institute for ASEAN and East Asia (ERIA) has come up with two project concepts to connect India with ASEAN (Kimura and Umezaki 2011). These are the Mekong–India Economic

Corridor (MIEC) and the Trilateral Highway connecting India with Myanmar and Thailand along the Asian Highway. While the major focus of the MIEC is to connect automotive industry in Bangkok with those in Chennai, India, the Trilateral Highway seeks to develop the North East region of India that is lagging behind the rest of the country. The economic and industrial corridor to be established under the MIEC is to constitute state-of-the art transportation infrastructure such as expressways and high-speed railways that connect major industrial agglomerations, modern airports, special processing zones, and enabling policy frameworks. Both of these projects are consistent with the Master Plan on ASEAN Connectivity adopted in October 2010 because it seeks to promote connectivity not only within ASEAN but also the broader East Asia region, including India.

In order to enhance connectivity between South Asia and East Asia, in addition to ASEAN–India connectivity, it is also necessary to promote connectivity between South Asia, China, and ASEAN. One such project could be the Yunnan–Myanmar–India–Nepal–Tibet–Yunnan Economic Corridor or the old South-western Silk Road (Chapter 5). In July 2005, the Yunnan province, from where the old South-western Silk Road began, was identified by the Chinese government as a 'bridgehead' to enhance cooperation with the countries of the Greater Mekong Subregion.

With Myanmar opening up, this concept could be extended to link Kunming with Kolkata and the rest of South Asia. The proposed Circular Economic Corridor would also be consistent with Nepal's potential as a land bridge between the two giant economies of India and China (Lohani 2011; Pandey 2006). Finally, the concept would be consistent with the Chinese government's strategy of identifying bridgeheads for subregional cooperation with neighbouring countries and ultimately linking them as part of its Go West and 'New Silk Road' policies.[4]

---

[4] In addition to Yunnan Province, other 'bridgeheads' for subregional cooperation identified by the Chinese government are Guanxi Province for Pan-Beibu Gulf Cooperation and Xinjiang Province for Central Asian States. The Go West policy, or more formally the Western Development Program, was launched in 2000 focusing on six provinces (including Yunnan), five autonomous regions (including Tibet), and one municipality.

4

ICT DEVELOPMENT AND DIGITAL DIVIDE BETWEEN SOUTH ASIA AND EAST ASIA

As noted in the previous chapter, linking production hubs in various countries requires efficient service links including well-developed ICT infrastructure so that production blocks in a supply chain can be managed efficiently. This chapter has two objectives: to review the level of ICT development in South Asia and East Asia and to recommend policies that South Asian countries should implement to close the digital divide with East Asia and within their region.

The rest of this chapter is organized as follows. The next section reviews the linkages between ICT, economic development, and international trade, while the third section assesses the current state of ICT development in South Asia and East Asia with a view of examining the digital divide between the two regions. Three dimensions of ICT development are considered:

1. Physical access
2. Availability and affordability
3. ICT use

Finally, policies that South Asian countries should implement to close the digital divide with East Asia are outlined. These policies are grouped as national, regional (at the level of SAARC), and the broader pan-Asian policies.

ICT, Economic Growth, and International Trade

A number of studies have found that robust ICT infrastructure leads to increased productivity, economic growth, and international trade. At the micro level, increased broadband usage leads to positive network externalities including the reduction of excess inventories and optimization of supply chains (Atkinson et al. 2009). A study by the World Bank (Qiang and Rossotto 2009) has found that a 10 per cent increase in broadband penetration rate results in a 1.21 percentage points increase in the GDP growth rate in high-income countries and a 1.38 percentage point increase in low- and middle-income countries. Using panel data from the OECD during 2002–7, Koutrompis (2009) has also found a positive relationship between broadband penetration rate and GDP growth. Similarly, Fornfeld, Delauney, and Elixmann (2008), using data from European countries, have found a strong impact of broadband penetration on GDP, employment, and productivity. Aside from economic growth, several other studies have also established a positive relationship between broadband penetration and productivity (Fornfeld et al. 2008). Jebsen (2007) found that the use of mobile phone by fishermen in the Kerala, a state in India, led to substantial increase in both producer and consumer welfare.

Yushkova (2013) has argued that ICT development could lead to reduction in trading costs in a number of ways.

1. ICT contributes to greater transparency in markets and, therefore, reduces the search, matching, and communication costs.
2. ICT usage leads to the reduction of monitoring and management costs of firms.
3. ICT deployment could lead to the reduction of shipping costs in part due to the organizational changes and digitalization.
4. ICT usage may reduce the transit time of goods.

Digital Divide between South Asia and East Asia

A robust ICT infrastructure not only provides trade-enhancing benefits but also provides meaningful social and economic spillovers, such as reducing the digital divide within a country. Digital divide has three dimensions–physical access to ICT, availability and affordability of ICT, and ICT use. The data analysed in this section show the digital divide between South Asia and East Asia and within countries in a region.

Physical Access to ICT

One commonly used indicator of ICT diffusion is the mobile penetration rate defined as the number of mobile users (SIM cards issued) in a country divided by its population. These data shown in Figure 4.1 suggest that although the mobile penetration rate has been increasing steadily both in South Asia and East Asia (and its subregions including China, Japan, Korea, ASEAN+6, and CLMV) during the period

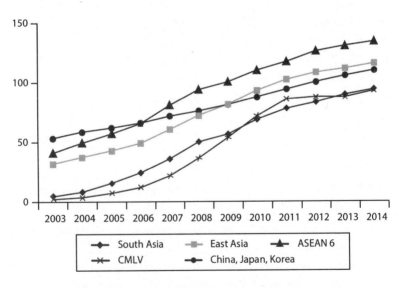

Figure 4.1   Mobile Phone Penetration Rate (Per 100 Population) (2003–14)
Source: Business Monitor International Database, 2015.

2003–14, the digital gap between the two regions has remained more or less unchanged. The gap (defined as the difference in mobile penetration rates between the two subregions) has averaged at 22 for the period 2008 to 2014.

The market penetration rates for individual South and East Asian countries in 2014 are shown in Figure 4.2. The data show that mobile penetration ratio averaged 116 in East Asia while it stood at 94 in South Asia. All East Asian countries except for China, Laos, and Myanmar had penetration rates that were higher than the South Asian average with the figure ranging from 154 for Singapore to 114 in Philippines. Within South Asia, Maldives had the highest mobile penetration rate of 181 followed by Sri Lanka with 104 while other countries were below the average of 94.

Reflecting the increasing trend of mobile phone penetration, the penetration of fixed-line telephone has been declining steadily in all Asian subregions (Figure 4.3). The lower cost of mobile phone ownership compared to a fixed-line telephone contributed to this decline.

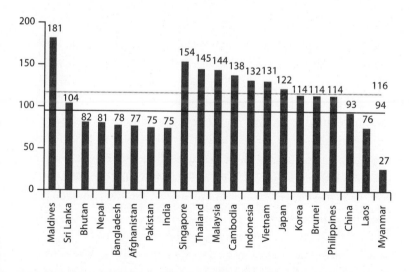

Figure 4.2 Mobile Phone Penetration Rate (Per 100 Population) (2014)
Source: Business Monitor International Database, 2015.
Note: 116 is the average for East Asia, while 94 is the average for South Asia.

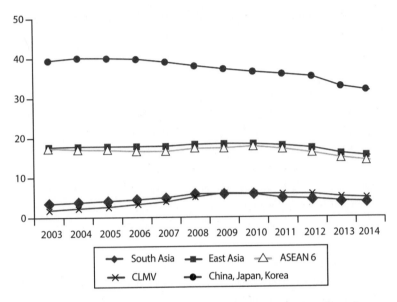

Figure 4.3   Fixed-line Telephone Penetration Rate (Per 100 Population) (2003–14)
Source: Business Monitor International Database, 2015.

Another commonly used indicator of access to ICT is the internet penetration rate. These data in Figure 4.4 also suggest a similar trend. Internet penetration rate has been increasing steadily in both South Asia and East Asia during the period between 2001 and 2013. The data also show that the internet divide between South Asia and East Asia has increased from 14 per cent in 2001 to 26 per cent in 2013. In 2013, the internet penetration in East Asia was 44 per 100 population, while in South Asia it was only 18. Within East Asia, China, Japan, and Korea had the highest internet penetration rate (72 per 100 population) followed by ASEAN 6 (48), and the CLMV (16).

Household access to computers and the internet is another indicator of ICT development. Once again the data show a digital divide between South Asia and East Asia. The divide is more pronounced in the case of internet access rather than access to computers. Data show that China, Japan, and Korea have the highest proportion of total households with access to these technologies followed by ASEAN 6 (Figure 4.5).

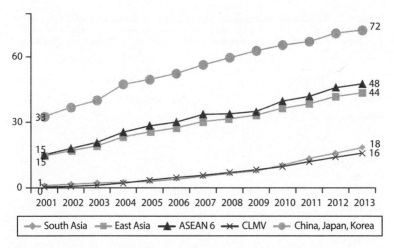

Figure 4.4 Internet Users (Per 100 Population) (2001–13)
Source: World Development Indicators, 2015.

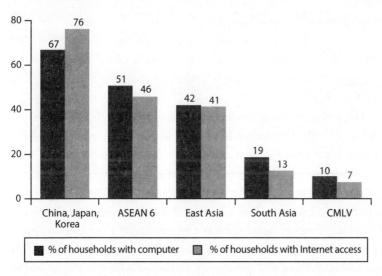

Figure 4.5 Household Accesses to Computer and Internet (2013)
Source: International Telecommunications Union (2014).

Availability and Affordability of ICT

Another dimension of ICT development is the availability and afford-ability of ICT. For mobile telephony service, network availability and quality are important determinants of uptake. The data in Table 4.1

Table 4.1   Population Covered by Mobile Cellular Network (2015)

Country	Percentage Network Coverage	Country	Percentage Network Coverage
East Asia		**South Asia**	
China	100	Afghanistan	90
Japan	100	Bangladesh	99
Korea	100	Bhutan	98
Brunei	97	India	93
Cambodia	99	Maldives	100
Indonesia	95	Nepal	85
Laos	98	Pakistan	86
Malaysia	96	Sri Lanka	98
Myanmar	79		
Philippines	99		
Singapore	100		
Thailand	97		
Vietnam	94		

Source: Data from World Development Indicators.

show that, aside from Myanmar in East Asia, a high proportion of the population is covered by mobile cellular networks in both South Asia and East Asia.

The cost of ICT services is another important determinant of access and use. If the cost of using an ICT service such as mobile phone is prohibitive, then the uptake of such service will be low. In response to calls for a global benchmark on ICT prices, the International Telecommunications Union (ITU) has since 2009 started to publish the ICT Price Basket (IPB) which measures the average cost of fixed-telephones, mobile phones, and fixed-band internet connections as a percentage of a country's monthly gross national income per capita. These data in Figure 4.6 suggest that the average costs of ICT services are higher in South Asia (5 per cent of monthly per capita GNI) than in East Asia (3 per cent). The cost of ICT services are the highest in Afghanistan where it accounts for 17.2 per cent of monthly per capita GNI and lowest in Singapore (0.3 per cent). In South Asia, the costs of ICT services are the cheapest in Sri Lanka (1 per cent of monthly per capita GNI) followed by Maldives (1.6 per cent of monthly per capita GNI).

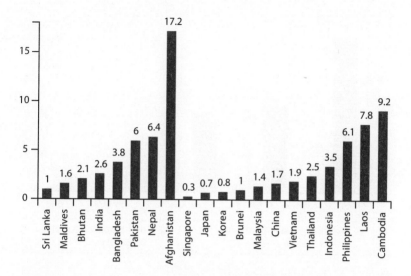

Figure 4.6 ICT Price Basket and Sub-Baskets (2013)
Source: International Telecommunications Union (2014).

ICT Use

According to ITU, access to broadband is a good proxy of ICT use in a country (ITU 2014). These data in Figure 4.7 show once again that South Asia lags behind East Asia on the use of ICT. The divide is more pronounced in the case of wireless broadband use (34 per cent) than fixed broadband use (9 per cent). On average, South Asia's broadband use pattern (both wireless and fixed) is comparable to that of the CLMV.

Overall Quality of ICT Infrastructure

Since 2008, the ITU has started to publish the ICT Development Index (IDI) that, among others, is a composite index assessing ICT access, affordability, and usage. This index can range from 0 to 10 (the higher the IDI value, the better). Figure 4.8 shows the IDI index for countries in South Asia and East Asia in 2013. The striking picture that emerges from Figure 4.8 is a stark digital divide between countries. On average, countries in East Asia have a relatively higher IDI index (4.9) than in

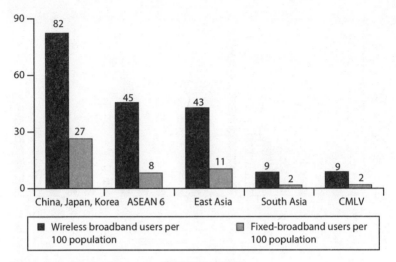

Figure 4.7 Various Measures of ICT Use (2013)
Source: International Telecommunications Union (2014).

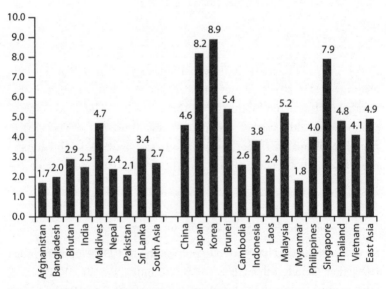

Figure 4.8 ICT Development Index (2013)
Source: International Telecommunications Union (2014).

South Asia (2.7). Korea, Japan, and Singapore lead not only regionally but also globally. Within South Asia, Maldives, Sri Lanka, and Bhutan have a higher IDI index than Pakistan, Bangladesh, and Afghanistan.

ICT and Education

The use of ICT is a function of a country's social sector development. Specifically, the relationship between ICT and education is important. This is because education provides the skills required for creating, adapting and utilizing such ICT technologies. There are a large number of studies focusing on the discussion about the digital divide across countries. In general, many of these studies suggest that the higher the literacy rate, the larger the ICT penetration rate (Quibria et al. 2002 and Robinson et al. 2003). For instance, in their regression exercises covering more than 100 countries, Quibria et al. (2002) show that the relationship between computer usage and education is statistically significant at 1 per cent level with tertiary education. The same is true for internet use. Secondary education is also significant at 1 per cent level for telephone. Using a framework developed by DiMaggio and Hargittai (2001), Robinson et al. (2003) found that respondents with college education possess added advantages over high-school–educated respondents in using the Internet to derive occupational, educational, and other benefits.

Given the strong evidence of complementarity between ICT use and the relevant education levels, if the South Asian countries aspire to exploit the significant opportunities offered by new ICT, particularly the creation of new industries, they need to focus on bringing up the overall literacy rate of the population. Not examining this dimension and merely suggesting ICT development alone without investing in education may not achieve the desired goals.

Recommended Policy Actions in South Asia

South Asian countries could consider a number of policy actions at the national, regional, and Pan-Asian level to reduce the digital gap with East Asia and within their own region.

National Policies

Individual country policies that could be considered by the South Asian countries are summarized in Table 4.2. These policy

Table 4.2 Policy Measures to Promote Supply and Demand of ICT Services

Bangladesh

Access	Affordability	Use
Encourage further investment in undersea cable communication links to overcome bottlenecks in the country's ICT infrastructure.	Reduce tax on ICT goods. In Bangladesh, a 57.8 per cent tax is added to the cost of ICT goods and services over and above the universal 15 per cent VAT.	Focus on scaling-up e-government applications with large citizen interface such as those related to land records.
Provide needed framework focused on facilitating innovation, healthy competition, and removing barriers to efficient delivery of service to customers in addition to implementing the broad vision spelt out in the Digital Bangladesh policy.	Reconsider the imposition of a 1 per cent surcharge on cell phone use.	Build capabilities and skills among the youth in the field of ICT.

Bhutan

Access	Affordability	Use
Further enhance development of the ICT industry such as through continued support of the Thimpu Technology Park and other similar initiatives.	Expand internet access service to rural areas and make it affordable through price regulation.	Continuously support ICT training programmes (such as through READ Bhutan) to increase ICT literacy among the population
Use the Bhutan–Bangladesh power grid which is fitted with optical ground ware to carry Internet Protocol (IP)-Transit bandwidth back to Bangladesh and therefore improve Bhutan's international bandwidth.	Formulate the right policies to open the Bhutanese telecom market to encourage competition in the sector.	Prioritize use of mobile channels to deliver government services (m-government services) and support m- or e-payment facilities.

India		
Access	**Affordability**	**Use**
Support investments aligned with India's 100 Smart Cities Mission.	Foster investment in mobile broadband across the country by ensuring that the business environment is built on trust and certainty.	Improve access to e-government channels including e-healthcare, e-education, e-agriculture, technology for financial inclusion, technology for justice, and technology for security among other things.
Implement roadmaps and plans under the Digital India Master Plan especially those related to building broadband highways, universal access to mobile connectivity, and increasing access to the Internet via multi-service centres especially in rural areas.	Ensure availability of spectrum at reasonable cost.	Improve human resources related to ICT training and skills upgrading.
Finish the deployment of the National Optical Fibre Network project.	Continue implementation of targeted subsidy for students to fund use of tablets for education.	Update the legal framework governing cybersecurity to instil trust in the country's ICT infrastructure.

(Cont'd)

Table 4.2 (Cont'd)

Maldives		
Access	Affordability	Use
Mandate open access to the dominant operator's backbone network to encourage market entry of new players.	Issue another license for Internet services to bring down cost.	Give the responsibility of maintaining the '.mv' domain to a neutral body such as the Communications Authority of Maldives.
Implement provisions of the National Broadband Plan, especially those related to infrastructure sharing and interconnection of service providers.	Support roll out of the government's push to roll out a basic broadband package within an affordable price range.	Encourage development of local content in partnership with educational institutes, NGOs, other government agencies, and so forth.

Nepal		
Access	Affordability	Use
Use Rural Telecom Development Fund to provide telecom services to rural areas.	Provide subsidies to operators interested to bring ICT services in rural areas.	Improve ICT literacy, especially in rural areas.
Assess readiness of critical infrastructure in response to natural disasters.	Review the provision that requires 20 billion rupees renewal fees associated with cellular mobile license and basic telephone service license.	Allocate state budget to develop use of ICT within government.

Pakistan

Access	Affordability	Use
Increase utilization rate of the Universal Service Fund (about $1 billion) to provide access infrastructure in underserved areas.	Reduce or eliminate usage tax on telecom.	Make available local contents that are relevant to the people especially from the rural areas such as information on farming, setting up a business, and so on.
Increase the number of telecentres that are being set up across the region from the originally planned 500 by 2018.	Fully implement the Telecom Service Retail Tariff Regulations 2015 to ensure affordability and transparency in pricing of mobile tariff rates.	Formulate comprehensive e-government Master Plan down to the province level to encourage use of e-government services.
Support roll-out of fibre-back connectivity to the country's backbone network.	Adapt Pakistan's Telecom Policy to be in-line with current best practices in various areas of regulation including competition to broaden affordability to access of telecom services.	Ensure that all stakeholders are consulted regarding the passage of Electronic Crimes Bill 2015 to instil trust and confidence in the ICT infrastructure of the country.

(Cont'd)

Table 4.2 *(Cont'd)*

	Sri Lanka	
Access	Affordability	Use
Ensure independence of the Telecoms Regulatory Commission and transparency in its operation.	Desist from imposing technology-specific taxes	Improve ICT education in schools
Ensure sustainability of government projects such as the current free Wi-Fi programme.	Improve regulatory action to reduce price of international connectivity where the Sri Lanka Telecom holds control over submarine cable stations keeping IP transit cost high.	Continuous support of government's eNABLE project which targets improving ICT use and access to disabled and marginalized groups.

Source: Data from World Bank, ITU and various national publications.

recommendations are classified under three headings—those seeking to enhance access, affordability, and use of ICT—and were derived from various publications of the ITU, World Bank, and various think tanks.

Broadly, these policies aim to stimulate ICT development through supply-push and demand-pull strategies. To enhance the supply of ICT infrastructure, governments can lead the way in several ways.

1. They can ensure that effective market competition is in place in the telecom and ICT sector. Kim et al. (2010) have noted that in the area of broadband market promotion, market competition is a critical element as it helps to bring down the cost of ICT services.
2. Governments can facilitate access to the right-of-way. By lowering the barriers and costs of accessing right-of-way associated with the construction of ICT networks, the government can increase incentives and encourage the private sector to invest in ICT networks.
3. Where market forces and competition are not adequate, governments can fund or co-fund network roll-out through public-private partnership models.
4. Finally, governments can also play a leading role in the area of encouraging the adoption of ICT services and applications. This can be done by promoting the awareness and attractiveness of using ICT services, improving digital literacy, spearheading efforts to develop local content, expanding access of ICT services to underserved communities, connecting schools to broadband networks, and providing targeted subsidies to encourage ownership of ICT devices among others.

In order to enhance access to ICT by their citizens, most South Asian countries have adopted ICT Master Plans and Broadband Plans (Table 4.2). These plans outline the vision of the governments, objectives, and strategies of countries for ICT development. The challenge facing many countries in the region is implementing these strategies, ensuring that targets are met, and making sure that funding is available. Coordination across various agencies and sectors is also necessary in implementing the plans and so is stakeholder participation and strong political support. Several key projects to improve access to ICT are also identified in Table 4.2. For example, Bangladesh needs to encourage further investment in undersea communications link and India needs to support investments aligned with its Smart City projects. Table 4.3 also highlights policies recommended to enhance use of ICT both in the public (for example, through rollout of e-governance projects) and the private sectors.

Regional Policies

At the regional level, South Asian countries must participate in effectively implementing the Revised SAARC Plan of Action on Telecommunications. This action plan adopted by the SAARC Communications Ministers in 2004 seeks to:

1. Promote cooperation in the enhancement of telecommunication links and utilization of information technologies within the SAARC region
2. Minimize disparities within and among member states in the telecommunications field
3. Harness telecommunication technology for the social and economic upliftment of the region through infrastructure development by optimal sharing of available resources and enhanced cooperation in technology transfer, standardization, and human resource development
4. Evolve a coordinated approach on issues of common concern in international telecommunications forums

The recent establishment of the SAARC Working Group on Telecommunications and ICT is a step in the right direction and, hopefully, these will lead to a SAARC ICT Master Plan similar to the ASEAN ICT Master Plan (Box 4.1).

Outside of SAARC, various regional mechanisms exist to facilitate knowledge exchange and networking for policymakers in the region. One such mechanism is the South Asian Telecommunication Regulator's Council (SATRC) that was formed in 1997 and has been meeting regularly ever since. SATRC meetings have high levels of representation from the regulatory bodies in South Asian countries. Through various working groups within SATRC, the body is able to provide policy recommendations on cross-regional issues such as mobile roaming and coordination in the use of the mobile spectrum. Since 2005, SATRC has developed action plans to coordinate its work. The current action plan, Phase V, focuses on policy coordination in regulation and in capacity-building. SATRC has been instrumental in harmonizing ICT standards and radio frequency coordination. It has focused on regional mobile roaming which could eventually pave the way for affordable roaming prices in the region.

Pan-Asian Efforts

Asian countries should also participate effectively in the Asian Information Superhighway (AIS) initiative of UNESCAP. The AIS initiative aims to develop a fibre-optic network along rights of ways of UNESCAP's Asian Highway project that links various countries of Asia. This initiative seeks to enhance the availability and affordability of broadband internet connection across Asia and the Pacific by strengthening the underlying internet infrastructure in the region. Work on the AIS is ongoing and a regional framework including norms and principles is presently under negotiation. Funding issues have also to be resolved.

Box 4.1   ASEAN ICT Master Plan (2015)

The ASEAN ICT Masterplan was launched in 2011 to encourage greater cooperation among ASEAN member countries through the use of ICT. Specifically, the AIM 2015 vision is to harness ICT to create an inclusive, vibrant, and integrated ASEAN. The AIM 2015 spells out three pillars, and three foundations to support four key outcomes (Figure 4.9).

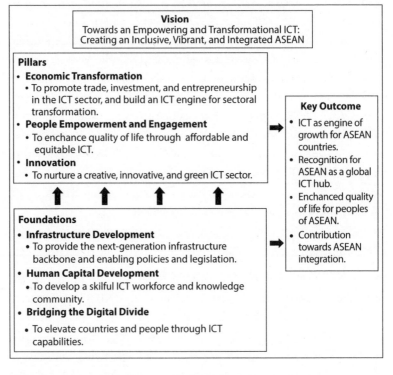

Figure 4.9   ASEAN ICT Master Plan (2015)
Source: Authors.

According to the Midterm Review of the ASEAN ICT Masterplan in 2013, 29 action points had been implemented of which 62 per cent had been completed, 24 per cent were ongoing, and 14 per cent were at risk of being unfulfilled. One of the reasons for the latter include unrealistic timelines.

5

REVIVAL OF THE SILK ROADS IN ASIA

The Silk Roads refer to the historical network of land-based trading routes that connected Asia with the Middle East, North Africa, the Mediterranean, and Europe. Although traffic on the Silk Roads comprised little more than camel caravans trudging through wind-swept deserts and frigid mountain passes, at that time there was no alternative form of connectivity between Asia and Europe. Vasco da Gama sailed around the Cape of Good Hope and landed in Calicut on the Malabar Coast of India in 1498. The Dutch, the Spanish, the French, and the British followed suit only later. The Silk Roads began to be used roughly a century before the birth of Christ. With a rich history spanning about 1,600 years, trade on the Silk Roads started to decline after the collapse of the Mongol Empire in the fourteenth century. Eventually, the invention of the steam engine and steamships during the Industrial Revolution led to a sharp decline in shipping costs and the Silk Roads lost out further to the Southern Ocean Corridor connecting Europe and Asia. The situation has now started to change.

As discussed in the section on 'Need for Actions to Revive the South-western Silk Road', trading costs—which are defined as the real costs to export and import—are higher, on average, in South Asia than in East Asia. ADB and ADBI (2015) have also found that reducing trading costs could have a positive impact on trade and investment relationships and economic welfare. This chapter, therefore, focuses on land connectivity in Asia with a view to reducing trading costs.

The rest of the chapter is organized as follows: the next section briefly reviews the history of the Silk Roads and highlights the reasons for its decline. It also argues that there were actually two Silk Roads in Asia—the Northern Silk Road and the less well-known South-western Silk Road (SSR) which connected South/Central Asia with southern China and present-day ASEAN. The third section high-lights the various factors—economic, security, and political—that have led to the revival of land connectivity in Asia and the actions that are presently being taken to revive the Silk Roads.[1] The fourth section finds that while efforts to promote the Northern Silk Road, which are driven mainly by the Go West and the New Silk Road policies in China,[2] are on track, more actions are required to revive the SSR or connectivity between South Asia/Central Asia, southern China, and East Asia. Finally, the summary and policy implications are presented.

History of the Silk Roads and the Reasons for their Decline

There were actually two major Silk Roads. The Northern Silk Road began from the present-day Xi'an in China. Further west, in Dunhuang, it branched into two routes which converged in Kashgar, before continuing on to the Mediterranean and Europe (Figure 5.1).

There was also a less well-known SSR which began in the Yunnan province of China. The SSR had four sections: the Sichuan–Yunnan–Burma–India Road which began in Chengdu, the capital of Sichuan, and then proceeded to Kunming and Dali in Yunnan province before entering Burma and India; the Yunnan–Vietnam Road; the

---

[1] Chapter 6 conducts a Perception Survey of opinion leaders to access the relative strengths of these factors.

[2] Also referred to as 'One Belt, One Road' policy and the 'Belt and Road Initiative'.

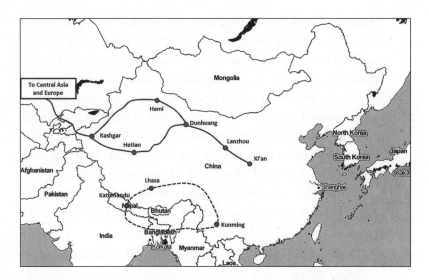

Figure 5.1 The Northern Silk Road and South-western Silk Road (SSR)
Source: Authors.
Note: Map not to scale and does not represent authentic international boundaries.

Yunnan–Laos–Thailand–Cambodia Road; and the Yunnan–Tibet Road (Yang 2009). Singhal (1969) and Frank (1998) have, in addition, alluded to trade over two overland routes through Nepal and Tibet to China. The SSR was, therefore, a circular road connecting South Asia and Central Asia with southern China and present-day ASEAN. It began in Yunnan, passed through Myanmar, India, Nepal, and Tibet and looped back to Yunnan.

The Silk Roads witnessed their zenith during the Mongol Empire in mid-thirteenth century when political stability allowed more trade in the region. There were significant complementarities in trade: merchandise that did not seem valuable to the Mongols and the Chinese (for example, silk, lacquerware, porcelain) was often seen as valuable by the West and the Mongols, in turn, received large amounts of luxurious goods from Europe: dates, saffron, and pistachio nuts from Persia; jade, almonds, indigo, and frankincense from Central Asia. India supplied paper, sandalwood, and cotton to the West. Marco Polo travelled the Silk Road to China at that time.

Trade on the Silk Roads started to decline after the fourteenth century for a number of reasons. After the collapse of the Mongol Empire, Genghis Khan's descendants converted to different religions and waged wars against each other, disrupting trade on the Silk Roads. The isolationist foreign policies of the Ming and the subsequent Qing dynasties of China also did not help. The sharp lowering of shipping costs which began with the invention of the steam engine during the Industrial Revolution also led to an increase in Europe's maritime trade with Asia on the so-called Southern Ocean corridor (Baldwin 2006). This corridor began in the Mediterranean, continued past South Asia, through the Straits of Malacca, and up the East Asian coast to Korea and Japan.

Reasons for the Revival of the Silk Roads and Actions Being Taken

Although sea transport is expected to be the dominant form of connectivity in the foreseeable future, the case for reviving land connectivity has increased for a number of economic, security, and political reasons. The first reason is the implementation of the Western Development Strategy or the Go West policy in China. More recently, China has also launched the New Silk Road policy. As is well known, China's economic reforms, which began in 1978, focused on the eastern coastal region of the country. In particular, special economic zones (SEZs) were established in four major coastal cities to attract foreign direct investment with liberal incentives. This policy proved to be a huge success and made the country the fastest-growing country in the world for a long period of time. Such a development strategy, however, led to the widening of economic disparity between the coastal region and the rest of the country, specially the inner western part of the country. The Go West policy was implemented in 2000 partly to address this economic disparity. The two key components of the policy were:

1. To build basic infrastructure such as transport system, power generation, gas and oil pipelines, telecommunication system, and environmental conservation

2. To attract private sector investment including FDI in the western region (Phanisham 2006; Zhong 2002).

The New Silk Road policy has two components (Szczudlik-Tatar 2013; MFA 2013). The first is the New Silk Road Economic Belt announced during President Xi Jinping's visit to Central Asia in September 2013 which seeks to jointly develop energy and transport infrastructure projects with neighbouring countries, first in Central Asia and then in South Asia. The second is the Maritime Silk Road policy which seeks to promote connectivity with the countries in Southeast Asia. As part of its Go West and New Silk Road policies, China has also established several bridgeheads for subregional connectivity such as the Yunnan province for Greater Mekong Subregion and India, Guangxi Province for Pan-Beibu Gulf Cooperation, and the Xinjiang province for cooperation with Central Asia.

China has achieved success in the above areas. Mainly because of these efforts, cities in inner provinces, such as Kunming, Chongqing, Chengdu, Xi'an, and Xining have emerged as major metropolitan cities with urban infrastructure projects paralleling some of those in the coastal areas. A number of expressways have been constructed from the coastal cities of Shanghai and Beijing to the inner provinces (Figure 5.2). These include the Shanghai-Xi'an, Shanghai–Chongqing–Kunming, Shanghai–Kunming, and Beijing–Lhasa Expressways.[3] The Beijing–Lhasa expressway has also been completed up to Xining, the halfway point, and the progress is expected to be quick (*The Economist* 2012).

[3] China's highways have grown rapidly in total length from 271 km in 1990 to 85,000 km in 2011 making this the world's largest national freeway system. The US Interstate Highway system—started in 1956 and considered complete in 1991—totals 75,932 km and is not expected to grow much. China, on the other hand, will expand its expressway system and is intent on connecting all provincial capitals and cities with populations over 200,000. The new highways and the economic growth they will drive will help close the gap with the US (Lee 2013). China's railway network was 27,000 km in 1949, now it is more than 110,000 km.

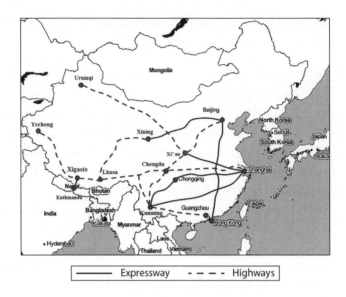

Figure 5.2   Infrastructure Development in China: Highways and Expressways
Source: Authors.
Note: Map not to scale and does not represent authentic international boundaries.

Of particular note is Lhasa's emergence as a major transportation hub in western China. There are five major highways that converge in Lhasa: Kunming–Lhasa, Shanghai–Chengdu–Lhasa, Beijing–Lhasa Expressway, Yecheng–Lhasa, and the Friendship highway that connects Kathmandu (Nepal) with Lhasa. Also, the Beijing–Tibet Railway has reached Xigaste, and is to be extended soon to reach the border with Nepal.

Figure 5.3 shows the key existing and proposed railway lines and pipelines in China. In addition to the north–south railway lines— some of which are high-speed—connecting the major cities of the country, China has built the east–west lines to connect far-flung cities like Urumqi and Kasghar to Xi'an and the major coastal cities. A trans-Karakoram corridor has also been proposed through Pakistan (Figure 5.3). As already mentioned above, the Beijing–Tibet railway has also been operational for a number of years. A new railway line from Chengdu to Tibet is under construction. The east–west line has also been extended to Moscow, using Central Asia as an economic

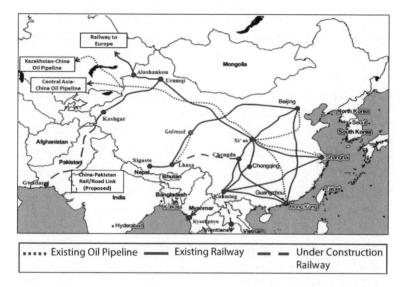

Figure 5.3 Infrastructure Development in China: Railways and Pipelines
Source: Authors.
Note: Map not to scale and does not represent authentic international boundaries.

corridor, and then on to Duisburg (in Germany) to become the China–Europe railway line (Figure 5.3).[4] Hewlett-Packard (HP) has been using this line to ship Chinese-assembled laptops to Europe from its Chongqing factories since 2011. Logistics company DHL also runs regular express trains to Europe from Chengdu. In July 2013, this railway line was extended to Zhengzhou, the largest inland manufacturing base for the Taiwanese electronics from the Foxcon Technology Group, to export mainly Apple products directly to Germany via Moscow. It takes around 21 days to reach Europe by rail, while seaborne transport between China and Europe takes around five weeks, with much longer delay times. Transport from inland China to Europe by rail costs about 25 per cent more than by sea, but for these

---

[4] This railway line was built in 2011 by a group of private companies. It is called the Yuxinou line and is 11,000 kilometres long, 2,000 kilometres shorter that the Shanghai–Germany line.

companies, the benefits of speed appear to outweigh the extra costs (Bradsher 2013; SGI 2013). China plans to build railroads not only in its country but also across the length and breadth of Africa, Eurasia, and Southeast Asia.

The rationale for Go West and the New Silk Road policies are not solely economic. China has also been trying to reduce its exposure to security risks and possible disruptions to its oil and resources supply from off its eastern coastal regions and beyond by building east-west pipelines such as the Kazakhstan–China and Central Asia–China pipelines (Figure 5.3). The Sino-Burma gas pipeline has been inaugurated. In both goods and energy trade, the overland transport corridor is unlikely to account for more than 5–7 per cent of China's total trade with Europe for a long time in the future. It will, however, certainly curtail China's over-reliance on the sea-lanes in the South and East China Seas (SGI 2013).

The second reason for the revival of land connectivity in Asia is the LEP in South Asia, specially India, and presently also in Myanmar. As part of their economic reform program, these countries have sought to improve connectivity with ASEAN and China to enhance trade and investment with each other. The ongoing bilateral/trilateral connectivity projects are summarized in Appendix A5.1. In addition, India is actively seeking to enhance ASEAN-India connectivity through two projects, namely, the Mekong–India Economic Corridor (MIEC) and the Trilateral Highway connecting India and Myanmar with Thailand (Kimura and Umezaki 2010) (Figure 5.4).[5] While the first project focuses on connecting production blocks and supply chains in Southeast Asia, specially the automotive industry in Bangkok, with those in Chennai (India) by sea and land, the second project focuses on the development of the North East region of India, which is relatively under-developed. One major component

---

[5] India has also established the ASEAN–India Center at Research and Information System for Developing Countries (RIS), New Delhi, to drive these projects.

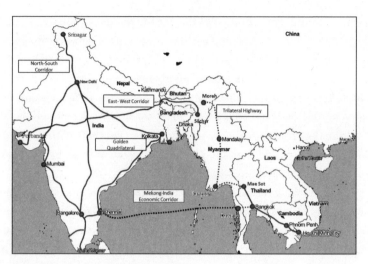

Figure 5.4   ASEAN–India Connectivity
Source: Authors.
Note: Map not to scale and does not represent authentic international boundaries.

of the MIEC is the $8.6 billion Dawei deep-sea port.[6] The ADB is the implementing body for the MIEC and it stands ready to bring together the stakeholders and provide technical assistance and co-financing. This role is similar to the one the ADB played in the GMS and the Central Asia Regional Economic Cooperation (CAREC) subregional cooperation efforts. In May 2013, the leaders of India and China endorsed the BCIM Economic Corridor and established a joint study group to explore ideas further (Ministry of External Affairs, Government of India 2013). Subsequently, ministerial-level talks under the BCIM framework were initiated in December 2013 transforming the Track II initiative to a Track I process.

The third reason is the encouraging but gradual political and economic reforms in Myanmar, a node between South Asia and East Asia, which has provided a boost to improving connectivity between South Asia and East Asia. Both China and India are actively involved. Chinese strategists have written about the 'Malacca Dilemma' with the Straits

---

[6] This project is presently facing financing difficulties.

being a natural choke point and the need to find an alternative route.[7] The 1,100-kilometre gas pipeline component of the Sino-Burma pipelines project from Kyaukphyu, a port in Myanmar, to Kunming became operational in 2013. This year, an oil pipeline that is expected to meet about 10 per cent of China's oil import demand will open along the same route. Roads and railways are to follow suit. Work on the Kaladan Multimodal Project seeking to connect Kolkata in India with Sittwe in Myanmar by sea and then the North East region of India by river and road transport is also ongoing (Appendix A5.1).

Finally, looking forward, in order to realize the potential of dynamic complementarities associated with the newer theories of trade pioneered by Jones and Kierzkowski (1990), there is a need to strengthen connectivity between South Asia and East Asia. Under the traditional theory of comparative advantage, developing countries produced labour-intensive goods which they then exchanged for relatively capital- and skill-intensive goods produced by the more advanced countries. All separate tasks involved in producing a good, however, were done entirely in one country. Under the newer theories, production is sliced and diced into separate fragments and production of parts and components are located in production blocks around the world which are linked by efficient service links. The type of service link required for supply-chain trade depends on the sector being considered. For bulky items, sea freight is still the most cost-effective way of moving goods. For less bulky and high value-added parts and components, road transportation could be more cost-effective, especially among neighbouring countries.

Need for Actions to Revive the South-western Silk Road

As discussed above, under the Go West and the New Silk Road policies of China, a large number of actions have already being taken

---

[7] Roughly 80 per cent of China's crude oil imports pass through the straits. The other strategic projects for China's oil imports are the proposed China–Pakistan Economic Corridor passing through some of the highest and most landslide-prone mountains (Figure 5.3), the proposed Kunming–Laos–Thailand Railway (Figure 5.3), and pipelines with Central Asian countries and Russia.

to revive the Northern Silk Road. These actions have resulted in encouraging results. The situation is, however, different in the case of the SSR. The ASEAN–India connectivity projects and the BCIM Economic Corridor are parts of the old SSR. In addition, efforts must be made to revive the Yunnan–Myanmar–India–Nepal–Tibet–Yunnan Economic Corridor. The perception survey in Chapter 6 supports this argument.[8] The survey also finds that the BIMSTEC is the appropriate mechanism to drive this process. Recently, India has highlighted that one of the focuses of the BIMSTEC should be 'promoting connectivity for seamless movement between India's Northeast, Myanmar, and Thailand on one side and with Bangladesh, Bhutan, Nepal on the other (Padmanabhan 2014).

Summary and Policy Implications

Summing up, contrary to the general belief, in the bygone era, there were not one but two Silk Roads—the Northern and the lesser well-known South-western Silk Roads. The latter connected South and Central Asia with southern China and the present day ASEAN. It began in the Yunnan province of China, passed through Myanmar, India, Nepal, and Tibet and looped back to Yunnan. After a gap of roughly five centuries, the case for reviving the Silk Roads has strengthened for economic, security, and political reasons. The focus has been mainly on reviving the Northern Silk Roads. A number of actions have also been initiated to revive the SSR. These include the various bilateral/trilateral projects, the projects under ASEAN–India connectivity, and the proposed BCIM Economic Corridor. In addition, efforts should be made to revive the Yunnan–Myanmar–India–Nepal–Tibet–Yunnan Economic Corridor or the old SSR.

A major finding of this chapter is that Maritime Asia, defined as the dynamic north–south coastal region from Korea to Indonesia, is starting to become more continental with expanding networks of roads, railways,

[8] Rana and Karmacharya (2015) have made the case for four Trans-Himalayan Economic Corridors to connect South Asia, Central Asia, and East Asia.

and pipelines. This finding is not a new one because Asia was an integrated and prosperous region of the world for much of human history. It was only during the colonial period and the few decades that followed India's independence that Asia was fragmented into the dynamic maritime Asia and the more closed and less prosperous South Asia (Rana 2012a). An important implication of this finding is that several regional institutions that focus solely on Maritime Asia are losing their relevance. There is a need to either expand membership of these institutions to bring in members from continental Asia—for example, India is not a member of the APEC—or to strengthen institutions in continental Asia such as the Shanghai Cooperation Organization (SCO).[9] Bubalo and Cook (2012) have also argued that in contrast to the situation in maritime Asia where the influence of the West was strong, the influence of India, China, and Russia in continental Asia is also expected to be strong. This has important implications for Asia's security.

[9] The SCO was established in 2001 with Russia, China, Kazakhstan, Uzbekistan, Kyrgyzstan, and Tajikistan as its founding members and India, Pakistan, Iran, and Mongolia as observers, with Sri Lanka and Belarus as dialogue partners.

APPENDIX A5.1
Bilateral and Trilateral Connectivity Projects

India/Myanmar: Tamu–Kalewa–Kalemyo Road

Project Description

The 160-kilometre-long Tamu–Kalewa–Kalemyo road was constructed by India in 2001 and is being used for Indo-Myanmar border trade through the Moreh–

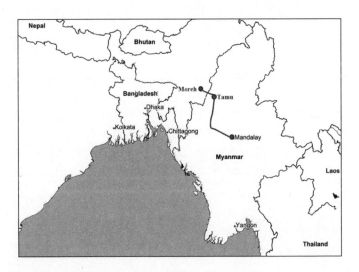

Figure A5.1   India/Myanmar: Tamu–Kalewa–Kalemyo Road
Source: Authors.
Note: Map not to scale and does not represent authentic international boundaries.

Tamu sector. From Kalemyo, there is also road connectivity to Mandalay, the second largest city in Myanmar. Along the 1643-kilometre-long Indo-Myanmar border, this is the only road that connects India and Myanmar. Eventually, there are plans to extend this road until Mae Sot in Thailand.

Project Benefits

This project aims to boost India's trade with Southeast Asia through Moreh and Namphalong in Myanmar.

Estimated Costs

The road was built by India at a cost of over Rs 1205 million.

Project Status

The project was completed in 2001.

India/Myanmar: Kaladan 'Multi-Modal' Project

Project Description

On 2 April 2008, the Indian government signed an agreement for this project with the Burmese military junta. The project will connect the eastern Indian

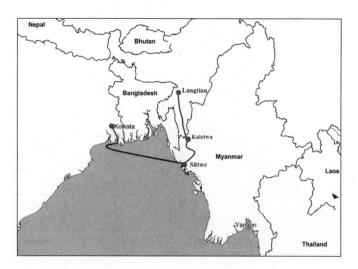

Figure A5.2   India/Myanmar: Kaladan 'Multi-Modal' Project
Source: Authors.
Note: Map not to scale and does not represent authentic international boundaries.

seaport of Kolkata with Sittwe port in Arakan State of Myanmar by sea; it will then link Sittwe to the landlocked region of Mizoram in northeastern India via river and road transport. The project has three phases, the first and second of which began in November 2010.

Project Benefit

It is expected that the transport system will be fully owned by the Myanmarese government, but it will be used primarily by Indian companies to increase trade with Southeast Asia and link the landlocked Mizoram region to the sea.

Estimated Costs

1. Redevelopment of Sittwe port and dredging the Kaladan waterway to Paletwa (Phases 1 and 2)—intially $68.24 million
2. Construction of highway between Palet.wa and the India–Burma border (Phase 3)—$49.14 million.

Project Status

The construction of the port and inland water transport (IWT) terminals at Sittwe and the construction of the IWT terminal at Paletwa started in 2010. In May 2012, the two sides reviewed the project and announced that the project will be completed by 2015 at a total cost of $500 million.

India/Bangladesh/Myanmar: Myanmar–Bangladesh–India Gas Pipeline

Project Description

The Myanmar–Bangladesh–India gas pipeline is an important component of India's energy security policy. It had stalled in the past because of the failure to accommodate Bangladesh's needs. But it is now being revived.

Project Benefit

The project will give India access to Myanmar's offshore gas resources.

Estimated Costs

USD 1 billion to be borne mostly by India and private sector partners and Bangladesh will receive USD 125 million in annual transit fees.

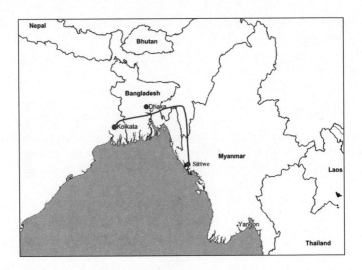

Figure A5.3   India/Bangladesh/Myanmar: Myanmar–Bangladesh–India Gas
Pipeline
Source: Authors.
Note: Map not to scale and does not represent authentic international boundaries.

Project Status

Slow progress in contrast to the Myanmar-China pipeline.

Myanmar/China: Kyaukpyu-Ramree Island–Kunming Pipeline

Project Description

An oil and gas pipeline connecting the natural deep sea port of Kyaukpyu,
Ramree Island, to China's southern city Kunming, in the Yunnan province.

The total length of the pipelines is expected to be in excess of 1,500 kilometres
for the oil pipeline and 1,700 kilometres for the gas pipeline, with around
800 kilometres of that across Burma. A railroad running adjacent to the pipelines is also planned.

Project Benefit

The project will decrease the reliance of China on the Malacca Straits through
which much of its oil and gas supply presently passes.

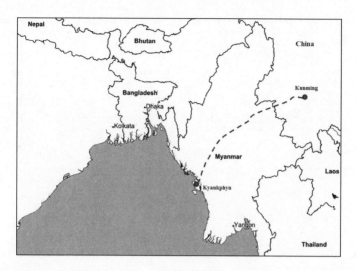

Figure A5.4 Myanmar/China: Kyaukpyu–Ramree Island–Kunming Pipeline
Source: Authors.
Note: Map not to scale and does not represent authentic international boundaries.

Estimated Costs

USD 2.5 billion—China National Petroleum Corporation will hold a 50.9 per cent stake and manage the project and Myanmar Oil & Gas Enterprise will own the rest.

Project Status

The gas pipeline became operational in June 2013 and the oil pipeline is nearing completion.

Myanmar/Thailand: 'Death Railway' Project

Project Description

Myanmar aims to restore the infamous 'Death Railway' to Thailand which was initially built by Japanese-held prisoners of war.

Project Benefit

Improved rail connectivity can facilitate the flow of goods and tourists between the two countries.

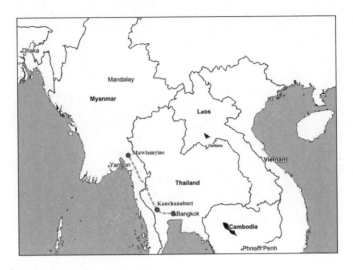

Figure A5.5   Myanmar/Thailand: 'Death Railway' Project
Source: Authors.
Note: Map not to scale and does not represent authentic international boundaries.

Project Costs

There is no information available on expected costs.

Project Status

Unknown.

India/Myanmar/China: Stilwell Road or Ledo Road

Project Description

Originally termed as Ledo Road, the 1,736-kilometre-long Stilwell Road was built during World War II from Ledo in Assam to Kunming so that the Western Allies could supply Chiang Kai-Shek's Kuomintang forces. It was renamed after General 'Vinegar' Joe Stilwell of the US Army in 1945. It winds its way from Ledo in Assam through Jairampur and Nampong in Arunachal Pradesh until it reaches the Pangsau Pass (a.k.a the 'Hell Pass') where it crosses into Myanmar. The road then weaves through upper Myanmar to reach Myitkyina before turning eastward to China where it culminates at Kunming, the capital of the

Yunnan province. Roughly 61 kilometres runs through India, 1,035 kilometres through Myanmar and 640 kilometres in China.

There are plans to rebuild the Stillwell Road. The Indian Chamber of Commerce, has described the potential gains from the reopening of the Stilwell Road as 'unimaginable'.

Project Benefit

The project would encourage greater overland trade especially between China and India.

Estimated Costs

Unknown.

Project Status

The contract has been awarded to China's Yunnan Construction and Engineering Group. But India fears that the road might help insurgents from Northeast India, many of whom have their hideouts in Myanmar.

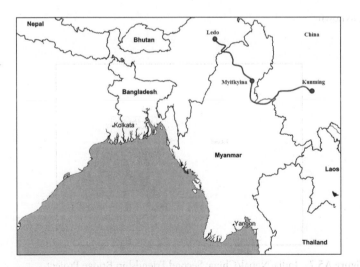

Figure A5.6   India/Myanmar/China: Stilwell Road or Ledo Road
Source: Authors.
Note: Map not to scale and does not represent authentic international boundaries.

India/Nepal/China: Second Friendship Bridge Project

Project Description

Nepal and China have agreed to construct another 'friendship bridge' in Rasuwagadhi on the Nepal–China border. The bridge—proposed to be located · along the Rasuwagadhi highway that stretches to the border with China—is expected to help the two countries expand their cross-border trade and transport, as it will link Nepal with major highways in that part of the northern neighbour. The 100-metre-long bridge will be constructed over the Trishuli River with Rs 100 million contributed by the Chinese.

Project Benefit

The project will connect China with Nepali markets and vice versa.

Estimated Costs

The project is estimated to cost China Rs 100 million and Nepal Rs 60 million.

Project Status

Unknown.

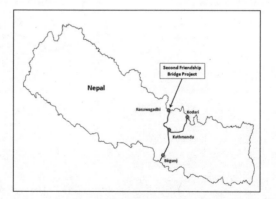

Figure A5.7   India/Nepal/China: Second Friendship Bridge Project
Source: Authors.
Note: Map not to scale and does not represent authentic international boundaries.

China–Nepal–India Railway Project

Project Description

In 2008, China and Nepal announced plans to connect Tibet with Nepal via a 770-kilometre-long rail link between Lhasa and the Nepalese border town Khasa, which is about 80 kilometres north of Kathmandu. It was also announced that a dry port near Tatopani on the Nepali side would be developed as well. China is also exploring the possibility of linking six additional highways with Nepal and developing cross-border energy pipelines. In 2008, China set up an advanced optical fibre cable network between Zhangmu and Kathmandu.

Project Benefit

The Lhasa–Khasa rail network will help Nepal diversify its trade and reduce dependence on India. Nepal faces several bottlenecks in its trade and energy supply chains due to poor connectivity in Nepal and the poor efficiency of Indian ports, which add to delays and higher costs for imported goods and delays in exports.

However, the southern expansion of China's rail networks has caused concern in India, particularly in security circles who argue that Chinese infrastructure projects serve dual purposes, both civilian and

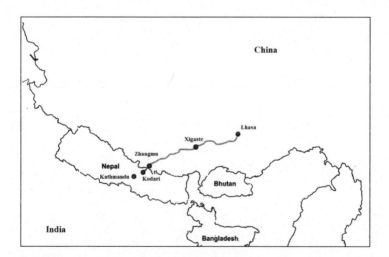

Figure A5.8   China–Nepal–India Railway Project
Source: Authors.
Note: Map not to scale and does not represent authentic international boundaries.

military. The initial plan was to connect Khasa to Lhasa, but due to the difficulty of terrain and the rugged mountains, the railway track has been directed to the Kerung of Rasuwa District. Kerung has been developed as a special economic zone.

Estimated Costs

USD 1.98 billion is the estimated cost.

Project Status

Unknown.

Figure A5.6   China–Nepal–India Railway Project

Source: Author

Note: Map not to scale and does not represent authentic international boundaries.

6

PERCEPTION SURVEY OF ASIAN OPINION LEADERS[1]

During the past two-and-a-half decades, economic linkages between South Asia and East Asia have grown at a rapid pace, albeit from a low base. Several reasons include the economic dynamism of the two regions, market-oriented open door policies of most East Asian countries, and the Look East policies adopted by the South Asian countries, most notably India. These trends are not new. From a historical perspective, Rana (2012a) has argued that during the first 18 centuries after the birth of Christ, based on the economic strengths of India and China, Asia was not only prosperous but also well-integrated. After a gap of nearly two centuries during which South Asia withdrew from the Asian scene and the focus shifted to East Asia, we are now starting to witness the re-emergence of an integrated and prosperous Pan-Asia. Despite the above trends, most authors who write on Asian regionalism focus only on the growing

---

[1] Perception surveys are frequently used to obtain online feedbacks on various options from a wide spectrum of stakeholders. These feedbacks are particularly useful in assessing the relative strengths of various options when it is difficult to use econometric techniques, for example, because of the difficulties in quantifying variables. International institution, such as the ADB, World Bank, APEC, and IMF conduct perception surveys on a regular basis.

trade and financial relationships among the East Asian countries, a phenomenon that picked up pace after the Asian financial crisis of 1997–8.

The major objective of this perception survey is to assess the views of the stakeholders in South Asia and East Asia on the relative strengths of the key findings of the earlier chapters of the book and to get their perspectives on the following factors:

1. Benefits and costs of economic integration between South Asia and East Asia
2. Preferred modalities and approaches of integration
3. Obstacles and barriers
4. Policy actions and institutional arrangements required

A special focus of the survey is on the reasons for the revival of land connectivity between South Asia and East Asia and the low level of integration in South Asia, and the role of South Asia in various East Asian regional initiatives. As far as the authors are aware, this is the first time that such a survey has been conducted.

The rest of this chapter is organized as follows. The survey methodology is outlined in the next section, then the survey results are presented in the following sections. The chapter concludes with some policy implications from the survey.

Survey Methodology and Responses

In conducting the perception survey, we identified a sample of 5,300 opinion leaders from 8 South Asian and 13 East Asian countries in five categories: government officials, academics, representatives from business sectors, media practitioners, retired bureaucrats, and international civil servants. The contact details of the opinion leaders were obtained from an earlier study of the authors supplemented by publicly available contact and mailing lists. The perception survey was conducted online for a period of five weeks from 4 September to

11 October 2013. Opinion leaders were contacted and invited to participate in the survey. Three reminders were also sent as a follow-up to respondents who did not reply.

Two sets of questionnaires were prepared to capture differences in regional perspectives, one for opinion leaders from South Asia and the other for those from East Asia.[2] Each questionnaire consisted of 16 questions that were further classified under eight categories. These included questions on costs and benefits of strengthening economic linkages between the two regions (two questions); the preferred modalities of regional cooperation (one question); the obstacles and barriers to enhancing economic linkages between the two regions (one question); the required policy actions to further enhance economic linkages between the two regions (one question); the initiatives to promote regional trade integration (three questions); the initiatives to promote macroeconomic policy coordination (two questions); and connectivity issues between the two regions (six questions). Two additional questions were also included in the questionnaire for South Asian opinion leaders asking for their view on the status of integration in South Asia. The questionnaires were in English and were designed to take no more than 15 minutes of the respondent's time.

At the end of five weeks we received a total of 390 responses, 203 responses from South Asia and 187 responses from East Asia, corresponding to 7 per cent of the sample. This response rate is reasonable for an online survey. The response rate could possibly have been higher had we used a professional survey firm followed by telephone calls to respondents. The budget for the study, however, restricted us from such an approach. Table 6.1 summarizes the number and percentage of responses by region and category. We had 57 per cent of the respondents from academia, 9 per cent from the business sector, 25 per cent from government officials, and 8 per cent from others

---

[2] The questionnaires are provided in Appendix A6.1.

Table 6.1 Survey Response Profile

	Academia		Business		Government		Others		Total
	Num	%	Num	%	Num	%	Num	%	Num
Afghanistan	0	0	0	0	1	100	0	0	1
Bangladesh	13	93	0	0	1	7	0	0	14
Bhutan	1	20	2	40	2	40	0	0	5
India	65	56	9	8	18	16	24	21	116
Maldives	1	33		0	2	67	0	0	3
Nepal	15	58	5	19	4	15	2	8	26
Pakistan	15	75	2	10	3	15	0	0	20
Sri Lanka	8	44	2	11	8	44	0	0	18
South Asia	118	58	20	10	39	19	26	13	203
China	19	90	0	0	2	10	0	0	21
Japan	11	79	0	0	2	14	1	7	14
Korea	2	50	0	0	2	50	0	0	4
Brunei	0	0	0	0	1	100	0	0	1
Cambodia	1	33	0	0	1	33	1	33	3
Indonesia	12	46	1	4	9	35	4	15	26
Laos		0	0	0	4	100	0	0	4
Malaysia	10	56	2	11	6	33	0	0	18
Myanmar	1	25	2	50	1	25	0	0	4
Philippines	15	58	1	4	10	38	0	0	26
Singapore	14	45	6	19	10	32	1	3	31
Thailand	6	55	1	9	4	36	0	0	11
Vietnam	14	58	3	13	7	29	0	0	24
East Asia	105	56	16	9	59	32	7	4	187
Total	223	57	36	9	98	25	33	8	390

Source: Data compiled by authors from survey responses.
Note: Others include media practitioners, retired bureaucrats, and international civil servants.

including media practitioners, retired bureaucrats, and international civil servants.

Among the 390 responses, 116 of them were from India accounting for about 30 per cent of the total responses, 31 responses or 8 per cent from Singapore, followed by 26 responses or 7 per cent each from Indonesia, the Philippines and Nepal. Countries with less than 10 responses included Afghanistan (one response), Bhutan (five responses), Maldives (three responses), Brunei (one response), Cambodia (three responses), Laos (four responses), Myanmar (four responses) and Korea (four responses).

Survey Results

Chapter 2 has made the case for a second round of LEP in South Asian countries. The five questions that follow focus on these issues and associated policies.

Costs of Strengthening Economic Linkages between South Asia and East Asia

We asked opinion leaders how they rate the costs of strengthening economic linkages between South Asia and East Asia. These costs include:

1. Possible loss of national sovereignty and loss of independence of national economic policies
2. Exposure to unfavourable shocks that might affect them
3. Loss of markets and increase in poverty
4. Weaker linkages with countries outside the region
5. Dilution of national identity and culture

Figure 6.1 summarizes the responses to this question. 19 per cent of the respondents felt that the most important cost of strengthening linkages between South Asia and East Asia is the exposure to unfavourable shocks emanating from the other region. The next most important cost is loss of markets and increase in poverty (13 per cent) followed by loss of national sovereignty (10 per cent) and weaker linkages with countries outside the region (10 per cent). Only 6 per cent of the respondents believed that closer integration between the two regions would lead to the dilution of national identity and culture.

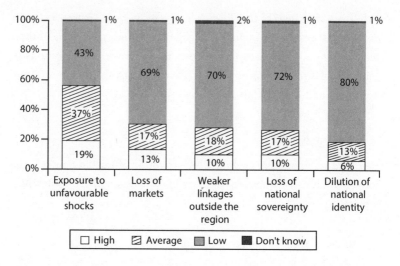

Figure 6.1   Costs of Strengthening Economic Linkages between South Asia and East Asia
Source: Authors.
Note: Values are based on total responses (387). The question was formulated as follows:
Question 1: Rate the costs for your country of strengthening economic linkages between South Asia and East Asia.

Benefits of Strengthening Economic Linkages between South Asia and East Asia

Figure 6.2 shows that most opinion leaders were of the view that faster and more resilient growth leading to a win-win situation for both regions (72 per cent) and deeper integration with the global economy (71 per cent) are the major benefits of strengthening economic integration between South Asia and East Asia. The latter implies that the concept of 'open' regionalism is valid and that both regionalism and globalization can proceed at the same time. The third-largest benefit of South Asia and East Asia integration is that it could lead to a stronger voice for Asia in various global forums such as the G20 (66 per cent). The alternative option of providing a regional platform to global international economic institutions (such as the International Monetary Fund and the World Bank) (41 per cent) and reduction of poverty and improvement of social indicators (39 per cent) are seen to be least beneficial.

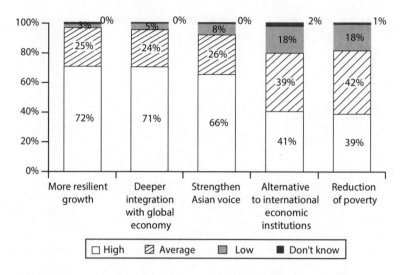

Figure 6.2 Benefits of Strengthening Economic Linkages between South Asia and East Asia

Source: Authors

Note: Values are based on total responses (387). The question was formulated as follows:

Question 2: Rate the benefits for your country of strengthening economic linkages between South Asia and East Asia.

Modalities of Regional Cooperation between South Asia and East Asia

Economic integration between South Asia and East Asia could be enhanced through various modalities or approaches. We asked the respondents to rate the various modalities for promoting regional coop-eration. Options considered were:

1. Signing and implementing new free trade and investment agreements
2. Creating new mechanisms to coordinate macroeconomic and finan-cial policies
3. Building regional infrastructure in transport, energy, and communi-cation to improve connectivity
4. Strengthening dialogues on matters of regional securities

We report both the aggregated (Figure 6.3) and disaggregated (Figures. 6.3a and 6.3b) results. Overall, most respondents felt

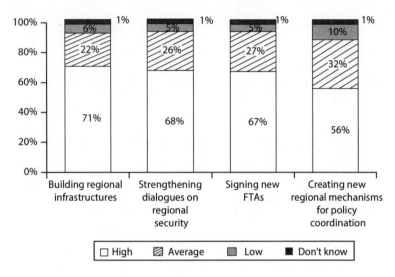

Figure 6.3 Modalities of Regional Cooperation between South Asia and East Asia
Source: Authors.
Note: Values are based on total responses (384). The question was formulated as Question 3: Rate the advantages for your country from participating in different regional cooperation initiatives with South Asia.

that improving connectivity between the two regions was the preferred modality for promoting economic cooperation between the two regions (71 per cent). The other modalities were strengthening regional security dialogues (68 per cent), followed by signing FTAs (67 per cent), and creating mechanisms for macroeconomic and financial policy coordination (56 per cent). Respondents from South Asia and East Asia have slightly different perceptions. The disaggregated sample data in Figures 6.3a and 6.3b suggest that unlike in South Asia, respondents in East Asia felt that strengthening dialogues on matters of regional security is the most significant modality to promote economic integration between the two regions (65 per cent). This, perhaps, is a reflection of the ongoing concern on territorial issues between several countries in East Asia and the thought that resolution of such issues could lead to greater economic integration between them.

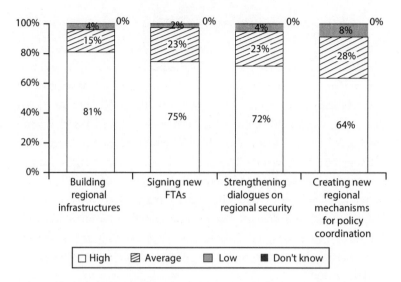

Figure 6.3a South Asian Responses to Modalities of Regional Cooperation between South Asia and East Asia

Source: Authors.

Note: Values are based on 201 responses from South Asia.

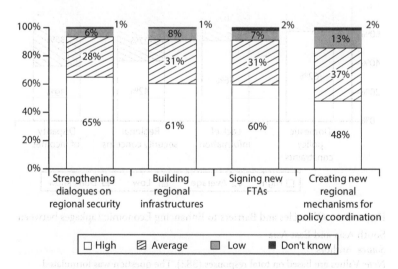

Figure 6.3b East Asian Responses to Modalities of Regional Cooperation between South Asia and East Asia

Source: Authors.

Note: Values are based on 183 responses from East Asia.

Obstacles and Barriers to Enhancing Economic Linkages between South Asia and East Asia

We also asked respondents to assess the potential obstacles and barriers to further economic integration between South Asia and East Asia. As shown in Figure 6.4, most respondents (62 per cent) felt that policy constraints behind the border, at the border, and beyond the border are the main obstacles to further economic integration between the two regions. The second key constraint is the lack of information on trading and investment opportunities and institutional gap (56 per cent), followed by regional security concerns (42 per cent) and disparity of income and development between countries (39 per cent). This finding suggests that the argument that income disparity reduces the potential for integration is not well-accepted.

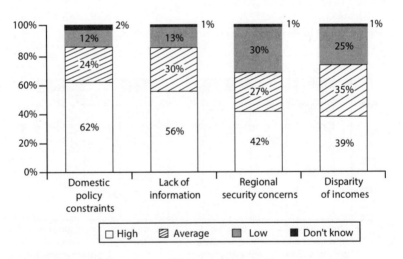

Figure 6.4   Obstacles and Barriers to Enhancing Economic Linkages between South Asia and East Asia
Source: Authors.
Note: Values are based on total responses (382). The question was formulated as Question 4: Assess the main obstacles to promoting your country's economic relations between South Asia and East Asia.

Required Policy Actions in South Asia

Given that inappropriate policies were the major constraint to the integration of South Asia and East Asia (Figure. 6.4), we were then keen to find out more about the policy actions that South Asian countries should implement to promote economic integration with East Asia. Figure 6.5 shows that 83 per cent of the respondents felt that South Asia should enhance physical connectivity, both national and regional, with East Asia. They should also take actions to improve the business environment by completing the reforms that they began in the 1990s (80 per cent). South Asian countries should also focus on reducing logistic costs including trade facilitation at the border (76 per cent) and on improving information communication and technology (ICT) system to facilitate management of supply chains

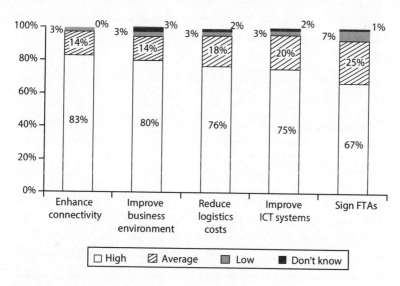

Figure 6.5   Required Policy Actions in South Asia
Source: Authors.
Note: Values are based on total responses (378). The question was formulated as follows:
Question 5: Rate the significance of policy actions that your country could consider to further enhance economic linkages with East Asia.

(75 per cent). Only 67 per cent of the respondents felt that South Asian countries should lobby to participate in various FTAs in East Asia. This finding suggests that most respondents prefer a market-led approach to integration between the two regions rather than regional cooperation policies such as lobbying to participate in regional trade cooperation in East Asia.

Survey Results: Economic Linkages between South Asia and East Asia

Going forward, economic integration between South Asia and East Asia will proceed along three tracks: cross-border trade, macroeconomic policy coordination, and physical connectivity. What is the role of South Asia in various initiatives to promote such integration with East Asia? Should South Asian countries join these initiatives in some way or should they establish initiatives of their own? Questions 6 to 8 of the questionnaire focused on these issues.

Initiatives to Promote Regional Trade Integration between South Asia and East Asia

Despite the preference for a market-led approach to integration (Question 5), Figure 6.6 shows that many respondents (85 per cent) in both regions felt that South Asian countries should join the present bandwagon in favour of FTAs and sign more free trade and investment agreements with East Asian countries. Only 6 per cent of the respondents said that South Asia should not sign more FTAs with East Asia.

While other South Asian countries are not yet involved, India is already active in negotiating the RCEP, which is an FTA between ASEAN+3 countries together with India, Australia, and New Zealand. We asked the opinion leaders to assess whether other South Asian countries should also join RCEP at some stage in the future? Figure 6.6a shows that close to 90 per cent of the respondents from non-participating countries actually feel that other South Asian countries should also join the RCEP at some stage in the future.

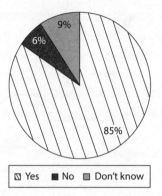

Figure 6.6 Initiatives to Promote Regional Trade Integration between South Asia and East Asia
Source: Authors.
Note: Percentage of respondents. Values are based on total responses (378). The question was formulated as follows:
Question 6: In order to enhance integration with East Asia (South Asia), should your country sign more free trade and investment agreements with East Asian (South Asian) countries?

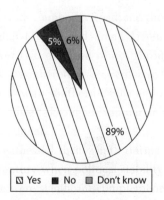

Figure 6.6a Per cent of respondents. Initiatives to Promote Regional Trade Integration between South Asia and East Asia—For Countries Not Participating in RCEP
Source: Authors.
Note: Values are based on 82 non-participating countries. The question was formulated as follows:
Question 6a: India is already involved in negotiating the RCEP, which is a trade agreement among 16 members of the East Asia Summit grouping. Should your country also join the negotiation at some stage?

Over one-half of our respondents felt that the case for pan-Asian FTA comprising all South Asian and East Asian countries is strong. As shown in Figure 6.6b, Support for pan-Asian trade integration is, however, stronger in South Asia than in East Asia. These findings are consistent with the computable general equilibrium analysis in Francois and Wignaraja (2009), which supports pan-Asian trade integration.

Initiatives to Promote Macroeconomic Policy Coordination between South Asia and East Asia and the Possible Role for South Asia

In the aftermath of the Asian financial crisis of 1997–8, East Asian countries have come up with a number of initiatives to promote macroeconomic policy coordination among each other to prevent and manage a crisis. These include the ERPD under which the finance ministers, central bank governors and their deputies hold dialogues with each other, and the ASEAN+3 CMIM. Should India be represented in some capacity in the ERPD and the CMIM? As shown in Figure 6.7, over three quarters of the respondents (79 per cent) felt that India should

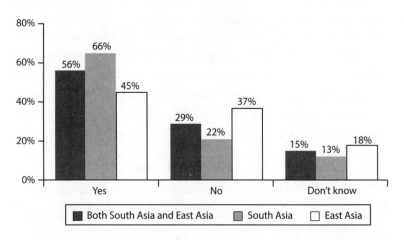

Figure 6.6b Pan-Asian Free Trade Agreement
Source: Authors.
Note: Values are based on total responses (378). The question was formulated as follows:
Question 6b: In your opinion, is the case for a Pan-Asian free trade agreement comprising all East Asian and South Asian countries strong?

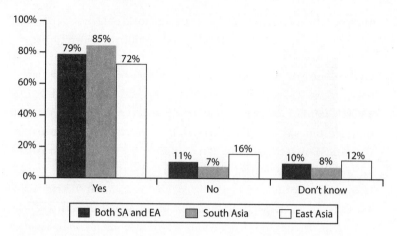

Figure 6.7 Initiatives to Promote Macroeconomic Policy Coordination in East Asia

Source: Authors.

Note: Values are based on total responses (376). The question was formulated as follows:

Question 7: In your opinion, should India, the largest country in South Asia, be represented in some capacity in the ERPD and CMIM?

be represented. Only 11 per cent of the responses are negative. While 85 per cent of the responses from South Asia are positive, a slightly lower support of 72 per cent is found in East Asia. This finding supports Sussangkarn (2010) and Rana (2012a) who propose to strengthen the participation of India in ERPD and CMIM.

Figure 6.7a shows the responses to the question on India's role in the East Asian financial architecture. These highlight that India's participation in the ERPD and CMIM would strengthen Asia's voice in the G20. Again, we see stronger positive responses from South Asia than East Asia, with South Asia reporting 82 per cent of positive responses compared to 71 per cent from East Asia.

Connectivity between South Asia and East Asia

Historically, land routes or the famous Silk Roads were the major forms of transportation between South Asia and East Asia. In addition to the Northern Silk Road which connected China with Central Asia

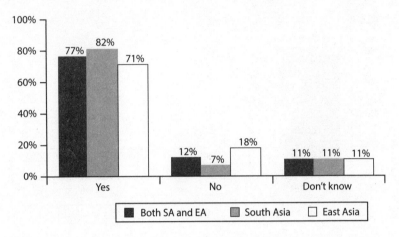

Figure 6.7a   Initiatives to Promote Macroeconomic Policy Coordination in East Asia
Source: Authors.
Note: Values are based on total responses (376). The question was formulated as follows:
Question 7a: Could India's participation in the ERPD and CMIM strengthen Asia's voice in various global forums such as the G20?

and Europe, as argued in Chapter 5, there was the lesser-known South-western Silk Road which connected South Asia with China and the ASEAN countries.

The Silk Roads were replaced by sea routes after the invention of steam engines and steam ships in the nineteenth century. But now, various factors have led to the revival of land connectivity in Asia. In this section, we asked opinion leaders to rate the factors that have contributed to such a revival. Figure 6.8 shows that majority of the respondents (70 per cent) felt that the reason for this revival of land connectivity in Asia is the growing importance of supply chains and fragmented trade. The Look East policies of South Asian countries (69 per cent) are also viewed as a key contributing factor. This shows a strong awareness among the respondents on the emerging newer ways of producing goods. Surprisingly, economic reforms in Myanmar (59 per cent) and China's Go West policies (48 per cent) are seen to be relatively less important.

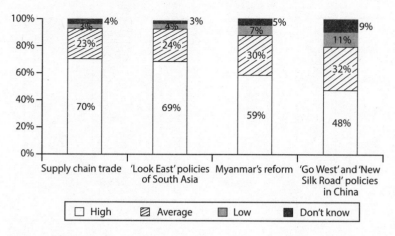

Figure 6.8 Factors That Have Revived the Case for Land Connectivity
Source: Authors.
Note: Values are based on total responses (372). The question was formulated as
follows:
Question 8: Rate the following factors that have revived the case for land and air
connectivity between South Asia and East Asia.

In addition to connectivity among its ten member countries, the
Master Plan on ASEAN connectivity also emphasizes the importance
of ASEAN's connectivity with neighboring countries such as India and
China and the other members of the East Asia Summit. At the request
of the East Asia Summit, ERIA has developed two projects for ASEAN–
India connectivity, namely, the Mekong–India Economic Corridor
(MIEC) and the Trilateral Highway connecting India and Myanmar with
Thailand (Kimura and Umezaki 2011). As shown in Figure 6.8a, more
than half of the respondents (56 per cent) are aware of these projects.

In addition, a large number of respondents (81 per cent) felt that
there was a need to consider projects to connect South Asia–China–
ASEAN such as the Bangladesh–China–India–Myanmar or the BCIM
Economic Corridor and the Yunnan–Myanmar–India–Nepal–Tibet–
Yunnan Economic Corridor or the old South-western Silk Road (72 per
cent). A large number of respondents (71 per cent) felt that trilateral
cooperation between India–Nepal–China should also be supported to
improve connectivity in Asia. Also, many opinion leaders felt that the

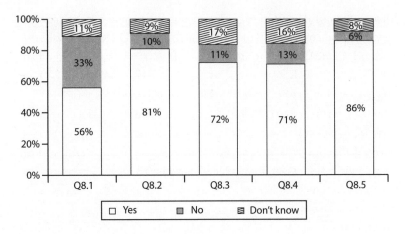

Figure 6.8a   Answers to Questions 8.1 to 8.5
Source: Authors.
Note: Values are based on total responses of 372. The questions were formulated as follows:

1. Question 8.1: Are you aware of the MIEC and the Trilateral Highway projects which seek to connect India with ASEAN?
2. Question 8.2: Do you think that Asia needs to consider infrastructure projects to connect South Asia–ASEAN–China such as the Bangladesh–China–India–Myanmar or BCIM Economic Corridor?
3. Question 8.3: Do you think that Asia needs to consider infrastructure projects to connect South Asia–China–ASEAN such as Yunnan–Myanmar–India–Nepal–Tibet–Yunnan Economic Corridor or the old South-western Silk Road?
4. Question 8.4: Do you think trilateral cooperation between India–Nepal–China should be promoted?
5. Question 8.5: In your opinion, should BIMSTEC be more active in developing and implementing regional infrastructure projects?

BIMSTEC which comprises Bangladesh, India, Myanmar, Sri Lanka, Thailand, Bhutan, and Nepal should play a more active role in fostering regional connectivity in Asia.

Survey Results: Economic Integration in South Asia

Before World War II, South Asia was a relatively well-integrated region with about 20 per cent of its total trade being intra-regional. Soon after the partition of India and Pakistan in 1947, the level of intra-regional trade in South Asia fell to about 4 per cent and sub-sequently to 2 per cent by 1967 (Rana 2012). With the economic reforms of the early 1990s, intra-regional trade in South Asia started to increase slightly and it presently stands at about 5 per cent of total trade. However, the region remains the least integrated region in the world. What was the reason for this? Could greater integration between South Asia and East Asia revive economic integration in South Asia? In order to answer these questions, two additional questions were posed to opinion leaders from South Asia. A large number of South Asian respondents (93 per cent) felt that political rivalries, border disputes, and suspicions in the region are the major factors for the low level of integration in South Asia (Figure 6.9).

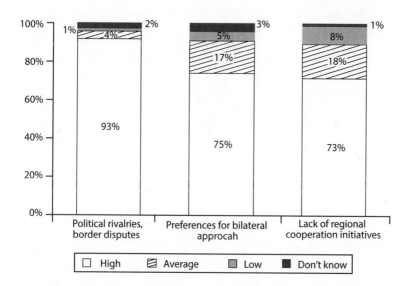

Figure 6.9 Factors That Led South Asia to Become One of the World's Least Integrated Regions
Source: Authors.
Note: Values are based on 190 responses from South Asia. The question was formulated as follows:
Question 9: South Asia, which once was a fairly well-integrated region, is now one of the least integrated. Rate the following factors which you think could have led to this development.

Other factors responsible are the preferences of several countries in the region for bilateral approaches as compared to regional ones (75 per cent) and the lack of regional cooperation initiatives in the region (73 per cent).

A large majority of our respondents (95 per cent) are of the view that increased economic linkages between South Asian countries with East Asian countries could lead to a win-win situation for both regions and also to the revival of economic integration in South Asia (Figure 6.9a).

The survey results present a fairly positive assessment of economic integration between South Asia and East Asia and its prospect. Many respondents, about three quarters of them, believe that the benefits of South Asia and East Asia integration would be faster and there would

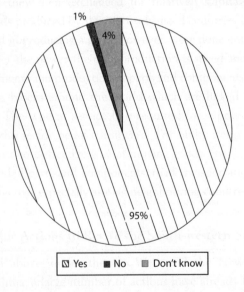

Figure 6.9a Economic Integration with East Asia as a Win-win Situation for Both Regions
Source: Authors.
Note: Percentage of respondents. Values are based on 190 responses from South Asia. The question was formulated as follows:
Question 9a: Could increased economic linkages with East Asia lead to a win-win situation for both regions and also revive economic integration in South Asia?

be more resilient economic growth in the two regions leading to a win-win situation for both. A similar number of respondents also felt that integration of the two regions would be a good example of open regionalism and also lead to deeper integration with the rest of the global economy. Roughly four out of five respondents feel that integration between South Asia and East Asia should be market-led (through improved connectivity and improved business environment). Less than two-thirds favoured a regional cooperation policy to promote integration (namely, South Asia lobbying to participate in various regional trade cooperation efforts in East Asia).

Over one-half of the respondents also felt that the case for a pan-Asian FTA comprising all South Asian and East Asian countries was strong and that the South Asian countries should sign more FTAs and investment agreements with their East Asian counterparts. All South Asian countries should also seek to join the ongoing negotiations for the RCEP.

Nearly four out of five respondents felt that India should be represented in some capacity at the ERPD and CMIM and that this would help enhance Asia's voice in the G20. The survey also establishes the important role of improved connectivity in transport, energy, and communication in promoting South Asia and East Asia integration. Nearly three out of four respondents felt that improved connectivity should be the major modality for promoting such integration. The survey found that the growing importance of supply chain trade and the Look East policies in South Asia were the major factors that had revived the case for land connectivity between South Asia and East Asia. Many respondents felt that the case for ASEAN–India connectivity, as well as South Asia–China–ASEAN connectivity (by reviving the old South-western Silk Road) was strong and that the BIMSTEC should play a greater role in this regard.

Finally, a large number of respondents (over 90 per cent) felt that political rivalries, border disputes, and suspicions in the region were the major reasons why South Asia, which was once a fairly well-integrated region of the world, had become one of the least integrated regions. Roughly, a similar number of respondents felt that closer economic linkages between the two regions could lead to a revival of economic integration in South Asia.

The above findings have a number of policy implications. First, economic integration between South Asia and East Asia should be promoted using market-led approaches including improved connectivity, which reduces trading costs. Second, in addition to ASEAN–India connectivity, connectivity between South Asia, China, and ASEAN should also be promoted. Nepal has a role to play in this regard. Next, just as they did when the East Asia Summit was formed, ASEAN and ASEAN+3 should invite India to join the ERPD and to pledge funds to the CMIM. Finally, in addition to India, which is already involved in negotiating the RCEP, at some stage in the future, ASEAN and ASEAN+3 must invite other South Asian countries to join the RCEP

APPENDIX A6.1

Questionnaires Used for Perception Survey of Asian Opinion Leaders on Linkages between South Asia[1] and East Asia[2]

Questions for Opinion Leaders from East Asia

Thank you for accepting our invitation. We appreciate your participation in our online survey.

During most of human history, Asia was not only a prosperous but also a well-integrated region of the world with strong economic and cultural linkages between South Asia and East Asia. After a break of roughly two centuries of colonization, we are once again witnessing the re-emergence of a prosperous and integrated Asia or the renaissance of Asia.

Against this background, the objective of this perception survey is to assess the views and perspectives of Asian opinion leaders on the costs and benefits, the potential modalities, and the policies required to enhance economic linkages between South Asia and East Asia.

This research is part of a project entitled 'Economic Integration between East and South Asia' supported by an Academic Research Fund (Tier 1), Nanyang Technological University (NTU).

---

[1] South Asian countries are: Afghanistan, Bangladesh, Bhutan, India, Maldives, Nepal, Pakistan, and Sri Lanka.

[2] East Asian countries are: Brunei, Cambodia, China, Indonesia, Japan, Laos, Malaysia, Myanmar, Philippines, Singapore, Korea, Thailand, and Vietnam.

☐ By clicking this box, I give my consent to take part in this survey.

All information that you provided will be used solely for the purposes of this research. The information you provided will be clubbed with information provided by other respondents and will not be used in an identifiable manner. Participation in this survey is voluntary and if you choose to withdraw, you may withdraw at any time. However, we hope that you would complete the survey which would take no more than 10 minutes of your time.

Thank you once again for your participation. Should you have further questions, please feel free to contact us at isdrojunio@ntu.edu.sg.

Respondent's Profile

Occupation:

Government	1
Business	2
Academia	3
Media	4
Others (please specify)	5

Country of Citizenship:

Brunei	1
Cambodia	2
China	3
Indonesia	4
Japan	5
Laos	6
Malaysia	7
Myanmar	8
Philippines	9
Singapore	10
Korea	11
Thailand	12
Vietnam	13

Email [_____] **Address:**

(Each respondent stands a chance to win an iPad mini 16 GB. Please provide an email address so that we can contact you accordingly.)

Costs of Strengthening Economic Linkages with South Asia

1. Rate the costs for your country of strengthening economic linkages with South Asia.

Costs	5 (Very High)	4 (High)	3 (Moderate)	2 (Low)	1 (Very Low)	99 (Don't Know)
Possible loss of national sovereignty and loss of independence of national economic policies.						
Exposure to unfavourable shocks that might affect South Asia (such as financial instability).						
Loss of markets and increase in poverty.						
Weaker linkages with countries outside the region.						
Dilution of national identity and culture.						

Please select one answer in each row.

Benefits of Strengthening Economic Linkages with South Asia

2. Rate the benefits for your country of strengthening economic linkages with South Asia.

Benefits	5 (Very High)	4 (High)	3 (Moderate)	2 (Low)	1 (Very Low)	99 (Don't Know)
Faster and more resilient growth and win-win situation for both regions.						
Reduction of poverty and improvement of social indicators.						
Alternative option of a regional platform to global international economic institutions such as the International Monetary Fund and World Bank.						
Stronger voice of Asia in various global forums such as the G20.						
Deeper integration with the global economy.						

Please select one answer in each row.

Modalities of Regional Cooperation with South Asia

3. Rate the advantages for your country from participating in different regional cooperation initiatives with South Asia.

Advantages	5 (Very High)	4 (High)	3 (Moderate)	2 (Low)	1 (Very Low)	99 (Don't Know)
Signing and implementing new free trade and investment agreements.						
Creating new mechanisms to coordinate macroeconomic and financial sector policies.						
Building regional infrastructure in transport, energy, and communication to improve connectivity.						
Strengthening dialogues on matters of regional security.						

Please select one answer in each row.

Obstacles and Barriers to Enhancing Economic Linkages between East Asia and South Asia

4. Assess the main obstacles to promoting your country's economic relations with South Asia.

Obstacles and Barriers	5 (Very High)	4 (High)	3 (Moderate)	2 (Low)	1 (Very Low)	99 (Don't Know)
Disparity of income and development between countries.						
Policy constraints behind the border, at the border, and beyond the border.						
Lack of information on opportunities and institutional gap.						
Regional security concerns due to conflicts.						

Please select one answer in each row.

Required Policy Actions in South Asia

5. Rate the significance of policy actions that South Asian countries could take to further enhance economic linkages with East Asia.

Policy Actions	5 (Very High)	4 (High)	3 (Moderate)	2 (Low)	1 (Very Low)	99 (Don't Know)
They should improve business environment by completing the reform process begun in the early 1990s.						

(Cont'd)

(*Cont'd*)

Policy Actions	5 (Very High)	4 (High)	3 (Moderate)	2 (Low)	1 (Very Low)	99 (Don't Know)
They should improve their ICT systems to reduce communication and coordination costs to manage supply chains.						
They should reduce logistic costs including at-the-border trade facilitation.						
They should enhance physical connectivity including regional connectivity.						
They should lobby to participate in various regional trade and financial cooperation efforts in East Asia.						

Please select one answer in each row.

Initiatives to Promote Regional Trade Integration in East Asia and the Role of South Asia

6.1 In order to enhance integration with East Asia, should South Asian countries sign more free trade and investment agreements with East Asian countries? (Please select one answer)

Yes	1
No	2
Don't Know	99

6.2 India is already involved in negotiating the Regional Comprehensive Economic Partnership (RCEP) which is a trade agreement among 16 members of the East Asia Summit grouping. Should other South Asian countries also join the negotiation at some stage? (Please select one answer)

Yes	1
No	2
Don't Know	99

6.3 In your opinion, is the case for a Pan-Asian free trade agreement comprising all East Asian and South Asian countries strong?

Yes	1
No	2
Don't Know	99

Initiatives to Promote Macroeconomic Policy Coordination in East Asia and the Possible Role of South Asia

7.1 East Asian countries have two initiatives in the area of macroeconomic policy coordination:

a. The ASEAN+3 Economic Review and Policy Dialogue (ERPD) to review global, regional and national macroeconomic and financial conditions and risks and to develop common positions on topics of interest
b. The Chiang Mai Initiative Multilateralism (CMIM) which is the $240 billion crisis fund to address short-term liquidity needs in the event of a crisis or contagion.

In your opinion, should India, the largest country in South Asia, be represented in some capacity in the ERPD and CMIM?

Yes	1
No	2
Don't Know	99

7.2 Could India's participation in the ERPD and CMIM strengthen Asia's voice in various global forums such as the G20?

Yes	1
No	2
Don't Know	99

Connectivity Issues

8.1 At present, a large proportion of trade between East Asia and South Asia is in the form of sea freight. But the case for land and air connectivity has also increased for several reasons.

Rate the following factors that have revived the case for land and air connectivity between East Asia and South Asia.

Initiatives	5 (Very High)	4 (High)	3 (Moderate)	2 (Low)	1 (Very Low)	99 (Don't Know)
'Go West' policy of China since 2005.						
'Look East' policies of South Asian countries.						
Encouraging but gradual political and economic reforms in Myanmar, the node for South Asia-East Asia connectivity.						
Growing importance of supply chain trade which comprises mainly trade in parts and components.						

Please select one answer in each row.

8.2 In addition to connectivity among its 10 members, the Master Plan on ASEAN Connectivity also emphasizes the importance of ASEAN's connectivity with neighbouring countries such as India and China and the other members of the East Asia Summit (EAS). At the request of the EAS, the Economic Research Institute for ASEAN and East Asia (ERIA) has developed two projects for ASEAN–India connectivity, namely, the Mekong–India Economic Corridor (MIEC) and the Trilateral Highway connecting India and Myanmar with Thailand.

Are you aware of the MIEC and the Trilateral Highway projects which seek to connect ASEAN with India?

Yes	1
No	2
Don't Know	99

In addition, do you think that Asia needs to consider infrastructure projects to connect China–ASEAN–India such as:

Yes	1
No	2
Don't Know	99

8.3 The Bangladesh–China–India–Myanmar or BCIM Economic Corridor?

Yes	1
No	2
Don't Know	99

8.4 The Yunnan–Myanmar–India–Nepal–Tibet–Yunnan Economic Corridor or the old South-western Silk Road?

Yes	1
No	2
Don't Know	99

8.5 Do you think trilateral cooperation between India–Nepal–China should be promoted?

Yes	1
No	2
Don't Know	99

8.6 In your opinion, should BIMSTEC, which is a regional grouping comprising Bangladesh, Bhutan, India, Myanmar, Nepal, Sri Lanka, and Thailand, be more active in developing and implementing regional infrastructure projects?

Yes	1
No	2
Don't Know	99

-End-

-Thank you for your participation-

Perception Survey of Asian Opinion Leaders on Linkages Between South Asia[3] and East Asia[4]

Questions for Opinion Leaders from South Asia

Thank you for accepting our invitation. We appreciate your participation in our online survey.

During most of human history, Asia was not only a prosperous but also a well-integrated region of the world with strong economic and cultural linkages between South Asia and East Asia. After a break of roughly two centuries of colonization, we are once again witnessing the re-emergence of a prosperous and integrated Asia or the renaissance of Asia.

Against this background, the objective of this perception survey is to assess the views and perspectives of Asian opinion leaders on the costs and benefits, the potential modalities, and the policies required to enhance economic linkages between South Asia and East Asia.

---

[3] South Asian countries are: Afghanistan, Bangladesh, Bhutan, India, Maldives, Nepal, Pakistan, and Sri Lanka.

[4] East Asian countries are: Brunei, Cambodia, China, Indonesia, Japan, Laos, Malaysia, Myanmar, Philippines, Singapore, Korea, Thailand, and Vietnam.

This research is part of a project entitled 'Economic Integration between East and South Asia' supported by an Academic Research Fund (Tier 1), Nanyang Technological University (NTU).

☐ By clicking this box, I give my consent to take part in this survey.

All information that you provided will be used solely for the purposes of this research. The information you provided will be clubbed with information provided by other respondents and will not be used in an identifiable manner. Participation in this survey is voluntary and if you choose to withdraw, you may withdraw at any time. However, we hope that you would complete the survey which would take no more than 10 minutes of your time.

Thank you once again for your participation. Should you have further questions, please feel free to contact us at isdrojunio@ntu.edu.sg.

Respondent's Profile

Occupation

Government	1
Business	2
Academia	3
Media	4
Others (please specify)	5

Country of Citizenship

Afghanistan	1
Bangladesh	2
Bhutan	3
India	4
Maldives	5
Nepal	6
Pakistan	7
Sri Lanka	8

Email [＿＿＿＿＿＿＿＿＿＿] **address:**

(Each respondent stands a chance to win an iPad mini 16GB. Please provide an email address so that we can contact you accordingly.)

Modalities of Strengthening Economic Linkages with East Asia

1. Rate the costs for your country of strengthening economic linkages with East Asia.

Costs	5 (Very High)	4 (High)	3 (Moderate)	2 (Low)	1 (Very Low)	99 (Don't Know)
Possible loss of national sovereignty and loss of independence of national economic policies.						
Exposure to unfavourable shocks that might affect East Asia (such as financial instability).						
Loss of markets and increase in poverty.						
Weaker linkages with countries outside the region.						
Dilution of national identity and culture.						

Please select one answer in each row.

Benefits of Strengthening Economic Linkages with East Asia

2.   Rate the benefits for your country of strengthening economic linkages with East Asia.

Benefits	5 (Very High)	4 (High)	3 (Moderate)	2 (Low)	1 (Very Low)	99 (Don't Know)
Faster and more resilient growth and win-win situation for both regions.						
Reduction of poverty and improvement of social indicators.						
Alternative option of a regional platform to global international economic institutions such as the International Monetary Fund and World Bank.						
Stronger voice of Asia in various global forums such as the G20.						
Deeper integration with the global economy.						

Please select one answer in each row.

Modalities of Regional Cooperation with East Asia

3. Rate the advantages for your country from participating in different regional cooperation initiatives with East Asia.

Advantages	5 (Very High)	4 (High)	3 (Moderate)	2 (Low)	1 (Very Low)	99 (Don't Know)
Signing and implementing new free trade and investment agreements.						
Creating new mechanisms to coordinate macroeconomic and financial sector policies.						
Building regional infrastructure in transport, energy, and communication to improve connectivity.						
Strengthening dialogues on matters of regional security.						

Please select one answer in each row.

Obstacles and Barriers to Enhancing Economic Linkages between South Asia and East Asia

4. Assess the main obstacles to promoting your country's economic relations with East Asia.

Obstacles and Barriers	5 (Very High)	4 (High)	3 (Moderate)	2 (Low)	1 (Very Low)	99 (Don't Know)
Disparity of income and development between countries.						
Policy constraints behind the border, at the border, and beyond the border.						
Lack of information on opportunities and institutional gap.						
Regional security concerns due to conflicts.						

Please select one answer in each row.

Required Policy Actions in South Asia

5. Rate the significance of policy actions that your country could consider to further enhance economic linkages with East Asia.

Policy Actions	5 (Very High)	4 (High)	3 (Moderate)	2 (Low)	1 (Very Low)	99 (Don't Know)
Improving business environment by completing the reform process begun in the early 1990s.						

(Cont'd)

(*Cont'd*)

Policy Actions	5 (Very High)	4 (High)	3 (Moderate)	2 (Low)	1 (Very Low)	99 (Don't Know)
Reducing communication and coordination costs to manage supply chains by improving ICT.						
Reducing logistic costs including 'at the border' trade facilitation.						
Enhancing physical connectivity including regional connectivity.						
Lobbying to participate in various regional trade and financial cooperation efforts in East Asia.						

Please select one answer in each row.

Initiatives to Promote Regional Trade Integration in East Asia and the Role of South Asia

6.1 In order to enhance integration with East Asia, should your country sign more free trade and investment agreements with East Asian countries? (Please select one answer)

Yes	1
No	2
Don't Know	99

6.2 (**Only for respondents who are not from India**) India is already involved in negotiating the Regional Comprehensive Economic Partnership (RCEP) which is a trade agreement among 16 members of the East Asia Summit grouping. Should your country also join the negotiation at some stage? (Please select one answer)

Yes	1
No	2
Don't Know	99

6.3 In your opinion, is the case for a Pan-Asian free trade agreement comprising all East Asian and South Asian countries strong?

Yes	1
No	2
Don't Know	99

Initiatives to Promote Macroeconomic Policy Coordination in East Asia and the Possible Role for South Asia

7.1 East Asian countries have two initiatives in the area of macroeconomic policy coordination:

1. The ASEAN+3 Economic Review and Policy Dialogue (ERPD) to review global, regional, and national macroeconomic and financial conditions and risks and to develop common positions on topics of interest.
2. The Chiang Mai Initiative Multilateralism (CMIM) which is the $240 billion crisis fund to address short-term liquidity needs in the event of a crisis or contagion.

In your opinion, should India, the largest country in South Asia, be represented in some capacity in the ERPD and CMIM?

Yes	1
No	2
Don't Know	99

7.2 Could India's participation in the ERPD and CMIM strengthen Asia's voice in various global forums such as the G20?

Yes	1
No	2
Don't Know	99

Connectivity Issues

8.1 At present, a large proportion of trade between South Asia and East Asia is in the form of sea freight. But the case for land and air connectivity has also increased for several reasons.

Rate the following factors that have revived the case for land and air connectivity between South Asia and East Asia.

Initiatives	5 (Very High)	4 (High)	3 (Moderate)	2 (Low)	1 (Very Low)	99 (Don't Know)
'Go West' policy of China since 2005.						
'Look East' policies of South Asian countries.						
Encouraging but gradual political and economic reforms in Myanmar, the node for South Asia–East Asia connectivity.						
Growing importance of supply chain trade which comprises mainly trade in parts and components.						

Please select one answer in each row.

8.2 In addition to connectivity among its 10 members, the Master Plan on ASEAN Connectivity also emphasizes the importance of ASEAN's connectivity with neighbouring countries such as India and China and the other members of the East Asia Summit (EAS). At the request of the EAS, the Economic Research Institute for ASEAN and East Asia (ERIA) has developed two projects for ASEAN–India connectivity, namely, the Mekong–India Economic Corridor (MIEC) and the Trilateral Highway connecting India and Myanmar with Thailand.

Are you aware of the MIEC and the Trilateral Highway projects which seek to connect India with ASEAN?

Yes	1
No	2
Don't Know	99

In addition, do you think that Asia needs to consider infrastructure projects to connect India–ASEAN–China such as:

8.3 The Bangladesh–China–India –Myanmar or BCIM Economic Corridor?

Yes	1
No	2
Don't Know	99

8.4 The Yunnan–Myanmar–India–Nepal–Tibet–Yunnan Economic Corridor or the old south-western Silk Road?

Yes	1
No	2
Don't Know	99

8.5 Do you think trilateral cooperation between India–Nepal–China should be promoted?

Yes	1
No	2
Don't Know	99

8.6 In your opinion, should BIMSTEC, which is a regional grouping comprising Bangladesh, Bhutan, India, Myanmar, Nepal, Sri Lanka, and Thailand, be more active in developing and implementing regional infrastructure projects?

Yes	1
No	2
Don't Know	99

Additional questions for South Asian Opinion Leaders

9.1 South Asia which once was a fairly well-integrated region of the world is now one of the least integrated.

Rate the factors below which you think could have led to this development.

Reasons	5 (Very High)	4 (High)	3 (Moderate)	2 (Low)	1 (Very Low)	99 (Don't Know)
Lack of regional cooperation initiatives in South Asia.						
Political rivalries, border disputes, and suspicions in the region.						
Preferences of several countries for bilateral approaches as compared to regional ones.						

Please select one answer in each row.

9.2 Could increased economic linkages with East Asia lead to a win-win situation for both regions and also revive economic integration in South Asia?

Yes	1
No	2
Don't Know	99

-End-

-Thank you for your participation-

7

MONETARY INTEGRATION IN ASEAN+3
A Perception Survey of Opinion Leaders[1, 2]

Since the Asian financial crisis of 1997–8, ASEAN+3 (East Asia) countries have made encouraging progress in promoting monetary integration (ADB 2008; Rana 2010). This includes the establishment of the ASEAN+3 ERPD, under which the finance ministers of the 13 member countries meet once a year and their deputies semi-annually to:

1. Assess global, regional, and national conditions and risks
2. Review financial sector developments and vulnerabilities
3. Exchange views and opinions on topics of mutual interest

---

[1] Reprinted with permission from Pradumna Bickram Rana, Wai-Mun Chia and Yothin Jinjarak, 'Monetary Integration in ASEAN+3: A Perception Survey of Opinion Leaders,' *Journal of Asian Economics* 23, no. 1 (2012): 1–12. Copyright (2016) by Elsevier.

[2] Although this chapter focuses on monetary integration in East Asia, it is relevant to policymakers in India and other South Asian countries because one of the key recommendations of Chapter 3 is that India (and subsequently other South Asian countries, as appropriate) should participate in the macroeconomic policy coordination and monetary integration efforts in East Asia. The survey results in Chapter 6 also support this recommendation.

Steps have also been taken to monitor short-term capital flows and to develop early-warning systems of currency and banking crises. Most recently, the ASEAN+3 Macroeconomic Research Office was established in Singapore as the regional surveillance unit of the ASEAN+3. According to the information posted on the website of the ASEAN Secretariat, AMRO will:

1. Monitor, assess, and report on the macroeconomic situation and financial soundness of the ASEAN+3 countries
2. Assess macroeconomic and financial vulnerabilities in any of the ASEAN+3 countries and provide assistance in timely formulation of policy recommendations to mitigate such risks
3. Ensure compliance of the parties requesting swaps with the lending covenants under the CMIM agreement

Progress has also been achieved in establishing regional financing arrangements to address short-term liquidity needs of the countries in the event of a crisis. The bilateral swaps under the Chiang Mai Initiative of 2000 have been multi-lateralized under the CMIM, establishing a $120 billion crisis fund for the region.

The next and a deeper phase of monetary integration is the coordination of exchange rates.[3] The increasing level of trade integration in ASEAN+3 has led to a greater synchronization of output and business cycles in the region, thereby enhancing the benefits of macroeconomic policy coordination including the introduction of the regional monetary unit (Rana et al. 2012). Many have, therefore, called for some sort of exchange rate coordination among the ASEAN+3 countries (IIMA 2010; ADB 2008). One such call is the one made by the ASEAN+3 Research Group in recent years (2006/7 and 2007/8) for the RMU,

---

[3] There is an ascending order of intensity of efforts to promote monetary integration in the sense that they involve progressively increasing constraints on the amount of discretion that individual countries can exercise in the design of macroeconomic policies. By level of intensity, these efforts have ranged from economic review and policy dialogue to establishing regional financing arrangements and eventually towards coordinating exchange rate policies.

a regional basket currency. This is because the RMU could strengthen the regional surveillance process and could eventually also facilitate exchange rate coordination in the region. Despite the calls made by the ASEAN+3 Research Group and others for the introduction of RMU, there has been no action as yet. What are the practical considerations in introducing the RMU?

In order to identify these issues, we undertook a perception survey of ASEAN+3 opinion makers. This chapter outlines the various roles that the RMU could play in enhancing monetary integration in ASEAN+3 and presents the survey methodology and results. The last section presents the conclusions of Chapter 7.

Roles of the RMU

An RMU in East Asia could have several purposes. First, like the Euro in Europe, it could be the single currency for East Asia leading to the establishment of a monetary union. This idea is not totally new and has been suggested, among others, by academics like Nobel Laureate Robert Mundell (*Asia Times Online* 2001) and politicians like Mahathir (Dongsheng 2006) and Arroyo (*Nikkei Weekly* 2003). However, the recent developments in the eurozone suggest that the viability of single currency requires not only close monetary coordination but also close fiscal union. The East Asian region is, therefore, perhaps not yet ready for a single currency.

Second, RMU could be a parallel currency in the region. Rejecting the idea of a single currency for the region at the present time, Eichengreen (2006) has proposed that governments create an RMU as a parallel currency based on a weighted average of Asian currencies, and allow it to circulate alongside existing national currencies. Official RMUs would be created in exchange for swaps of a portion of participating central banks' international reserves, and RMUs would be used in transactions among member banks, as well as in denominating bond issuances. Monetary unification in this case would be driven by the market rather than politicians, as the RMU gains acceptance as a common regional currency among market participants.

Third, RMU could be an alternative international reserve asset. This idea has become popular especially after the global economic crisis of 2008–9 and the ongoing sovereign debt crisis of 2010 in Europe which has raised questions regarding the value of the US dollar and the Euro. As is well-known, Zhou (2009), the governor of the People's Bank of China, has proposed the creation of a new supranational currency to establish a more symmetric international reserve asset.

Fourth, a much less ambitious purpose than the ones above, is to have RMU as a numeraire or unit of account. 'Official RMU' could be used for surveillance purposes as an indicator of relative currency values to make sure that countries are avoiding competitive devaluations among each other and are converging their polices for deeper integration. Countries could also use the RMU to peg their currencies and bring about stability which would be beneficial for intra-regional trade. Also, the use of the RMU as a component of an Asian monetary system, similar to the role that the European currency unit (ECU) played within the European monetary system (EMS), is an attractive concept in East Asia to enhance monetary integration.

Private RMU could be used by exporters and importers and market participants to denominate economic transactions such as in invoicing, deposit-taking, lending, hedging, and issuing bonds in a more stable reference currency. This draws from the experience of the ECU, which was initially adopted in 1975 as the unit of account for the European Community's budget, but which was taken up by market participants, particularly those attracted by opportunities for diversification and regulatory arbitrage. Banks handled ECU deposits and governments eventually issued ECU bonds.

In the context of CMIM and the establishment of the AMRO, another purpose of the official RMU could be to serve as the unit of account for contributions and withdrawals by member countries. This would mirror the role of the special drawing right (SDR) in the operations of the IMF. The multiples that can be withdrawn from the fund could also be linked to the deviation of the RMU rate of a member from the official rate, with those countries tracking the RMU being awarded higher multiples and those with divergent policies being awarded lower multiples. Such a system, as suggested by Montiel (2004), could lead to a convergence of exchange rates in the region.

The global economic crisis of 2008–9, the ongoing sovereign debt crisis in Europe, and the progress in monetary integration in East Asia have greatly enhanced the case for the introduction of RMU in East Asia. The ADB-led initiative to create an RMU index was suspended in 2006. A study by Kawai (2010) shows that, in the post-crisis period, East Asian countries are attracting large amounts of private capital and the best policy option for the region is to allow a collective appreciation of their currencies vis-à-vis the US dollar and the Euro, while maintaining the stability of intraregional rates.

Survey Methodology and Results

The objectives of our perception survey were to assess the views of a broad range of ASEAN+3 opinion leaders on the following points.

1. How can the RMU help deepen the ASEAN+3 economic integration process?
2. What are the practical difficulties and constraints in introducing the RMU?
3. What new institutional arrangements are required to resolve these issues and promote the RMU to deepen ASEAN+3 economic integration?

Survey Methodology

The perception survey used a stratified sample of 1691 ASEAN+3 opinion leaders divided into three categories: government officials (mainly from ministries of finance, trade, and foreign affairs), academia, and representatives of the financial sector. We did not include the non-financial business sector because they would be less familiar with the various institutional arrangements to promote integration and as they are new and are still evolving. The sample covered the 13 member countries of the ASEAN+3 broken down into 2 groups—the Plus 3 countries (China, Japan, and Korea) and the 10 ASEAN countries.

We conducted an online survey where the names and contact details of opinion leaders were obtained mainly from the list of ASEAN+3 deputies and ASEAN+3 Research Group members provided by the ASEAN Secretariat. They were supplemented by the mailing list of S. Rajaratnam School of International Studies and personal files of the authors.

The survey questionnaire comprised 2 parts and 23 questions— 9 questions on economic integration in ASEAN+3 and the role of RMU, CMIM, AMRO, ASEAN+3 Research Group, and AMF and 14 questions on purposes, weights, and practical issues of RMU. To increase the likelihood of responses, the questionnaire was designed to take 10–15 minutes of the respondent's time.

Survey Results

Interviews were conducted from 1 November 2010 to 26 December 2010 using an online survey. Opinion leaders were contacted and invited to participate in the survey. After sending the invitations, we also followed up with the respondents who did not reply by sending them a number of reminders. At the end of eight weeks, a total of 218 responses were collected, corresponding to 12.9 per cent of the sample. This response rate was slightly lower than the response rate of 14.7 per cent for a perception survey conducted by the Asian Development Bank in 2007. At that time, the ADB had noted that the 14.7 per cent response rate was 'considered as a quite high response rate for this type of surveys'. Had we used a professional surveying firm and follow-ups with telephone calls like the ADB, the response rate would certainly have been higher. Table 7.1 shows the breakdown of responses by region, country, and category.

The majority of opinion leaders who responded to the survey were based in the ASEAN countries. ASEAN countries account for 70.2 per cent of the total respondents while the Plus 3 countries account for the remaining 29.8 per cent. The majority of the respondents were from Singapore (19.7 per cent) followed by Japan (17.4 per cent) and Malaysia (12.8 per cent). There was only one respondent from Laos and none from Myanmar. There were low response rates from Vietnam (3.2 per cent), Brunei (2.8 per cent), and Cambodia (1.8 per cent).

Table 7.1   Survey Responses Profile

		Government Official	Researcher/ Academia	Private Financial Sector	Total
Plus 3	China	2	9	2	13
	Japan	3	31	4	38
	Korea	2	12	0	14
	Subtotal	**7**	**52**	**6**	**65**
	Indonesia	7	24	3	34
	Malaysia	4	22	2	28
	Philippines	2	13	4	19
	Singapore	6	29	8	43
	Thailand	4	7	0	11
ASEAN	Vietnam	2	5	0	7
	Cambodia	1	3	0	4
	Brunei	2	4	0	6
	Laos	0	1	0	1
	Myanmar	0	0	0	0
	Subtotal	**28**	**108**	**17**	**153**
Grand total		**35**	**160**	**23**	**218**

Source: Data compiled by authors from survey responses.

We did not translate the questionnaire into various languages like the ADB survey did. The response rate could have been higher if we had translated the survey into other languages. Reflecting the bias in the list made available to us by the ASEAN Secretariat, academia comprised 73.4 per cent of the respondents followed by government officials (16.1 per cent) and representatives of the private financial sector (10.6 per cent).

While there were 218 responses to the first 9 questions, question 10 which requested a ranking by the opinion leaders of the six purposes of RMU confused many and only 148 responses were obtained for question 11 onwards.

Assessment of Economic Integration in ASEAN+3 and the Role of RMU   The survey results show that although the interest of policy makers in promoting regional cooperation started only after the Asian financial crisis and is, therefore, fairly recent, 36 per cent of the respondents felt that the intensity of economic integration within ASEAN+3 was strong. Of the rest, 43 per cent felt that the intensity was average and 20 per cent felt that it was weak, as shown in Figure 7.1. Additionally, the data in Figure 7.1 also show that a relatively high proportion of 45 per cent of the opinion makers who responded felt strongly that the introduction of the RMU could increase economic integration within ASEAN+3.

Awareness of CMIM and Plans to Establish AMRO   As part of their regional self-help financing mechanism, in 1998, the ASEAN+3 finance ministers had launched the CMI comprising bilateral swaps among each other. The bilateral swaps under the CMI were multi-lateralized in March 2010 to form the CMIM which comprises a $120 billion crisis

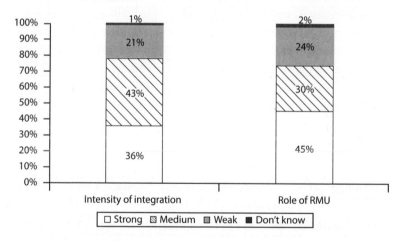

Figure 7.1   Assessment of Economic Integration in ASEAN+3 and the Role of RMU
Source: Authors.
Note: Values are based on total responses (200) and are rounded to the nearest integers. The question was formulated as follows:
Question 1: Estimate the intensity of the current level of economic integration within the ASEAN+3 countries.
Question 2: Assess the possible role of RMU in enhancing economic integration among the ASEAN+3 countries.

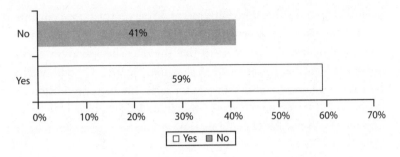

Figure 7.2 Awareness of the CMIM and Plans to Establish AMRO
Source: Authors.
Note: Percentage of respondents answering 'Yes' or 'No'. Values are based on
total responses (200) and are rounded to the nearest integers. The question was
formulated as follows:
Question 3: Are you aware of the CMIM and plans to establish AMRO early
next year?

fund. Also, the ASEAN+3 has established the AMRO in Singapore to
serve as an independent regional surveillance unit for the ASEAN+3
Finance Ministers Process. As shown in Figure 7.2, the survey results
show that 59 per cent of the respondents were aware of the CMIM
and plans to establish the AMRO. Over 41 per cent of the respondents were, however, unaware of these new institutional arrangements,
suggesting regional integration issues are new not only to the general
public but also to quite a few opinion makers.

Assessment of the ASEAN+3 Research Group   The ASEAN+3
Research Group is a network of research institutes from the 13 countries
that supports the ASEAN+3 Finance Ministers Process by conducting
research on topics identified by the ministers. As shown in Figure 7.3,
although 58 per cent of the respondents were aware of the ASEAN+3
Research Group and its activities, a large percentage of 42 per cent
were not.

Future of AMRO and CMIM   Figure 7.4 shows that 69 per cent of
the respondents felt strongly that the decision to establish the AMRO

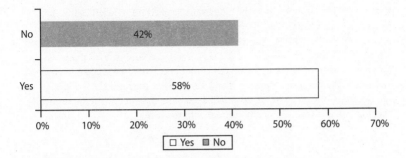

Figure 7.3   Awareness of the ASEAN+3 Research Group
Source: Authors.
Note: Percentage of respondents answering 'Yes' or 'No'. Values are based on
total responses (200) and are rounded to the nearest integers. The question was
formulated as follows:
Question 4: Are you aware of the ASEAN+3 Research Group which is a network
of research institutions that supports the ASEAN+3 Finance Ministers Process
(including the Economic Review and Policy Dialogue, the Chiang Mai Initiative,
and the ASEAN+3 Asian Bond Market Initiative)?

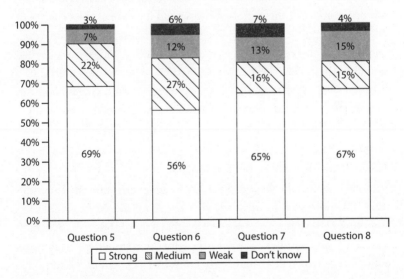

Figure 7.4   Future of AMRO and CMIM
Source: Authors.
Note: Values are based on total responses (200) and are rounded to the nearest
integers. The questions were formulated as follows: Please select an answer from
each row (5: Very strong, 1:Very weak, 0: Don't know).

Question 5: In your opinion, is the establishment of AMRO a significant step towards strengthening regional surveillance in the region?
Question 6: So far, CMIM, whose size at present is $120 billion, has not been used. Do you think that this will change as the capacity of AMRO is strengthened?
Question 7: In your opinion, should the CMIM and AMRO be merged to create an institution like the Asian Monetary Fund sometime in the future?
Question 8: If the Asian Monetary Fund is established, sometime in the future, it should work in a complementary manner with the IMF.

was a significant step towards enhancing regional economic integration. Also, 65 per cent of the respondents were of the view that, sometime in the future, the CMIM and AMRO should be merged together to create an institution similar to the once proposed Asian Monetary Fund (AMF). It was strongly felt by 67 per cent of the respondents that if the AMF were to be established in the future, it should work in a complementary manner with the IMF and regional institutions should not try to replace global ones. Additionally, a majority of 56 per cent of the respondents actually felt that although CMIM, whose size at present is $120 billion, has not been used, the use of CMIM would increase as the capacity of AMRO is strengthened. This is encouraging because, in late 2008, when countries in the region (for example, Korea and Singapore) needed liquidity, they had relied either on national reserves or entered into bilateral swap arrangements with non-regional and regional countries outside of the CMIM (Korea had entered into bilateral swap arrangements with the US and China, and Singapore with the US and Japan).

When Can the AMF Be Established?   In general, as shown in Figure 4.5, it is of the view that the AMF cannot be established anytime soon. Of those who felt strongly that the AMF should be established sometime in the future, 34.3 per cent felt that it should be established only after 2020 and another 52.1 per cent felt that it should be established sometime between 2016 and 2020. Only 10.1 per cent of the respondents felt that it should be established before 2015.

Assessment of ASEAN+3 Economic Integration by Plus-3 and ASEAN Respondents   Some interesting results are derived by splitting

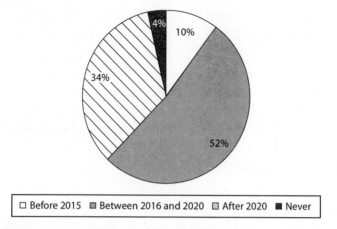

Figure 7.5 Establishment of Asian Monetary Fund
Source: Authors.
Note: Values are based on total responses (169) and are rounded to the nearest integers. The questions were formulated as follows:
Question 9: Answer this question only if your answer to Question 8 is 'Strong' or 'Very strong'. When do you think an Asian Monetary Fund can be established?

the sample into two. We find that Plus-3 (China, Japan, and Korea) opinion leaders are more optimistic about ASEAN+3 economic integration and institutions than ASEAN opinion makers. This can be seen in Figures A7.1–A7.5 (a) and (b) in Appendix A7.1.

1. 45 per cent of Plus-3 leaders felt strongly that the intensity of ASEAN+3 economic integration was high as opposed to 32 per cent of ASEAN leaders.
2. 52 per cent of Plus-3 leaders felt strongly that RMU could enhance ASEAN+3 integration, compared to 41 per cent of ASEAN leaders.
3. 69 per cent of Plus-3 leaders were aware of CMIM and AMRO as opposed to 55 per cent of ASEAN leaders.
4. 71 per cent of Plus-3 leaders were aware of the ASEAN+3 Research Group as compared to 53 per cent of ASEAN opinion leaders.
5. 78 per cent of Plus-3 leaders felt strongly that the establishment of AMRO was a significant step as opposed to 65 per cent of ASEAN leaders.

6. 60 per cent of Plus-3 leaders felt strongly that AMRO could strengthen CMIM as opposed to 54 per cent in ASEAN.
7. Nearly three-fourths of Plus-3 opinion leaders felt that an AMF should be established sometime in the future as opposed to only 60 per cent in ASEAN.

The above finding supports the comments made by some that it was the Plus-3 countries and not so much ASEAN that is driving regional integration institutions such as CMIM, AMRO, and AMF.

Purposes of RMU   After conducting a number of studies in 2006 and 2007/8, the ASEAN+3 Research Group had highlighted the following six reasons or purposes for calculating the RMU. These include:

1. Regional surveillance in ASEAN+3
2. Denominator of official transactions (such as budget for AMRO, unit of account for AMRO operations)
3. Denominator of private transactions (such as trade, bond, and bank deposit denomination),
4. Reference basket currency (like the European Currency Unit in the European Monetary System)
5. New international reserve asset
6. Single currency for Asia

How would the ASEAN+3 opinion leaders rank the purposes in terms of their urgency for the ASEAN+3 economic integration process?

Table 7.2 shows that the respondents felt that regional surveillance was the most urgent purpose for introducing the RMU, followed by RMU as a denominator of official and private transactions. According to the survey, the fourth urgent purpose for introducing the RMU was to serve as a reference basket like the ECU in the EMS, followed by RMU as a new international reserve asset. The least urgent of the six purposes was RMU as a single currency for the region which is, at best, a very long-term objective because of the need for economic convergence.

Table 7.2 Assessment of the Purposes of RMU

Purposes	Degrees of Urgency					
	6	5	4	3	2	1
Regional Surveillance	70%	11%	6%	9%	1%	4%
Denominator of Official Transactions	9%	40%	22%	16%	9%	5%
Denominator of Private Transactions	2%	11%	40%	22%	20%	4%
Reference Basket Currency	10%	22%	16%	38%	11%	3%
New International Reserve Asset	5%	15%	11%	10%	47%	12%
Single Currency for Asia	5%	1%	5%	5%	12%	72%

Source: Calculated by the authors.

Note: Values are based on total responses (148). The questions were formulated as follows:

Question 10: After conducting a number of studies, in 2008, the ASEAN+3 Research Group had highlighted the following reasons or purposes for calculating the RMU. Rank the purposes according to what you think is the most urgent for ASEAN+3 and should be done at the soonest by ASEAN+3 (6: most urgent to 1: least urgent):

(a) Regional surveillance in ASEAN+3

(b) Denominator of official transactions (such as budget for AMRO, unit of account for AMRO operations)

(c) Denominator of private transactions (such as trade, bond and bank deposit denomination)

(d) Reference basket currency (like the European Currency Unit in the European Monetary System)

(e) New international reserve asset

(f) Single currency for Asia

Weights for RMU Given that all 13 ASEAN+3 countries (including Cambodia, Laos, Myanmar, and Vietnam) have, after extended negotiations, agreed to contribute to the CMIM, CMIM weights would have been a good measure to determine the value of the RMU. But Figure 7.6 shows that only 35 per cent strongly felt that this was so, 44 per cent felt that weights based on GDP and/or trade were more appropriate, and 21 per cent of the respondents said that they did not know. A possible explanation for this finding could be that the agreement on CMIM

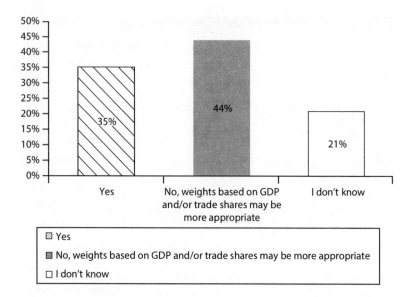

Figure 7.6   Using CMIM Weights to Calculate the RMU
Source: Authors.
Note: Percentage of respondents. Values are based on total responses (148) and are rounded to the nearest integers. The questions were formulated as follows: Question 11: A number of studies conducted by the ASEAN+3 Research Group have shown that the choice of weights (such as GDP and intra-regional trade or a combination of the two) does not make much difference in calculating the value of the RMU. But given that now all 13 ASEAN+3 countries have agreed to contribute to the CMIM, in your opinion, should CMIM weights be used to calculate the RMU?

is fairly new and even the ASEAN+3 opinion leaders may still be unfamiliar with it and its potential implications.

Is There a Need to Calculate Different Types of RMU?   A frequently encountered issue on the RMU is whether one type of RMU is good enough for all purposes or whether there is a need to calculate different types of RMU for different purposes. From Figure 7.7, it is shown that the majority of the respondents, that is, 55 per cent of them felt strongly that there was a need for RMU with regional weights for ASEAN+3 surveillance and policy coordination; 44 per cent of the respondents also strongly felt that there was a need for an RMU-plus-US-dollar-and-Euro-weighted

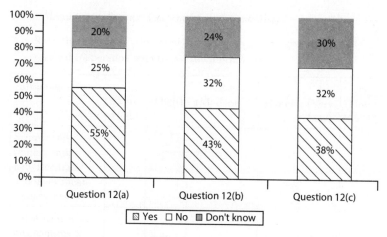

Figure 7.7   Different Types of RMU
Source: Authors.
Note: Percentage of respondents. Values are based on total responses (148) and are
rounded to the nearest integers. The questions were formulated as follows:
Question 12: Do you think that there is a need for calculating different types of RMU?
(a) RMU for ASEAN+3 surveillance and policy coordination
(b) RMU plus US dollar and Euro weighted basket for extra ASEAN+3 stability
(c) Core RMU comprising only the convertible ASEAN+3 currencies for private
sector transactions

basket for extra-ASEAN+3 stability; and 37 per cent felt that there was
a need for a core RMU comprising only the convertible ASEAN+3 currencies for private sector transactions.

Should AMRO Calculate and Publicize the RMU?   The ADB-led
initiative of creating an RMU/ACU index in 2006 was suspended
in the same year due to the Plus-3 position that currency weights in
RMU/ACU should not be decided by the ADB. Now that the AMRO
is to be established soon, should the AMRO calculate the RMU and
publicize it on a daily basis?

Figure 7.8 shows that over two-thirds of the respondents felt that
the AMRO should be tasked with calculating the RMU and publicizing
it on a daily basis. 17 per cent of the respondents said no and another
16 per cent said that they did not know.

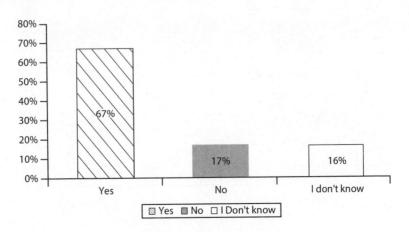

Figure 7.8   Calculation and Publication of RMU
Source: Authors.
Note: Percentage of respondents. Values are based on total responses (148) and are
rounded to the nearest integers. The questions were formulated as follows:
Question 13: Now that AMRO is to be established soon, do you think AMRO
should calculate the RMU and publicize it on a daily basis?

Should AMRO Use RMU and RMU Divergence Indicators?   As shown
in Figure 7.9, nearly two-thirds of the respondents felt that the AMRO
should indeed use the RMU and RMU divergence indicators for
regional surveillance, the key activity of AMRO. This would, among
other benefits, bring about intra-regional exchange rate stability. As
shown in Figures 7.10 and 7.11, many also felt that the AMRO budget
and the operations of AMRO and CMIM should be denominated in the
RMU like Special Drawing Rights (SDRs) in the IMF.

**Practical Issues in Calculating and Publicizing RMU for Regional
Surveillance**   As already mentioned above, in 2008, the ASEAN+3
Research Group had recommended that 'RMU for regional surveillance purpose should start immediately'. But this has not happened
yet. Why? What were the practical issues in calculating and publicizing
RMU for regional surveillance? Were they political, technical, institutional, or simply inertia?

Our survey result show that over three-quarters of the respondents strongly felt that the issue was political namely deciding which

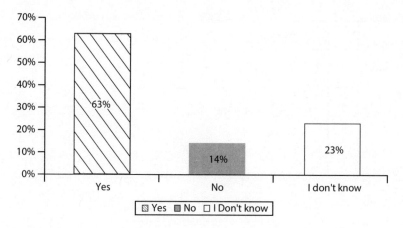

Figure 7.9 Use of RMU and RMU Divergence Indicators for Regional Surveillance
Source: Authors.
Note: Percentage of respondents. Values are based on total responses (148) and are rounded to the nearest integers. The questions were formulated as follows:
Question 14: Should AMRO use RMU and RMU Divergence Indicators for regional surveillance and policy coordination in ASEAN+3?

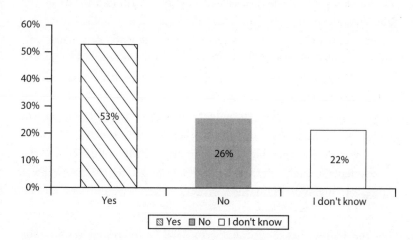

Figure 7.10 Contributions to AMRO Budget Denominated in RMU
Source: Authors.
Note: Percentage of respondents. Values are based on total responses (148) and are rounded to the nearest integers. The questions were formulated as follows:
Question 15: Should contributions to the budget of AMRO by the individual ASEAN+3 countries be denominated in RMU?

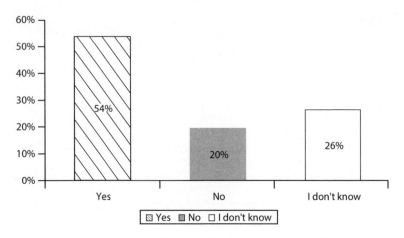

Figure 7.11   AMRO and CMIM Operations be Denominated in RMU
Source: Authors.
Note: Percentage of respondents. Values are based on total responses (148) and are rounded to the nearest integers. The questions were formulated as follows: Question 16: Should the operations of AMRO and CMIM be denominated in RMU like the SDR in the IMF?

countries to include in the basket (Figure 7.12). Two-thirds of the participants strongly believed that the constraint was institutional— absence of a suitable institution to calculate the RMU on a daily basis and to publicize it (in 2006, ADB was requested by the ASEAN+3 to suspend its work on calculating and publicizing the RMU and so there was an institutional gap).

Over one-half of the respondents strongly felt that the issue was technical, namely, choice of weights, choice of the base year, and level of integration not being high enough to justify RMU. 44 per cent of the respondents strongly felt that the issue was inertia, that is, the inertia of officials to maintain the status quo.

Do You Think That the Private Sector Will Be Interested in Using the RMU?   Figure 7.13 shows the survey results of how respondents see the usage of RMU in the private sector. Close to two-thirds of the respondents felt that the private sector would be interested in denominating selected transactions (such as trade, bank deposits, and bond issues) in RMU but only after official use of RMU strengthens.

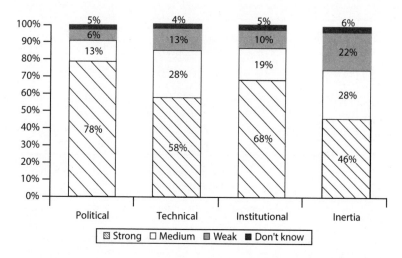

Figure 7.12   Practical Issues in Calculating and Publicizing RMU for Regional Surveillance

Source: Authors.

Note: Values are based on total responses (147) and are rounded to the nearest integers. The questions were formulated as follows: In 2008, the ASEAN+3 Research Group had recommended that 'RMU for regional surveillance purpose should start immediately'. But this has not happened yet. In your opinion, why has this happened? Estimate the intensity of the following constraints to calculating and using the RMU for surveillance purpose (5: Very strong, 1: Very weak, 0: Don't know).

Question 17:- Political: deciding which countries to include in the basket.

Question 18: Technical: choice of weights, choice of the base year, level of integration not high enough to justify RMU.

Question 19: Institutional: absence of a suitable institution to calculate the RMU on a daily basis and to publicize it (in 2006, ADB was requested by the ASEAN+3 to suspend its work on calculating and publicizing the RMU and so there is an institutional gap);

Question 20: Inertia: simple inertia of officials to maintain the status quo.

Do You Think That RMU Should Be Used to Stabilize Exchange Rates in ASEAN+3?   In the EMS, countries had stabilized their exchange rate around the ECU. Should RMU be used for such purposes in ASEAN+3? From Figure 7.14, nearly 60 per cent of the respondents said yes, but only after economic integration deepens further in the region, not right now.

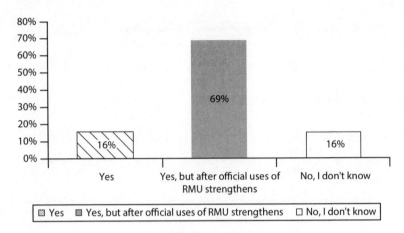

Figure 7.13   Do You Think That Private Sector Will be Interested in Using the RMU?

Source: Authors.

Note: Percentage of respondents. Values are based on total responses (147) and are rounded to the nearest integers. The questions were formulated as follows: Question 21: Once the RMU is calculated and publicized, do you think that the private sector in ASEAN +3 will be interested in denominating selected transactions (such as trade, bank deposits, bond issues) in RMU?

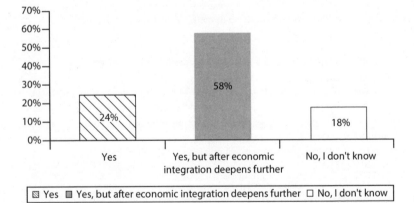

Figure 7.14   RMU to Stabilize Exchange Rate in ASEAN+3

Source: Authors.

Note: Percentage of respondents. Values are based on total responses (147) and are rounded to the nearest integers. The questions were formulated as follows: Question 22: Because of growing economic interdependence among countries, some analysts have suggested that ASEAN+3 should stabilize their exchange rates around the RMU like the European Monetary System? Do you agree?

Do You Think That Asia Needs a Single Currency? Survey results in Figure 7.15 show that nearly 60 per cent of the respondents felt that the creation of a single currency for ASEAN+3 could be useful in enhancing economic integration, but that the single currency was possible only in the longer term.

Additional Comments from the Respondents The survey questionnaire had provided a box where the respondents could offer additional comments. These focused on:

1. The usefulness of RMU (both the positives and the negatives)
2. Weights for RMU
3. RMU for private sector
4. RMU versus Euro

Selected comments are summarized in Table 7.3.

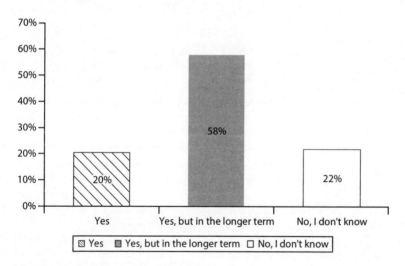

Figure 7.15 A Single Currency in Asia
Source: Authors.
Note: Percentage of respondents. Values are based on total responses (147) and are rounded to the nearest integers. The questions were formulated as follows:
Question 23: Some have also suggested that the creation of a single currency for ASEAN+3 sometime in the future could be useful in enhancing economic integration. Do you agree?

Table 7.3 Some Additional Comments

Respondents' Comments	
Usefulness of RMU: Some positive comments	• RMU is very useful, but could have bottlenecks because of the political will of different countries. • The RMU is useful as a focal point for discussion and learning to work with each other. • We should begin to use RMU for surveillance even on a trial basis immediately. • RMU is very important since it will promote economic growth within member countries. • It is good for surveillance purposes. It can be used for other purposes only if economic integration in the region deepens.
Usefulness of RMU: Some negative comments	• Political will among the participants is crucial. A strong leader may provide the necessary rallying points for the establishment of RMU. Defining the weights to be used is also a sensitive topic that should be resolved. • Political obstacles among the Plus-3 countries must be addressed first. • There is a risk that RMU will be ineffective like the SDR. It needs to be desired by the market. Therefore, RMU's effectiveness is likely to depend on whether renminbi (RMB) is included and RMB is freely convertible. • Some Asian countries still have political systems that are too unpredictable to make them reliable partners to integrate monetary affairs in this group. • It will take a long time because of the diversity in culture, history, politics, and economy. It is a complicated issue, but it is worth trying to go into this direction. • Different countries have differing economic priorities that will make consensus on the RMU difficult to achieve. • Whether RMU is practically needed for East and Southeast Asia remains an open question. • Harmonization of the statistical system among the ASEAN+3 is also a key to the success of the practical application of RMU. • It is strongly recommended that RMU initiative be discussed at the Business Chambers level.

(Cont'd)

Table 7.3 (*Cont'd*)

Weights for RMU	• The use of CMIM weights as a base for RMU calculation is questionable due to its non-economical nature. The adoption of RMU for any purposes is hindered by the wide variety in exchange rate regimes among member countries.
	• Currency basket weight should reflect the member country's share in CMIM. The only difficulty to establish RMU is the political willingness in APT.
RMU and private sector	• Private use shall be the key for RMU success.
	• The lead will have to be taken by the official sector.
	• It is strongly recommended that the RMU initiative to be discussed at the Business Chambers level.
	• As RMU is an artificial currency, RMU should give confidence by very strong official commitments to use it.
	• If there are no currency markets for RMU vis-à-vis other major currencies, including forward markets, the private sector will simply not be interested.
RMU and Euro	• After the disastrous results of the EURO experiment, it is surprising that there is still talk of RMU at all. One should learn from others' mistakes.
	• RMU will only be relevant to Asia if the Euro succeeds as an alternative to the US dollar as a global reserve currency.

Source: Compiled by authors.

Overall Summary and Recommendations The survey results present a fairly positive assessment of the economic integration process in ASEAN+3 and its prospects in the future. Over one-third of the ASEAN+3 opinion leaders who responded felt strongly that the level of economic integration in their region was high. They also felt that newly established institutions could strengthen the ASEAN+3 economic integration process further. Nearly half of the respondents felt that the introduction of the RMU could further accelerate the integration process. Nearly two-thirds of the respondents strongly felt that the decision to establish the AMRO was a good one and that, with AMRO, the usage of CMIM would increase in the future. They also felt that the AMF should be established in the longer term (sometime after 2016) and that the AMF should complement the IMF and not substitute for it. ASEAN+3 opinion leaders are optimistic about ASEAN+3 economic integration and institutions than ASEAN leaders supporting the view of some that new institutions were driven mainly by the Plus-3 countries. The respondents felt, however, that greater publicity needed to be given to the work of the CMIM, AMRO, and ASEAN+3 Research Group so that there will be a greater awareness and appreciation of their work and their contribution to the economic integration process.

The respondents strongly felt that regional surveillance was the most urgent purpose for introducing the RMU, followed by RMU as a denominator of official and private transactions. The next urgent purpose of introducing the RMU was to serve as a reference basket like the ECU in the EMS. The major practical difficulties and issues in introducing the RMU were political and institutional. The latter issue could be alleviated by the establishment of the AMRO, if AMRO should decide to calculate and publicize the RMU on a daily basis and use it for regional surveillance. The political issue can be addressed by greater efforts to convince countries that CMIM weights which includes all 13 members countries is the best option. AMRO contribution and budget, and AMRO and CMIM operations should also be denominated in RMU. Private sector demand for RMU would increase only after official use of RMU increases. Eventually, RMU could also be considered as a reference basket currency for ASEAN+3. However, RMU as a single currency for ASEAN+3 is still a long time off, if ever.

This chapter has number of policy implications. The first is that the introduction of RMU could contribute significantly to deepening economic integration in ASEAN+3 by strengthening the ERPD and eventually by leading to greater coordination of exchange rates. So could the CMIM and the AMRO. The second is that, eventually, AMRO should be tasked by the ASEAN+3 to calculate the RMU using CMIM weights and publicize it on a daily basis. The third is that ASEAN+3 could denominate the AMRO budget, CMIM and AMRO contributions and operations, in the RMU to provide more stable currency values.

APPENDIX A7.1

Perception from ASEAN and Plus 3

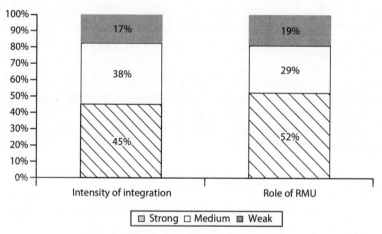

(a) China, Japan, and Korea. Total responses: 58

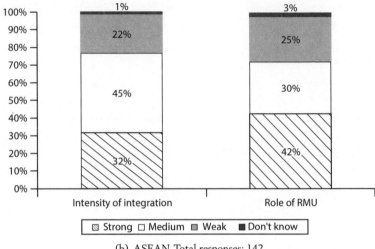

(b) ASEAN. Total responses: 142

Figure A7.1   Assessment of Economic Integration in ASEAN+3 and the Role of RMU

Source: Authors.

Note: Values are based on total responses (200) and are rounded to the nearest integers. The question was formulated as follows:

Question 1: Estimate the intensity of the current level of economic integration within the ASEAN+3 countries

Question 2: Assess the possible role of RMU in enhancing economic integration among the ASEAN+3 countries.

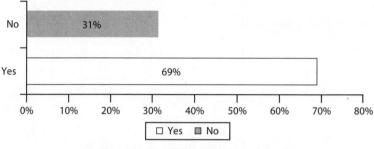

(a) China, Japan, and Korea. Total responses: 58

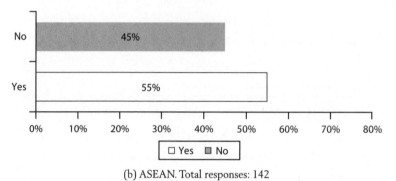

(b) ASEAN. Total responses: 142

Figure A7.2   Awareness of the CMIM and Plans to Establish AMRO
Source: Authors.
Note: Percentage of respondents answering 'Yes' or 'No'. Values are based on total responses (200) and are rounded to the nearest integers. The question was formulated as follows:
Question 3: Are you aware of the CMIM and plans to establish AMRO by early next year?

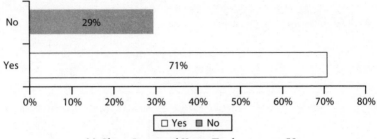

(a) China, Japan, and Korea. Total responses: 58

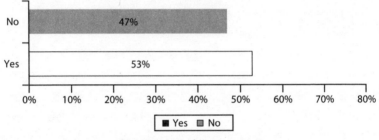

(b) ASEAN. Total responses: 142

Figure A7.3   Awareness of the ASEAN+3 Research Group
Source: Authors.
Note: Percentage of respondents answering 'Yes' or 'No'. Values are based on
total responses (200) and are rounded to the nearest integers. The question was
formulated as follows:
Question 4: Are you aware of the ASEAN+3 Research Group which a network
of research institutions that supports the ASEAN+3 Finance Ministers Process
(including the Economic Review and Policy Dialogue, the Chiang Mai Initiative,
and the ASEAN+3 Asian Bond Market Initiative)?

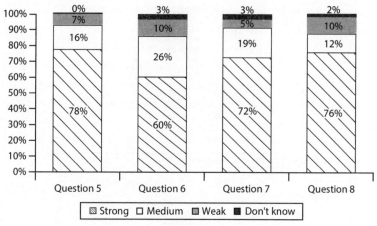

(a) China, Japan, and Korea. Total responses: 58

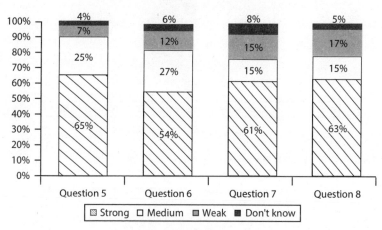

(b) ASEAN. Total responses: 142

Figure A7.4   Future of AMRO and CMIM

Source: Authors.

Note: Values are based on total responses (200) and are rounded to the nearest integers. The questions were formulated as follows:

Please select an answer from each row (5: Very strong 1: Very weak, 0: Don't know).

Question 5: In your opinion, is the establishment of AMRO a significant step towards strengthening regional surveillance in the region?

Question 6: So far, CMIM, whose size at present is $120 billion, has not been used. Do you think that this will change as the capacity of AMRO is strengthened?

Question 7: In your opinion, should the CMIM and AMRO be merged to create an institution like the Asian Monetary Fund sometime in the future?

Question 8: If the Asian Monetary Fund is established, sometime in the future, it should work in a complementary manner with the IMF.

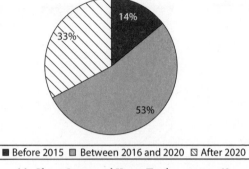

(a) China, Japan, and Korea. Total responses: 49

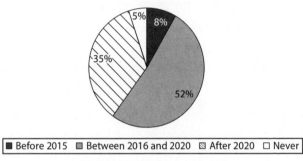

(b) ASEAN. Total responses: 120

Figure A7.5   Establishment of Asian Monetary Fund
Source: Authors.
Note: Values are based on total responses (169) and are rounded to the nearest integers. The questions were formulated as follows:
Question 9: Answer this question only if your answer to Question 8 is 'Strong' or 'Very strong'. When do you think an Asian Monetary Fund can be established?

REFERENCES

ADB (Asian Development Bank). 2004. 'Monetary and Financial Integration in East Asia', Manila: Asian Development Bank.

———. 2008. 'Emerging Asian Regionalism: A Partnership for Shared Prosperity', Manila: Asian Development Bank.

———. 2009. 'India 2039: An Affluent Society in One Generation', Manila: Asian Development Bank.

———. 2012. 'Asian Economic Integration Monitor', Manila: Asian Development Bank.

———. 2014a. 'Asian Development Outlook 2014 Update: Asia in Global Value Chains', Manila: Asian Development Bank.

———. 2014b. 'Asian Development Outlook: Fiscal Policy for Inclusive Growth', Manila: Asian Development Bank.

———. 2015. 'Asian Development Outlook 2015 Update'. Manila: Asian Development Bank.

ADBI (Asian Development Bank Institute). 2014. *Connecting South Asia and Southeast Asia: Final Report*. Tokyo: Asian Development Bank Institute.

ADB and ADBI (Asian Development Bank and Asian Development Bank Institute). 2015. *Connecting South Asia and East Asia*. Tokyo: Asian Development Bank Institute.

Afghanistan Government. 2013. *Afghanistan National Development Strategy 2008–2013*. http://www.undp.org.af/publications/KeyDocuments/ANDS_Full_Eng.pdf.

Ando, M. 2006. 'Fragmentation and Vertical Intra-industry Trade in East Asia,' *North American Journal of Economics and Finance* 17, No. 3: 257–81.

————. 2010. 'Machinery Trade in East Asia, and the Global Financial Crisis.' ERIA Discussion Paper Series No. 10, Economic Research Institute for ASEAN and East Asia, Jakarta.

Ando, M. and F. Kimura. 2005. 'The Formation of International Production and Distribution Networks in East Asia.' In *International Trade in East Asia*, Vol. 14, NBER-East Asia Seminar on Economics, edited by T. Ito and A.K. Rose. Chicago: University of Chicago Press.

Arnold, J. 2009. 'The Role of Transport Infrastructure, Logistics, and Trade Facilitation in Asian Trade.' In *Pan-Asian Integration: Linking East and South Asia*, edited by J. Francois, P.B. Rana, and G. Wignaraja. UK: Palgrave Macmillan.

Asia Times Online. 2001. 'After European, now Asian Monetary Union?' *Asia Times Online*, 4 September.

Athukorala, P. 2010. 'Production Networks and Trade Patterns in East Asia: Regionalization or Globalization?' ADB Working Paper Series No. 56, Asian Development Bank, Manila.

Athukorala, P. and J. Menon. 2010. 'Global Production Sharing, Trade Patterns, and Determinants of Trade Flows in East Asia.' ADB Working Paper Series No. 41, Asian Development Bank, Manila.

Athukorala, P. and N. Yamashita. 2006. 'Production Fragmentation and Trade Integration: East Asia in a Global Context.' *North American Journal of Economics and Finance* 17, No. 3: 233–56.

Atkinson, R., D. Castro, and S. Ezell. 2009. *The Digital Road to Recovery: A Stimulus Plan to Create Jobs, Boost Productivity and Revitalize America*. Washington, D.C.: The Information Technology and Innovation Foundation.

Aturupane, H., Y. Savchenko, M. Shojo, and L. Kurt. 2014. 'Sri Lanka: Investment in Human Capital.' South Asia: Human Development Sector Discussion Paper Series No. 69. Washington D.C.: World Bank.

Baldwin, R. 2006. 'Globalization: The Great Unbundling(s)', Geneva: Graduate Institute of International Studies.

————. 2012. 'Global Supply Chains: Why They Emerged, Why They Matter, and Where They are Going.' CTEI working paper. Centre for Trade and Economic Integration, Geneva.

————. 2013, 'Multilateralizing 21st Century Regionalism,' *Vox*, 20 January, http://www.voxeu.org/article/multilateralising-21st-century-regionalism.

Baru, S. 2014. *The Accidental Prime Minister*. India: Penguin Books India.

Bhagwati, J. and A. Panagariya. 2013. *Why Growth Matters: How Economic Growth in India Reduced Poverty*. New York: Public Affairs.

National Statistics Bureau, Bhutan, 2014, 'Bhutan-Poverty Assessment 2014', http://documents.worldbank.org/curated/en/2014/01/20197512/bhutan-poverty-assessment-2014.

Bradsher, K. 2013. 'Hauling New Treasure along the Silk Road.' *New York Times*, 20 July.

Breusch, S. and A. Pagan. 1979. 'A Simple Test for Heteroscedasticity and Random Coefficient Variation.' *Econometrica* 47, No. 5: 1287–94.

Bubalo, A. and M. Cook. 2012. 'Horizontal Asia.' In *Renaissance of Asia: Evolving Linkages between South Asia and East Asia*, edited by P.B. Rana, 75–88. Singapore: World Scientific Publishers.

Chibber, A. 2006. 'Overview.' In *Reform and Growth: Evaluating the World Bank Experience*, edited by K. Peters and B. Yale. Washington D.C.: World Bank.

———. 2013. 'India's Missed Reforms.' *Business Standard*, 2 November.

Chongvilaivan, A. 2012. 'Thailand's 2011 Flooding: Its Impact on Direct Exports and Global Supply Chains.' UNESCAP Asia-Pacific Research and Training Network on Trade (ARTNeT) Working Paper No. 34, UNESCAP ARTNeT, New York.

Chongvilaivan, A. and S. Thangavelu. 2012. 'Does Outsourcing Provision Lead to Wage Inequality? New Evidence from Thailand's Manufacturing Industries.' *Review of International Economics* 20, No. 2: 364–76.

Christiansen, L., M. Schindler, and T. Tressel. 2009. 'Growth and Structural Reforms: A New Assessment.' IMF Working Paper WP/09/284, International Monetary Fund, Washington D.C.

De, P. 2010. 'South Asia: Trade Integration after the Global Crisis.' International Bank for Reconstruction and Development Background Paper, World Bank, Washington D.C.

Debroy, B., A. Tellis, and R. Trevor. 2014. *Getting India Back on Track: An Action Agenda for Reform*. Delhi: Random House India.

DeLong, B. 2003. 'India since Independence: An Analytical Growth Narrative.' In *In Search of Prosperity: Analytical Narratives of Economic Growth*, edited by R. Dani. Princeton, NJ: Princeton University Press.

Devarajan, S. and I. Nabi. 2006. 'Economic Growth in South Asia: Promising, Un-equalizing, Sustainable?'. Washington, D.C.: World Bank.

DiMaggio, P. and E. Hargittai. 2001. 'From the "Digital Divide" to "Digital Inequality": Studying Internet Use as Penetration Increases.' Working paper No. 15, Center for Arts and Cultural Policy Studies, Woodrow Wilson School, Princeton University, Princeton, NJ.

Dongsheng, S. 2006. 'Asian Currency Unit still a Dream.' *People's Daily Online*, 16 November.

Dowling, M. and P. Rana. 2010. *Asia and the Global Economic Crisis: Challenges in a Financially Integrated World*. UK: Palgrave Macmillan.

Economic Research Institute for ASEAN and East Asia. 2010. The Comprehensive Asia Development Plan, ERIA Research Project Report FY 2009, No. 4–1.

Eichengreen, B. 2006. 'The Parallel Currency Approach to Asian Monetary Integration.' *American Economic Review* 96, No. 2: 432–6.

Fornfeld, M., G. Delaunay, and D. Elixmann. 2008. 'The Impact of Broadband on Growth and Productivity.' Study on the behalf of the European Commission, MICUS Management Consulting, Germany.

Francois, J. and G. Wignaraja. 2009. 'Pan-Asian Integration: Economic Implications of Integration Scenarios.' In *Pan-Asian Integration: Linking East and South Asia*, edited by J. Francois, P.B. Rana, and G. Wignaraja. UK: Palgrave Macmillan.

Frank, AG. 1998. *Reorient: Global Economy in the Asian Age*. Berkeley: University of California Press.

Fujita, M. and N. Hamaguchi. 2012. 'Japan and Economic Integration in East Asia: Post-disaster Scenario.' *Annals of Regional Science* 48, No. 2: 485–500.

Golub, S., R. Jones, and H. Kierzkowski. 2007. 'Globalization and Country-specific Service Links.' *Journal of Economic Policy Reform* 10, No. 2: 63–88.

Government of India. 2014. Available at www.makeinindia.org.

Hiratsuka, D. 2011. 'Production Networks in Asia: A Case Study from the Hard Disk Drive Industry.' ADBI Working Paper No. 301, Asian Development Bank Institute, Tokyo.

Humphrey, J. and H. Schmitz. 2000. 'How Does Insertion in Global Value Chains Affect Upgrading in Industrialized Clusters?', UK: Institute of Development Studies, University of Sussex.

Institute for International Monetary Affairs. 2010 'Possible Uses of Regional Monetary Units-Identification of Issues for Practical Use.' Unpublished, Institute for International Monetary Affairs, Tokyo.

International Labour Organization. 2013. *Decent Work Country Programme: 2013–2017*. Nepal: International Labour Organization.

International Telecommunications Union. 2014. 'Measuring the Information Society Report.' http://www.itu.int/en/ITUD/Statistics/Documents/publications/mis2014/ MIS2014 without _Annex_4.pdf.

IMF (International Monetary Fund). 2014a. *IMF Country Report*. No. 14/128. Afghanistan: IMF.

———. 2014b. *IMF Country Report*. No. 14/214. Nepal: IMF.

———. 2014c. *IMF Country Report*. No. 14/1. Pakistan: IMF.

———. 2015. 'Staff Report for the 2015 Article IV Consultation.' www.imf.org.

Islam, M.S. and R. Khanam. 2014. 'Trade Performance of Bangladesh with East: An Evaluative Study.' *Asian Journal Management Sciences & Education* 3, No. 4: 1–18.

Jebsen, R. 2007. 'The Digital Provide: Information (Technology), Market Performance, and Welfare in the South Indian Fisheries Sector.' *Quarterly Journal of Economics* 122, No. 3: 879–924.

Jha, S. and J. Zhuang. 2014. 'Governance Unbundled.' *Finance and Development* 51, No. 2: 24–7.

Jones, R.W. and H. Kierzkowski. 1990. 'The Role of Services in Production and International Trade: A Theoretical Framework.' In *The Political Economy of International Trade: Essays in Honor of Robert E Baldwin*, edited by R.W. Jones and A.O. Krueger. Oxford: Blackwell.

———. 2001. 'A Framework for Fragmentation.' In *Fragmentation: New Production Patterns in the World Economy*, edited by S.W. Arndt and H. Kierzkowski. New York: Oxford University Press.

Kawai, M. 2010. 'Reform of the International Financial Architecture: An Asian Perspective.' *Singapore Economic Review* 55, No. 1: 207–42.

Keyfitz, N. and R.A. Dorfman. 1991. 'The Market Economy is the Best but not the Easiest', Unpublished.

Kim, Y., T. Kelly, and S. Raja. 2010. *Building Broadband: Strategies and Policies for the Developing World*. Washington D.C.: World Bank.

Kimura, F. and M. Ando. 2005. 'Two-dimensional Fragmentation in East Asia: Conceptual Framework and Empirics.' *International Review of Economics and Finance* 14, No. 3: 317–48.

Kimura, F. and A. Obashi. 2011. 'Production Networks in East Asia: What We Know So Far'. ADBI Working Paper Series No. 320, Asian Development Bank Institute, Tokyo.

Kimura F. and S. Umezaki. 2011. 'ASEAN-India Connectivity: The Comprehensive Asia Development Plan.' Phase II. ERIA Research Project Report No. 7, Economic Research Institute for ASEAN and East Asia, Jakarta.

Konana, P., J. Doggett, and S. Balasubramanian. 2004. 'Comparing India and China Growth Strategies: Chaotic or Planned?' http://faculty.mccombs.utexas.edu/prabhudev.konana/indiachina.pdf.

Koutrompis, P. 2009. 'The Economic Impact of Broadband on Growth: A Simultaneous Approach.' *Telecommunications Policy* 33: 471–85.

Lee, K.Y. 2013. 'Once China Catches Up: What Then?', Forbes Magazine, 17 September.

Lohani, P.C. 2011. *Nepal's Evolving Relations with India and China: Perspectives from Nepal*. New Delhi: Observer Research Foundation.

Maddala, S. 1983. *Limited Dependent and Qualitative Variables in Econometrics*. Cambridge, MA: Cambridge University Press.

Maddison, A. 2007. *Contours of the World Economy, 1–2030 AD*. UK: Oxford University Press.

Maira, A. 2012. 'The Reforms that Matter.' *The Times of India*, 29 September.

Malik, A. 2015. *Pakistan's Vision East Asia: Challenges and Opportunities*. Pakistan: Institute of Strategic Studies.

McKinnon, R. 1993. *The Order of Economic Liberalization: Financial Control in the Transition to Market Economy*. Baltimore: Johns Hopkins University Press.

Ministry of External Affairs, Government of India. 2013. *Joint Statement by India and China on the Visit of Chinese Premier Li Keqiang to India*, India.

MFA (Ministry of Foreign Affairs), Government of China. 2013. *President Xi Jinping Delivers Important Speech and Proposes to Build a Silk Road Economic Belt with Central Asian Countries*, China.

Montiel, P. J., 2004. 'Monetary and Financial Integration in East Asia', Asian Development Bank.

Navia, P. and V. Andres. 2003. 'The Politics of Second Generation Reforms.' In *After the Washington Consensus: Restarting Growth and Reform in Latin America*, edited by J. Williamson and P.P. Kuczynski. Washington D.C.: Institute of International Economics.

Nikkei Weekly. 2003. 'The Future of Asia', 9 June.

Padmanabhan, A. 2014. 'India Wants BIMSTEC to Focus on Five Key Areas.' *Odisha Sun Times*. http://odishasuntimes.com/35257/india-wants-bimstec-focus-five-key-areas/.

Panagariya, A. 2014. 'A Reform Agenda for India's New Government.' CD Deshmukh Memorial Lecture, National Council of Applied Economic Research, New Delhi.

Pandey, N., ed. 2006. *Nepal as a Transit State: Emerging Possibilities*. Kathmandu: Institute of Foreign Affairs.

Papke, L. and J. Wooldridge. 1996. 'Econometric Methods for Fractional Response Variables with an Application to 401(K) Plan Participation Rates.' *Journal of Applied Econometrics* 11, No. 6: 619–32.

Patnaik, I. and M. Pundit. 2014. 'Is India's Long-term Trend Growth Declining?' Asian Development Bank Working Paper No. 424, Asian Development Bank, Manila.

Phanisham, A. 2006. 'Economic Implications of China's "Go-West" Policy.' *ASEAN Economic Bulletin* 23, No. 2: 253–65.

Poddar, T. and E. Yi. 2007. 'India's Rising Growth Potential.' Global Economics Paper 152, Goldman Sachs, New York.

Qiang, Z. and M. Rossotto. 2009. 'Economic Impacts of Broadband.' In *Information and Communications for Development 2009: Extending Reach and Increasing Impact*, 35–50. Washington D.C.: World Bank.

Quibria, M.G., S.N. Ahmed, T. Tschang, and M.L. Reyes-Macasaquit. 2002. 'Digital Divide: Determinants and Policies with Special Reference to Asia.' ERD Working Paper No. 27, Asian Development Bank, Manila.

Rahman, A. 2014. 'Can I See Your Papers Please?' *Dhaka Tribune*, 21 October.

Rajendram, D. 2014. 'India's New Asia-Pacific Strategy: Modi Acts East.' Lowy Institute for International Policy, Sydney.

Rana, M. S. J. B. R. 2012. *South Asia Regional Economic Cooperation: From SARC to SAARC and Whither Next*. Sri Lanka: South Asia Policy and Research Institute.

Rana, P.B. 2009. 'Trade Intensity and Business Cycle Synchronization: The Case of East Asian Countries.' *Singapore Economic Review* 53, No. 2: 279–92.

———. 2011. 'Reform Strategies in South Asian Countries: A Comparative Analysis.' *South Asian Journal of Global Business Research* 1, No. 1: 96–107.

———. 2012a. *Renaissance of Asia: Evolving Linkages between South Asia and East Asia*. Singapore: World Scientific Publishers.

———. 2012b, 'The Next Steps in ASEAN+3 Monetary Integration,' *Vox*, 27 May, http://www.voxeu.org/article/next-steps-asean3-monetary-integration.

Rana, P.B. and B. Karmacharya. 2015. 'Nepal—A Connectivity-driven Development Strategy.' In *Connecting Asia: Infrastructure for Integrating South and Southeast Asia*, edited by G. Wignaraja, M. Plummer, and P. Morgan. UK: Edward Elgar.

Rana, P.B. and N. Hamid. 1995. 'Reform Strategies in Transitional Economies: Lessons from Asia.' *World Development* 23, No. 3: 1157–69.

Rana, P.B, T.Y. Cheng, and W.M. Chia. 2012. 'Trade Intensity and Business Cycle Synchronization: East Asia versus Europe.' *Journal of Asian Economics* 23, 701–6.

Refaqat, S., J. Lopez-Calix, H. Mukhtar, M. Ashraf, M. Waheed, and R. Ahmed. 2014. *Pakistan Development Update*. Washington D.C.: World Bank.

Robinson, J., P. DiMaggio, and E. Hargittai. 2003 'New Social Survey Perspectives on the Digital Divide.' *IT & Society* 1, No. 5: 1–22.

SGI (Stratfor Global Intelligence). 2013. *China's Ambitions in Xinjiang and Central Asia: Part 1.*' https://www.stratfor.com/analysis/chinas-ambitions-xinjiang-and-central-asia-part-1.

Shanti, N. 2014. 'Nepal Reaps Benefit of Regional Trade Policy Course in India.' *ANI*, September 13. https://in.finance.yahoo.com/news/nepal-reaps-benefit-regional-trade-112304368.html.

Singhal, D. P. 1969. *India and the World Civilization*, Vol. 1. East Lansing: Michigan State University Press.

Sussangkarn, C. 2010. 'The Chiang Mai Multilateralization: Origin, Development, and Outlook.' ADBI Working Paper Series No. 230, Asian Development Bank Institute, Tokyo.

Szczudlik-Tatar, J. 2013. 'China's New Silk Road Diplomacy.' PISM Policy Paper No. 34(82), Polish Institute of International Affairs, Poland.

Thangavelu, M. and A. Chongvilaivan. 2013. *Globalization, Outsourcing and Labour Development in ASEAN*. London: Routledge.

The Asia Foundation. 2011. *Afghanistan Labour Law Program*. San Francisco: The Asia Foundation .

The Economist. 2012. 'Get your Kicks on Route G6.' *Economist*, 22 December.

The United Nations Commodity Trade Statistics Database (UN Comtrade), 2012.

Transparency International. 2010. *Fighting Corruption in South Asia*. Berlin; Transparency International.

———. 2012. *Position Paper: Urgent Bills, Transparency and Human Rights*. Berlin: Transparency International.

———. 2014. *Position Paper: A Single Food Safety Regulatory Agency-An Imperative for Sri Lanka*. Berlin: Transparency International.

UNCTAD (United Nations Conference on Trade and Development). 2013a. *World Investment Report 2013*. Geneva: UNCTAD.

———. 2013b. *Global Value Chains and Development: Investment and Value Added Trade in the Global Economy*. Geneva: UNCTAD.

United Nations Development Programme. 2014. *Maldives Human Development Report 2014*. New York: United Nations Development Programme.

Wignaraja, G. 2016. *Production Networks and Enterprises in East Asia: Industry and Firm-level Analysis*. Berlin: Springer.

————. Forthcoming. 'Assessing the Experience of South Asia-East Asia Integration.' In *Integration in South Asia and East Asia: Economics of Regional Cooperation and Development*, edited by T.N Srinivasan and J. Menon. New Delhi: Oxford University Press.

Wignaraja, G., J. Kruger, and A.M. Tuazon. 2013. 'Production Networks, Profits, and Innovative Activity: Evidence from Malaysia and Thailand.' ADBI Working Paper Series No. 416, Asian Development Bank Institute, Tokyo.

Wilson, D. and R. Purushothaman. 2003. 'Dreaming with the BRICS: The Path to 2050.' Global Economic Paper No. 99, Goldman Sachs. New York.

World Bank. 2004. 'Trade Policies in South Asia: An Overview Report.' Paper No. 29929, World Bank, Washington D.C.

————. 2006. *Doing Business in 2006: Creating Jobs*. Washington, D.C.: International Bank for Reconstruction and Development, World Bank.

————. 2012. *Sri Lanka-Demographic Transition: Facing the Challenges of an Aging Population with Few Resources*. Washington, D.C.: World Bank.

————. 2014a. *Afghanistan Development Update*. Washington, D.C.: World Bank.

————. 2014b. *Afghanistan-Country Snapshot*. Washington, D.C.: World Bank. http://documents.worldbank.org/curated/en/2014/10/20305952/afghanistan-country-snapshot.

————. 2014c. *Bangladesh-Country Snapshot*. Washington, D.C.: World Bank. http://documents.worldbank.org/curated/en/2014/10/20305953/bangladesh-country-snapshot.

————. 2014d. *Bhutan-Country Snapshot*. Washington, D.C.: World Bank. http://documents.worldbank.org/curated/en/2014/10/20305893/bhutan-country-snapshot.

————. 2014e. *India-Country Snapshot*. Washington, D.C.: World Bank. http://documents.worldbank.org/curated/en/2014/10/20305633/india-country-snapshot.

————. 2014f. *Maldives-Development Update*. South Asia Region Poverty Reduction and Economic Management'. Washington, D.C.: World Bank. http://documents.worldbank.org/curated/en/2014/04/19402100/maldives-development-update.

————. 2014g. *Nepal-Country Snapshot*. Washington D.C.: World Bank. http://documents.worldbank.org/curated/en/2014/03/19435327/nepal-country-snapshot.

————. 2014h. *Nepal-Development Update*. South Asia Region Poverty Reduction and Economic Management, Washington, D.C.: World Bank.

http://documents.worldbank.org/curated/en/2014/04/19402140/
nepal-development-update.

———. 2014i. *Pakistan-Country Snapshot.* Washington, D.C.: World Bank.
http://documents.worldbank.org/curated/en/2014/03/19612873/
pakistan-country-snapshot.

———. 2014j. *Sri Lanka-Country Snapshot.* Washington D.C.: World Bank.
http://documents.worldbank.org/curated/en/2014/03/19435328/
sri-lanka-country-snapshot.

———. 2015. *Doing Business 2016: Measuring Regulatory Quality and Efficiency.*
Washington, D.C.: International Bank for Reconstruction and Development,
World Bank.

———. 2016. *Connecting to Compete 2016: Trade Logistics in the Global
Economy.* Washington, D.C.: The International Bank for Reconstruction and
Development, World Bank.

World Trade Organization. 2012. *Trade Policy Review: Nepal 2012.* Geneva:
World Trade Organization.

Xiaochuan, Z. 2009. 'Reform of the International Monetary System.' People's
Bank of China.

Yang, B. 2009. *Between Wind and Clouds: The Making of Yunnan.* New York:
Columbia University Press.

Yushkova, E. 2013. 'Impact of ICT on Trade in Different Technology Groups:
Analysis and Implications.' *International Economics and Economic Policy* 11,
No. 1: 165–77.

Zeddies, G. 2011. 'Determinants of International Fragmentation of Production
in European Union.' *Empirica* 38, No. 4: 511–37.

Zhong, Z. 2002. 'The Chinese Western Development Initiative: New
Opportunities for Mineral Investment.' *Resources Policy* 28, No. 3–4: 117–31.

INDEX

ABOUT THE AUTHORS

Pradumna B. Rana is associate professor and coordinator of International Political Economy Programme at the Centre of Multilateralism Studies of the S. Rajaratnam School of International Studies (RSIS) at the Nanyang Technological University (NTU), Singapore. He was senior director of the Asian Development Bank's (ADB's) Office of Regional Economic Integration, which spearheaded the ADB's support for Asian economic integration. Prior to that, he held various senior positions at ADB for many years. He has teaching and research experience at NTU, National University of Singapore (NUS), and Tribhuvan University (Nepal). He obtained his PhD from Vanderbilt University where he was a Fulbright Scholar. He has a Masters in Economics from Michigan State University and is a gold medallist from Tribhuvan University. His works have been published widely in the areas of Asian economic development and integration, economic policy reforms in transition economies, financial crises, and the evolving global economic architecture. These include 15 authored or edited books, over 25 chapters in books, and over 60 articles in international scholarly journals including *Review of Economics and Statistics, Journal of International Economics, Journal of Development Economics, Journal of Asian Economics, World Development, Developing Economies,* and *Singapore Economic Review.* He has edited *Renaissance of Asia: Evolving Economic Relations between South Asia and East Asia* (2012). He has co-authored *Asia and the Global Economic Crisis: Challenges in a Financially Integrated World* (2010) and *South*

Asia: Rising to the Challenge of Globalization (2009). He has co-edited *Pan-Asian Integration: Linking East and South Asia* (2009) and *National Strategies for Regional Integration: South and East Asian Case Studies* (2009). He was also the guest editor of the *Singapore Economic Review* special issue on 'Asian Economic Integration' (Volume 55, Number 1, March 2010) and is presently guest editing a special issue on 'ASEAN: Long-term Challenges and Vision'.

Wai-Mun Chia is associate professor of economics at the School of Social Sciences, NTU, Singapore. Her research covers topics in international macroeconomics, housing economics, and cost–benefit analysis. She is an associate editor of the *Singapore Economic Review*. She holds a PhD from NTU, an MSc from the London School of Economics (LSE), UK, and a BSc from the University of London, all in economics. Wai-Mun was also a consultant to various government agencies in Singapore including the Singapore Police Force, National Environment Agency, Land Transport Authority, Ministry of Community Development, Youth and Sports, and Building and Construction Authority.